American and British Pewter

AN HISTORICAL SURVEY

Edited by John Carl Thomas

Main Street/Universe Books

New York

Articles included in this volume are printed as they appeared originally in the following issues of *THE MAGAZINE* ANTIQUES:

Part I. Pewter Collector's Progress, August, 1964; An English Pewter Collection, August, 1969; Some British Pewter, June, 1946; More British Pewter, May, 1947; Some Scottish Pewter Measures, February, 1948; A Note on the Pewter of the Channel Islands, May, 1928; Pewter Pieces in an English Collection, August, 1947; Some Pewter of England, October, 1927; Further Notes on Commemorative Porringers, July, 1928; Royal Portraits and Pewter Porringers, January, 1958; An Old English Provincial Trade Guild, September, 1926.

Part II. Pewter at the Forum, English Influence in American Pewter, I, September, 1949; Pewter at the Forum, English Influence in American Pewter, II, September, 1949; American Pewter as a Collectible, November, 1930; Important Early American Pewter, September, 1939; An American Pewter Collection, July, 1957; American Pewter Tankards, September, 1938; The American Pewter Porringer, May, 1930; Unique Crown-Handled Porringers, January, 1948; Joseph Copeland, 17th-Century Pewterer, April, 1938; The Pewterers of Eighteenth-Century New York, October, 1970; A Pewter Discovery, January, 1951; Three Flagons Attributed to John Will, May, 1972; Concerning the Pewtering Bassetts, March, 1930; A Bassett Discovery, January, 1949; An American Silversmith and His Pewter, March, 1938; Cornelius Bradford, Pewterer, August, 1930; New Finds in Old Pewter by William Will, April, 1950; Some Pewter by William Will, February, 1952; Interchangeable Parts in Early American Pewter, February, 1963; A Flat-Top Tankard, April, 1950; Swedish Influence on American Pewter, March, 1955; I.C.H., Lancaster Pewterer, September, 1931; Richard Lee, Pewterer, June, 1934.

Part III. Marked American Pewter, May, 1926; Coffeepot? Teapot! June, 1945; Some Pewter of Little Importance, November, 1948; Samuel Pierce, Pewterer, and His Tools, February, 1927; Samuel Pierce, Jr., and the Small Eagle Die, July, 1957; William Calder, a Transition Pewterer, November, 1936; George Richardson, Pewterer, April, 1937; George Richardson, Pewterer, October, 1940; A Massachusetts Pewterer, January, 1924; Three Maine Pewterers, July, 1932; Ohio and Missouri Pewter Data, October, 1928.

First Edition

Library of Congress Catalog Card Number 76-5096

ISBN 0-87663-949-X, paperback edition
ISBN 0-87663-241-X, cloth edition

Published by Universe Books, 381 Park Avenue South, New York City 10016. Produced by The Main Street Press, 42 Main Street, Clinton, New Jersey 08809

Printed in the United States of America

American and British Pewter

Cover illustration: Quart tankards by, left, William
Kirby (w. 1760-1793), and, right, Frederick Bassett
(w. 1761-1780), New York. Photo by Taylor & Dull.

ANTIQUES Magazine Library

I   Needlework, An Historical Survey,
   Edited by Betty Ring

II   Philadelphia Furniture & Its Makers,
   Edited by John J. Snyder, Jr.

III   Chinese Export Porcelain,
   Edited by Elinor Gordon

IV   Lighting in America,
   Edited by Lawrence S. Cooke

V   Pilgrim Century Furniture
   Edited by Robert F. Trent

VI   American and British Pewter
   Edited by John Carl Thomas

Contents

INTRODUCTION   7

I   BRITISH PEWTER

Pewter Collector's Progress, *Robert M. Vetter*   13
An English Pewter Collection, *Christopher A. Peal*   18
Some British Pewter, *A. Sutherland-Graeme*   25
More British Pewter, *A. Sutherland-Graeme*   27
Some Scottish Pewter Measures, *Lewis Clapperton*   29
A Note on the Pewter of the Channel Islands, *Howard Herschel
    Cotterell*   31
Pewter Pieces in an English Collection, *Roland J. A. Shelley*   33
Some Pewter of England, Porringers with Busts of Sovereigns,
    Adolphe Riff   35
Further Notes on Commemorative Porringers, *Howard Herschel
    Cotterell*   39
Royal Portraits and Pewter Porringers, *Ronald F. Michaelis*   42
An Old English Provincial Trade Guild, *Howard Herschel
    Cotterell* and *Walter Graham Churcher*   47

II   AMERICAN PEWTER BEFORE 1800

Pewter at the Froum, English Influence in American Pewter, I,
    Charles F. Montgomery   53
Pewter at the Forum, English Influence in American Pewter, II,
    Percy E. Raymond   55
American Pewter as a Collectible, *P. G. Platt*   57
Important Early American Pewter, *Charles F. Montgomery*   62
An American Pewter Collection, *Dr. Robert Mallory III*   66
American Pewter Tankards, *Edward E. Minor*   70
The American Pewter Porringer, *Ledlie I. Laughlin*   73
Unique Crown-Handled Porringers, *Percy E. Raymond*   78
Joseph Copeland, 17th-Century Pewterer, *Worth Bailey*   80
The Pewterers of Eighteenth-Century New York, *Ledlie I. Laughlin*   83
A Pewter Discovery, *Adelbert C. Abbott*   88
Three Flagons Attributed to John Will, *Charles V. Swain*   89
Concerning the Pewtering Bassetts, *H. V. Button*   94
A Bassett Discovery, *Oliver Wolcott Deming*   96
An American Silversmith and His Pewter, *John W. Poole*   98
Cornelius Bradford, *Ledlie I. Laughlin*   100

New Finds in Old Pewter by William Will, *Paul M. Auman*   102
Some Pewter by William Will, *John J. Evans, Jr.*   104
Interchangeable Parts in Early American Pewter, *Charles V. Swain*   106
A Flat-Top Tankard, *J. J. Evans, Jr.*   108
Swedish Influence on American Pewter, *Eric de Jonge*   110
I. C. H., Lancaster Pewterer, *John J. Evans, Jr.*   113
Richard Lee, Pewterer, *Harold G. Rugg* and *the Editor*   117

III   AMERICAN PEWTER AFTER 1800

Marked American Pewter, *Charles L. Woodside*   123
Coffeepot? Teapot! *Percy E. Raymond*   128
Some Pewter of Little Importance, *Percy E. Raymond*   130
Samuel Pierce, Pewterer, and His Tools, *Julia D. Sophronia Snow*   132
Samuel Pierce, Jr., and the Small Eagle Die, *Marion* and *Oliver Deming*   137
William Calder, a Transition Pewterer, *Percy E. Raymond*   140
George Richardson, Pewterer, *Lura Woodside Watkins*   143
George Richardson, Pewterer, *Edward H. West*   146
A Massachusetts Pewterer, *John Whiting Webber*   148
Three Maine Pewterers, *Charles L. Woodside* and *Lura Woodside Watkins*   151
Ohio and Missouri Pewter Data, *J. G. Braecklein*   154

INDEX   157

Introduction

The metal alloy we know as pewter has served various needs of mankind for many centuries. At once an ancient metal and a modern one, its use predates the voyages of Christopher Columbus by more than a thousand years, and extends to present-day factories making pewter rowing trophies and bonbon dishes.

In its lengthy evolution, pewter has crisscrossed through the private, public, and religious lives of our ancestors. It has been used by the rich and the poor, young and old, clergyman and soldier. At different times in its history, pewter has been equally at home in the grand castles of European royalty and the rude log cabins of the American frontier. Pewter has been fashioned into vessels for use in the religious sacraments of baptism and communion, and mugs made of pewter were once commonplace in alehouses here and abroad.

It is, at least in part, this universal aspect of pewter that has awakened the strong interest of antiquarians and historians. No other metal has been so closely associated with the everyday lives of our forefathers, and in turn, can tell us more about them. A study of pewter is at the same time a study of changing fashions: of cultural and technological advances, and of matters related to the economy. In the texture of pewter from various periods, we may read something of the advances in metallurgy, and the design of an article made from pewter often exhibits the influence of one national culture on that of another.

The collector of pewter is attracted and satisfied by those same considerations, coupled with the pleasing combinations of metal and form, general availability, and reasonably simple documentation of the objects he may acquire.

That last element, ease of documentation, is of major importance to the beginning collector. Having purchased his first few pieces of pewter because they were pleasing to the eye or served a decorative purpose, the novice soon experiences the need to know more about those possessions. Who made them? How were they made? Those questions, along with others regarding the place and period of origin, often follow closely after the acquisition of some physical part of a bygone age. The object is there to see and touch, and one "feels" the hand of the early craftsman who produced it and those of successive generations of ownership.

Attaining the knowledge required to "read" the story embodied in each piece of pewter is one of the single most rewarding elements of collecting.

There exists, for the many who wish to better know their pewter, a fine library of reference books, incorporating many man-years of careful research and patient examination into informative volumes regarding every aspect of the metal. In addition, a great many articles on the subject of pewter have appeared in publications of a more general orientation, such as *The Magazine* ANTIQUES. These articles, especially when considered collectively, add much to our overall knowledge. *American and British Pewter* is designed to assemble some of the more illustrative of the ANTIQUES segments, providing a single volume which places emphasis on some areas not covered in depth by other bodies of text. In each of the articles contained in this anthology there is support for present opinion, or the foundation for future discovery, or both.

Another collection of articles from *The Magazine* ANTIQUES was published in 1972 under the title *National Types of Old Pewter*. That assembly of data concentrated on the stylistic variations of pewter produced in Britain and the countries of Europe. It has proved invaluable as a guide to those particular styles which influenced the design of pewter in some areas of colonial America.

The earlier writers of pewter reference works, each of them a pioneer in his own country, embodied the results of their research in books that became the foundations upon which all subsequent investigations have been based. H. J. L. J. Massé and H. H. Cotterell, writing in the first third of this century, provided substantial beginnings in the field of British pewter. Cotterell's *Old Pewter, Its Makers and Marks*, first published in 1929, exists even today as the best general standard reference to British pewter. It contains a body of over 6,000 entries regarding the individual pewterers, and illustrates a large percentage of the marks they used to identify their wares. The balance of the text, although still of fundamental interest, has been considerably improved upon by more recent authors.

Ronald F. Michaelis added much to the understanding of pewter in 1955, with the publication of *Antique Pewter of the British Isles*, and provided excellent photographic coverage of a wide array of forms in *British Pewter*, published in 1969.

The aesthetics of collecting, and likewise the realities, were treated by Christopher A. Peal in his *British Pewter and Britannia Metal—For Pleasure and Investment*, published in 1971. Combining those elements with an interesting and concise review of the periodic development of British pewter, Peal has provided an invaluable manual for beginning and advanced collectors alike.

The books mentioned above, and others of a highly specialized content such as *Pewter of the Channel Islands* by S. C. Woolmer and C. H. Arkwright, provide the student of pewter with a great variety of analytic tools and a carefully wrought history of the development of Britain's pewter industry. If fault is to be found with this total body of data, it is the absence of an updated version of Cotterell's list of pewterers and their marks.

Pewter made and used in America has received an even greater degree of attention by researchers than that of its European counterparts. Perhaps it is the relative newness of our own nation, and the consequent lack of a long and rich tradition, which drives us to pursue in great detail every element of our brief history. Whatever has been the reason for the enthusiastic investigation, the result, in terms of our present subject, is that we know each pewterer on an almost intimate level. We have gone beyond the study of regional differences in style to examine the subtle changes in form between individual shops within those regions. Even the passage, from one pewterer's shop to another, of a mould for a handle, or some other element of a total form, has not escaped observation by the advanced students of American pewter.

An excellent representation of this intense research is contained in the article entitled "Three Flagons Attributed to John Will," by Charles V. Swain, in Part II of this volume. Swain employs a detailed analysis of several parts of an individual piece of pewter, as well as a knowledge of styles, the histories of the individual pewterers, and records of ownership, to document fully his presentation.

Such in-depth investigations have led to a wider understanding and appreciation of the pewter in present-day collections and of the men who produced it. Swain's article is an extension of the increasingly sophisticated body of knowledge being made available by leading authorities in the field.

Some research had been published previously, but the appearance in 1924 of J. B. Kerfoot's *American Pewter* marked the beginning of intense study. Although much of the content is now completely out of date, the book stands as a monument to Kerfoot's enthusiasm and his ability to communicate it to the reader.

The truly definitive work on American pewter is Ledlie I. Laughlin's *Pewter in America: Its Makers and Their Marks.* This was first published in two volumes in 1940, and was reprinted in a single volume, containing marginal notes of corrections, in 1969. A third volume was added in 1971, incorporating all of the new data gathered since the original publication and attempting to correct and update the earlier edition. A history of the trade is included, along with notes regarding the several geographic areas of pewter production in America and a biographical sketch of each identified American pewterer. Every maker's mark known to Laughlin is represented by a photograph or a line drawing. It is a reference book of awesome proportions, having involved many years of study and preparation. That a book of such magnitude must contain a few errors is unavoidable, and that knowledge does not detract from its importance to every collector and student of American pewter. Laughlin enlarged our understanding and defined areas which need more study, thereby promoting further research and, as a result, contributing far more than he has included in his own writings.

The last major shortcoming in the literature on American pewter was eliminated by the publication, in 1973, of *A History of American Pewter,* by Charles F. Montgomery. Handsome photographs illustrate the development of forms, and the reader is challenged to see the influence of economic and social factors expressed in pewter objects. Also, by comparing the elements of design evident on a piece of pewter with similar manifestations in the designs of architectural elements and furniture, Montgomery guides the reader to a better understanding of the object through placement in a proper frame of historical reference.

For the past forty years, The Pewter Collectors Club of America has produced its *Bulletin* on a semi-annual basis. That in-house publication has been the medium through which a great many revelations about pewter have been passed to students and collectors. While some of the *Bulletin* inclusions have been self-contained research studies, others are fractional bits of data, or observations, shared amongst collectors, that eventually have been tied together to help form a complete survey of some particular area. Many of the authorities whose work is represented here in *American and British Pewter* have been frequent contributors to the P.C.C.A. *Bulletin.*

Many other books have been written on the subject of pewter, and all have contributed to the total body of knowledge. Those which are mentioned specifically are the ones which have had the greatest impact and best illustrate our progress in the field. Each of these represents a generation of research, and has formed a base for continued study which produced another such generation. For example, Kerfoot reported "Daniel Melvil" as a pewterer working in Newport, Rhode Island in 1788, and suspected that his initial working date might even be pre-Revolutionary. A total of four marks used by that pewterer were illustrated. Some sixteen years later, Laughlin corrected the name to David Melville; provided a family history commencing in 1691, with working dates for the pewterer of 1776-1793; and pictured a total of eight marks. At the same time, he presented several other pewterers named Melville and illustrated marks used by three of them. Proof that perhaps several more "generations" will pass before we achieve anything like perfection is indicated in volume III of *Pewter in America* (1971), where Laughlin incorrectly attributed a British mark to one of those same Melvilles.

Twentieth-century man, on balance, is an optimistic creature, and, for most purposes, that must be considered a happy state of affairs. When our optimism has been too enthusiastically employed in such areas as the study of antique pewter, however, it has resulted in misleading or totally incorrect assumptions. When those assumptions or "attributions" appear in print, they are often interpreted as "proofs," and one can easily see the problems which arise from that unfortunate sequence.

In Part III of this volume an article entitled "George Richardson, Pewterer," by Lura Woodside Watkins, claims that pewter made by that craftsman in Cranston, Rhode Island, *must* have been made before 1818. This was based on accurate information proving that Richardson had worked in Boston from 1818 to 1828 and on the *assumption* that a George Richardson who died in Boston in 1830 was the pewterer of the same name. Optimism about the dead man's identity had triumphed over reason, for an examination of the forms bearing Boston and Cranston marks should have shown that the styles employed in the Rhode Island work were definitely the later of the two groups. Three years after the publication of Watkins' article, Edward H. West corrected the situation, revealing Richardson's relocation to Rhode Island and his later death, in Providence, in 1848. The two articles are included here in their chronological sequence.

It is not absolutely clear whether the increased interest in collecting pewter has provided the stimulus for continually expanding research or if, as a result of excellent research and its resultant literature, the hobby has been made so much more interesting that many additional collectors have joined in. The chicken and egg argument lives on. Frankly, I suspect that both allegations are true and that collecting and research must continually interact in order for either element to be completely satisfactory.

Interest and activity involving pewter has increased dramatically over the past two or three decades. Specialties have developed, with some students and collectors directing their attention towards a particular national or regional area of pewter production and still others concentrating on a form, or a group of forms, such as porringers or pewter ecclesiastical wares. Studies and collections have even been formed around the work of a single pewterer.

Some of those specialties may be evident as one reads through the three portions of *American and British Pewter*, but the real purpose of this anthology is the general introduction of a field of study which has provided so much satisfaction over the years to its many devotees. I hope and expect that the enthusiasm of these writers and the beauty of the items they have illustrated will incite an even broader appreciation of early pewter.

I British Pewter

Some of the men of the Roman legions occupying Britain during the third and fourth centuries A.D. mined the rich deposits of tin in Cornwall and, adding lead to complete the alloy, produced pewter plates, bowls, ewers, and other vessels. Some 200 pieces of that Romano-British ware have been discovered and stand as the earliest examples of pewter presently known anywhere in the world.

Evidence indicates that pewter production ceased, along with many other crafts, at the time of the destruction of the Roman Empire and Europe's entry into the so-called "Dark Ages." In about the eleventh century, however, manufacture of pewter began anew in Britain and steadily increased in magnitude through the eighteenth century. Although facing severe competition from many other materials and declining in general use, pewter was still produced in major quantity through the middle of the nineteenth century, and many public houses still served beer and ale in pewter mugs only a decade before World War II.

From at least the fourteenth century onward a strong set of regulations governing the trade were administered by a craft guild. Ordinances were laid down in London in 1348 which established ethical practices as well as standards for both metal and workmanship. The Craft of Pewterers in London was given its first charter in 1473, and the powers conferred upon it included the control of the trade both in London and elsewhere in England.

Men were not allowed to practice as pewterers until a regulated apprenticeship had been completed and then only after proof had been established that the applicant had both the talent and the means to enter the business independent of his master. Goods of poor quality were confiscated by "searchers" from the guild, and the offending workman was often fined for his impropriety.

The exercise of strict controls was primarily responsible for the fine quality of British pewter and its employment as a standard of excellence everywhere. Pewterers in Europe often used marks such as "London" or "Englisches Zinn" to imply a ware of the best grade, and many American pewterers of the eighteenth century added a "London" mark to their better goods.

It was perhaps during the seventeenth and early eighteenth centuries that the finest of the British pewter was produced. The quality of the metal was undeniably superior at that time, and the forms produced were bold and expressive. Styles changed often in the century from 1610 to 1710, and each variation was brought to perfection by British pewterers. In Christopher A. Peal's article, "An English Pewter Collection," many of the styles of flagons, measures, and other forms of that period are explained and beautifully illustrated. Also, in "Some British Pewter" and "More British Pewter," A. Sutherland-Graeme pictures many examples from the same period, including a representation of the "wriggle-work" decoration employed by many pewterers on wares of the last quarter of the seventeenth century.

The eighteenth century brought new designs and increasing competition. Many British pewterers found an excellent market in the American colonies and exported vast amounts of pewter to the new settlements. Some forms, such as teapots, cream jugs, and sugar bowls, seem to have been made primarily for the American market and are seldom encountered in England today. There is evidence that some British pewterers even had separate "touch marks" which they placed on their export pieces. One such mark, a small shield enclosing the intials ["HI,"] was thought for many years to have been used by an unknown American pewterer. Many examples so marked had been found here, and none in England. It has been discovered, in only the past decade or so, that the mark was employed by Henry Joseph, a London craftsman, on goods intended for sale in America. William Eden was another "exporter," and Sutherland-Graeme also pictures items by that maker in "More English Pewter."

Measures were made throughout the whole period of pewter manufacture in England. Illustrations of some of the early forms are included in the articles cited above, and Lewis Clapperton and H. H. Cotterell review other types in "Some Scottish Pewter Measures" and "A Note on the Pewter of the Channel Islands." All of the types of measures discussed by writers in this section are collected with equal enthusiasm both in England and the United States. Measures have become an area of intense specialization by some collectors.

The so-called "commemorative porringers" discussed by Adolphe Riff, H.H. Cotterell, and Ronald F. Michaelis are amongst the most handsome of pewter forms. They are given some extra attention here, not only because of their great beauty and special historic interest, but also because of the lack of adequate discussion in other books owing to their considerable rarity.

The article "An Old English Provincial Trade Guild," by H. H. Cotterell and Walter G. Churcher, is fascinating in its revelations about the craft guild structure and its functions. Because these craft organizations were so important to the British pewter industry, an understanding of their workings is almost prerequisite to a study of pewter itself.

Pewter collector's progress

To become a collector of pewter
You certainly need no computer—
Just your heart and your mind
And some money, combined
With advice from a trusty old tutor.
R. M. V.

BY ROBERT M. VETTER

SOME FATAL DAY your attention is arrested by a salt, a plate, perhaps a spoon, made from a soft, semiprecious metal. You acquire the piece, and without even being aware of it you have entered upon the adventurous career of the pewter collector.

What makes old pewter so attractive? Compared with other collectible antiques, it is of little material value. Its subtle magic comes from mellow patina, fine surface texture, a capacity for producing soft reflections of light, not to mention an infinite variety of styles, shapes, and dimensions, diversity of use, and fascinating national and regional differences.

In the beginning, everything seems quite easy and you regard the first fruits of your passion as great finds and good bargains. If you are lucky they may be genuine. A marked piece will intrigue you into interpreting, and that leads you to consult advanced collectors, to study

1 Early pewter against background of Gothic carving. From left to right: ciborium, Dutch, c. 1600, height 8¾ inches; candlesticks, northwest German, c. 1500, height 13½ inches; council flagon, Swiss (St. Gallen), first half seventeenth century, height 18 inches; flagons, Austrian (Linz), second half sixteenth century. The oaken plank is French and bears the Bourbon arms. *Photographs by Karl Scherb, Vienna.*

the ever-increasing pewter literature, and to visit public collections in museums. The suasion of an experienced dealer may give you useful hints. Honest pewter is more apt to conjure up the taste and customs of olden times than more precious objects (excepting perhaps old furniture), and at this point you will already have had the experience of entering into the spirit of a bygone age.

Now your collection will develop in accordance with your individual disposition and taste. You may become a mono-collector, *e.g.*, of spoons or porringers; you may limit yourself to the products of one nation or one period; or you may acquire everything that appeals to your sense of beauty or curiosity, irrespective of origin or age. You may prefer plain household and tavern ware, or find only decorated objects worthy of your attention. Some collectors acquire large picturesque flagons and broad-rimmed chargers for decoration without consideration of where or when they were made.

Pewter offers infinite possibilities for expressing the collector's personality. No matter how you try to confine your efforts you will be faced with a baffling diversity, partly because the trade was followed by thousands of sometimes very self-willed masters whose disregard for the standards of custom and fashion have left delightful surprises for the attentive amateur.

Differences in quality are great and perfection is rare,

but you will soon find that quality goes before quantity and that it is wiser, occasionally, to invest your money in a single first-rate object than to spend it for a number of mediocre ones. Only objects which are beyond doubt will satisfy in the long run. Since your taste, knowledge, and critical sense will increase together with your collection, an occasional purge of earlier acquisitions will be beneficial. Such pruning should be merciless. It will furnish the means to buy something of "museum quality." Some good and even famous collections have, with moderate means, been built up on this principle.

The times are definitely gone when it was possible to pick up a good piece at the junk dealer's, to find it in a garret or in a farmhouse during your vacation. The

2

present-day collector must depend on what the antique trade offers or on what he may buy at auctions. Though it is, generally speaking, safe to trust an experienced *antiquaire* of repute, and buying at auction requires more time and study, the latter course is far more exciting. Either way, the acquisition of every additional item is an emotional adventure. Every true collector knows those vacillations between doubt and certainty which precede the act of buying—accompanied by qualms of conscience if money is short. However, it may safely be said that good pewter has so far proved a wise investment, and few collectors have occasion to regret the acquisition of a fine piece even at a stiff price. Rubbish only is dear. It is also true that desirable pieces have become quite rare, but this makes the hunt more exciting.

To clean or not to clean is a question which puzzles every collector. It is impossible to give an exhaustive answer here, but it may be said that this is a matter of taste and often of necessity. Just remember that a fine coat of patina took many years to form and cannot be replaced. Cleaning and possibly even repairing your own pieces will give you an intimate knowledge of the material and the finish applied by the old masters of the craft, and you will learn thereby to distinguish genuine pieces from fake.

Here we might mention four basic factors which the connoisseur (not only of pewter) must consider:

Style: all-important.

Material and technology: decisive.

Marking: very helpful but by no means decisive. Ever so many splendid specimens are unmarked, but fakes always bear some semblance of a touch.

Patina and wear and tear: not to be depended upon. The quasi-antique appearance given to fakes is sometimes quite deceptive, whereas perfectly bona fide pewter may have a new look. Close study in a good light helps to avoid deception.

Much could be said about advice from sympathetic or jealous fellow collectors (they may be one and the same), or about the indispensable card index which will be ever

3

4

5

2 French pewter, plain and ornate, from left to right: Paris *pichet,* or jug, height 15 inches; relief-decorated tankard, height 6 inches, from Strasbourg; salver, diameter 15 inches, probably from Paris; flask with chain, height 16 inches, from Lyons; all seventeenth century.

3 South German pewter, early eighteenth century. The four-guild (carpenters, gunsmiths, glaziers, and turners) flagon in the center, height 17 inches, bears touch of an Amberg (Bavaria) pewterer. The pair of church flagons, height 15 inches, hails from Protestant Württemberg. Transition from Renaissance to early baroque, tending toward the monumental.

4 Austrian pewter. Left: lavabo ewer, height 6⅛ inches, Vienna, c. 1700; plate, diameter 7½ inches, Innsbruck; drinking vessel (*biberon*), height 6¼ inches, dated 1697, Wels; small measure, Vienna; torch-bearing angels, second half eighteenth century. Closely related to the German but more sprightly.

5 Dutch pewter of the sixteenth, seventeenth, and eighteenth centuries. Left: so-called Rembrandt flagon from Amsterdam's beer porters' guild, dated 1648, height 10 inches; the spouted, so-called Jan Steen flagons (see ANTIQUES, February 1955, p. 138) are seventeenth century, height 7¾ inches; the bulbous flagon is the work of a Gouda pewterer about 1500, height 7¼ inches; the small plate, diameter 6¼ inches, bears the touch of a Utrecht master. Dutch pewter is plain, substantial, and of harmonious proportions.

6 Two weavers' guild tankards from Bremen, height 8¼ inches, dated 1666 and 1667; soup pot with strap handle from Lübeck, height 7¼ inches, eighteenth century; the engraved platter, diameter 14 inches, is a so-called *Schüsselring,* employed for protecting the table top from hot dishes, dated in touch 1715. "True and dark and tender is the North."

6

15

7

8

so helpful to a future auctioneer; but more important than either is consideration of the matter of display. A good piece may speak for itself, but its effect will be enhanced immeasurably if it is well placed. Enviable is the man who can show off his treasure against old oak paneling or place small groups on fine old furniture (but not on polished mahogany). Mixed with other metals such as brass or silver, pewter loses; but it gets on very well with gay old pottery.

Having arrived at the stage where our hypothetical tyro has, by sheer perseverance, become the proud owner of a splendid array of select pewter and learned to care for it and to show it off to best advantage, we turn our attention to the progress of the collector's mind. From the beginning he has been acquiring, through intimate contact with craftsmen of another day, the historical perspective we must have if we are not to overvalue the triumphs of modern science. His intellectual horizon has broadened in other ways as well: his critical sense has been sharpened and so have his other senses. He has established at least a nodding acquaintance with metallurgy, chemistry, and technology. He has studied esthetics, history, sociology, and folklore to understand certain phenomena. Still-life paintings of old masters give valuable hints with regard to age and use of certain types, so he has visited picture galleries and thereby entered the wonder-world of the fine arts.

In short, our inquisitive amateur has become broad- as well as pewter-minded. He has learned to see the world as through the crack of a door a little ajar, and to wonder at the ever-changing yet intrinsically invariable ways and means of human existence. Many prejudices have disappeared, tolerance has emerged, and finally true progress is achieved: he will even look at the treasures of his fellow collectors without envy.

Robert M. Vetter of Vienna has been a valued contributor to ANTIQUES since 1928 and is an honorary member of the Pewter Collectors' Club of America, which this year celebrates its thirtieth anniversary. The illustrations are from his own rich and varied collection.

9

10

11

12

7 Austrian pewter. Large flagon from Graz, dated in touch 1690, height 17 inches; the measure is Viennese, height 10 inches, eighteenth century; the large dish hails from Feldkirch, diameter 16 inches. Plain and stable.

8 British pewter. Monteith, height 8½ inches, over all diameter 16 inches, c. 1700; richly engraved tankard by William Eddon, London, height 7 inches, dated 1730; large hammered dish by Nicholas Kelk, London, 1641-1687, diameter 17 inches; salt without touch. All of excellent material and finish.

9 Rococo soup tureens, Frankfurt and Karlsbad. From left to right, width over all: 15 inches, 11¼ inches, 7¾ inches, 15¼ inches. The Louis XV fashion offered German pewter a last lease on life before the final collapse of the trade.

10 An early sixteenth-century spouted flagon from Cologne, height 10½ inches, and two small measures, height 4⅞ inches each. Long before the spouted and barred type became so popular in Switzerland it was used on the Rhine as a decanter for wine.

11 A sturdy kitchen salt of noble simplicity, dated 1694, height 9 inches, made by a Prague pewterer. Though in constant use for nearly 250 years it is still in perfect condition.

12 Guild sign of the bakers and millers of Landshut (Bavaria), size 15 inches by 22, made c. 1830. In the taverns, such signs were placed above the *Stammtisch* (the regular table) of the guild members so the traveling journeyman might know where to meet his fellow craftsmen.

An English pewter collection

BY CHRISTOPHER A. PEAL

COLLECTING ANTIQUE PEWTER in England is not easy; sometimes one feels that the native product has all gone abroad. In the 1930's there were many antique metal shops whose *décor* was dust and cobwebs (how much more attractive they were to collectors than the glossy shops of today!) and there was always the hope of discovering a real treasure. Lack of cash, time, and mobility kept my early efforts to a minimum, but intensive study resulted in first one excellent find and then another—and a collector was blooded. Some of the results of the ensuing thirty-five years of activity are shown here.

I recently inspected all known Romano-British pewter plates and hollow ware, some two hundred pieces, primarily to establish a datable series of rim types. This was futile, as dating evidence is extremely scarce: most specimens first reappear wrapped round the sharp end of a plow. However, the survey developed into total research, published in the *Proceedings* of the Cambridge Antiquarian Society (Vol. LX, 1967, pp. 19-37). Among many interesting facts this study established is the near certainty that the alloy pewter evolved under the Romans when they copied silverware in the tin of Cornwall. Accidentally or nefariously the tin was debased with lead, which proved easier to work than tin alone and more durable. The proportion of tin to lead varied wildly. Pieces are known with such extremes as 99.2 to 0.8 and 43 to 57, but the ratio 80 to 20 (very roughly) became normal. The majority of known pieces have been found in the Norfolk, Suffolk, and Cambridgeshire fen and fen edge of East Anglia (Fig. 1).

With the collapse of the Roman civilization and trade, manufacture of pewter in England apparently died. We do not know of it again until the twelfth- or thirteenth-century sepulchral chalices appear. A remarkable find is the bowl depicted in Figure 2, which is probably the earliest complete piece of native English pewter extant (the sepulchral chalices found when monks' graves are disturbed are all fragmentary). This bowl is in nearly perfect condition, although it is heavily oxidized. Because it is archaeologically so important I have not thought it wise to clean it. One deduces its function as a font bowl from its depth, the scratches down the sides caused by sliding it up and down over the stone font, and its state of preservation, protected in the cup of the font. The remarkable feature is the decoration round the rim. One must think of this piece in terms of twelfth-century rural perpetuation of traditional design, probably from the Celtic region.

My interest in any category wanes as its early period draws to a close; for plates this is about 1700. In its simplicity and dignity the "bumpy-bottom" type (Fig. 3, *left*) is particularly pleasing. So indeed is the rare triple-groove (not triple-reed) dish (*right*). A dish showing slightly more enterprising design is that with punched decoration around the broad rim, a late continuation of a Tudor style (*center*). A particularly interesting wriggled broad-rim plate (Fig. 4) is by TH of London, Number 17 on the London touch plates. This appears to be Thomas Haward (or Howard) who was fined for not serving as steward warden in 1671. The plate is inscribed, in English and Latin, *Honour is the reward of virtue 1671*.

Spoons are a fascinating form of pewterware, excellently discussed by F. G. Hilton Price in his pioneering

Fig. 1. Romano-British plate, c. 350 A. D.; diameter 15¼ inches. *All illustrations are from the author's collection; photographs by Michael Vesey Associates. Code numbers refer to* Cotterell, Old Pewter, Its Makers and Marks *(London, 1929).*

Fig. 2. Font bowl, twelfth or thirteenth century (?); diameter 15½ inches; no mark. Decorated around the rim with fantastic beasts, strapwork, stylized flowers, and buckles, in Anglo-Saxon chip carving, a treatment earlier than the medieval wriggling and, in fact, unique on pewter; stippled background. The base of the bowl has lightly traced arcs and circles as a guide for further decoration.

Fig. 3. *Left to right:* "Bumpy-bottom" dish, c. 1620; diameter 17¼ inches; mark indecipherable. Dish with punched decoration, c. 1680; diameter 20½ inches; mark, P (?). Triple-groove dish, c. 1680; diameter 18¼ inches; by George Smith; O.P. 4347.

Fig. 4. Plate with wriggle-work decoration, c. 1671; diameter 9½ inches; mark, TH (Thomas Haward or Howard); O.P. 5683.

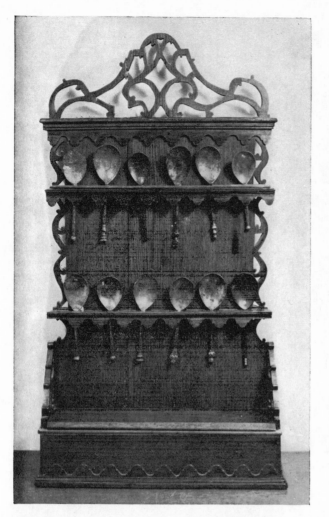

Fig. 5. Spoon rack, c. 1700; containing (*left to right, top section*): writhen-ball knop, c. 1450; gauntlet seal, c. 1600; stump end, c. 1400; horned headdress, c. 1450; lion sejant, c. 1560; lined ball, c. 1500; (*lower section*) peach-stone ball, c. 1520; melon, c. 1530; seal, c. 1550; alderman, c. 1620; maiden head, c. 1550; decorated slip top, c. 1520 (this bears bands of decoration at both top and bottom of stem, applied with the same punch).

Fig. 6. Salts. *Left to right*: Trencher, c. 1710; height 1½ inches; by G. Lowes of Newcastle; O.P. 2001. Base of bell salt, c. 1590; 3¾ inches; mark, HW. Octagonal-collar salt, c. 1670; 1¾ inches; no mark. Gadrooned capstan, c. 1700; 2¾ inches; mark, TL. Octagonal trencher, c. 1715; 1⅝ inches; no mark.

Old Base Metal Spoons (London, 1908). My collection contains examples of all save one of the types known to Price, and it has several not included in his study (Fig. 5). Because pewter is so soft and flexible it is a rather unserviceable alloy for spoons, and their use must have been confined to foods no stiffer than porridge. Pewter spoons were as personal possessions as toothbrushes are now; they were carried about and, fortunately for us, dropped. All old pewter spoons have been recovered from below—found in wells, drains, rivers, or accidentally dug up. The earliest appear to date from about 1400 and to have a thin four-sided stem. Later the stem becomes hexagonal. The fig-leaf bowl varies slightly but significantly in the next two hundred and fifty years. Spoons with a diamond or acorn knop seem to have been made throughout those two and a half centuries. Apostle spoons exist in pewter as well as in silver, but in most cases wear has made the cast emblems impossible to identify. The stump-end spoon is the only type with a stem that is circular in section and—excepting, of course, the slip top—with no knop. It is always small and, because of its tapering sides, easily distinguishable from the much more common and much later, heavier Dutch type. Almost all the knopped spoons are very rare indeed. The economy slip top came into use in Tudor times and is by far the most common type.

Salts are exceptionally rare in pewter. Styles changed quickly and salts were inexpensive, so they usually went to the pewterer to be melted down in part payment for new pieces. Perhaps the most interesting of the group shown here (Fig. 6, *second from left*), certainly the earliest, was found with a stone cannonball teed up in its cup, propping open the door of an antiques shop. It is Tudor and is the base of a bell salt which must have had two or even three sections above, in a lighthouse shape. It is exactly paralleled by the salts recovered from the Dutch Heemskirk expedition of 1596 and now in the Rijksmuseum, Amsterdam. Another great rarity is the octagonal-collar salt (*center*). I know of one or possibly two other genuine examples, but specimens not more than fifty years old are to be seen, here and there.

Coeval with the salts are the candlesticks (Fig. 7). The bell-based one (*center*) is Tudor. I am convinced

Fig. 7. Candlesticks. *Left to right*: Jacobean without drip pan, c. 1670; height 6½ inches to lip; mark, RB; O.P. 5452. Drip-pan or skirted candlestick, c. 1675; 6½ inches to lip; no mark. Bell base, c. 1590; 9 inches; no mark. Knopped stem, c. 1700; 5⅝ inches; no mark. Newcastle type, c. 1720; 6½ inches; by G. Lowes; O.P. 3001.

that the only other one I know, in the Victoria and Albert Museum and often depicted, has been tapped to its present shape falsely to give the base a flat rim. The drip-tray and the knopped sticks illustrated with it are well-known glamor types, but there appears to be no fellow for the simpler, no-tray specimen at the left. There are very few English pewter candlesticks made between about 1710 and the late 1700's; the specimen at the right is one of four of that period in my collection, representing what was apparently a Northumberland specialty.

Spoons and salts, for their interesting variety and rarity, are perhaps my favorites, but their fascination is surely equaled by that of the sometimes chunky, sometimes slender, and sometimes delicate baluster measures (Figs. 8, 9, 10). The series must have run from about 1500 to about 1820 and was made only in pewter. Sired by the leather bottle, the baluster has a low center of gravity and narrow neck ensuring stability, while its graceful curves give it great strength. In the eighteenth century, a few examples were made without lids. The wedge type (Fig. 8, *left* and *center*), so called because of the simple attachment on the lid, *must* have borne a thumbpiece—a ball or a hammerhead. Every single lidded tankard, flagon, or measure has a large, imposing thumbpiece; is it reasonable to accept such a miserable leverage as the wedge would afford to stubby thumbs? Both of those illustrated bear house marks as well as touch marks—one (*center*) a bull, cast or branded in the base; the other (*left*) a Saracen's head struck thrice on the lid and once inside the lip. This measure has the initials TD in the house mark, and also punched on the lid. In the early seventeenth century the Saracen's Head at Dunmow, Essex, was kept by a family named Deane, but unfortunately there is no record of a Deane whose given name began with T. One of my first acquisitions (*right*) is a half pint with simple early lines and early touch; unfortunately, the lid and thumbpiece are missing.

It bears a rose-and-crown house mark on the underside of the base, almost obscured because the base has been tapped up, no doubt to reduce its contents—for which mine host at ye Rose and Crown may have had a spell in the stocks or an uncomfortable time at the whipping post.

The baluster with ball thumbpiece appears in several forms, and an early North Country type in my collection (Fig. 9, *left*) has an "anti-wobble" flange under the lid (as have the late Scottish balusters). Hammerhead balusters are most desirable (*center* and *right*), and therefore popular with the fakers. Genuine heavy hammers are very, very scarce; the thin hammers are less worrying.

The range of measures with bud thumbpieces (Fig. 10) shows a most pleasing variety of detail. Though all were supposed to conform to the official standard, they vary, unaccountably, in capacity. A particularly rare type of ball thumbpiece (*front row, left*) seems to have been used for the smallest measure in the bud set, as genuine eighth-pint buds are even rarer.

Flat-lid tankards (Fig. 11) without wriggling are much harder to find than decorated ones, but of course they do not have the same appeal. That shown (*left*) has a very unusual chrysalis-inspired thumbpiece, and the ram's horn (*right*) is one of the few pieces extant made in the county of Norfolk, where I live. It may have been used as a measure, for it bears the mark of proving in Queen Anne's reign. Lidless tankards are scarcer still; a magnificent specimen is shown in Figure 12.

21

Fig. 8. Wedge baluster measures. *Left to right*: Pint, c. 1600; height 5¾ inches; marks, 1 (?) and Saracen's-head house mark. Pint, with initials *B/WM*, c. 1640; 7¾ inches; mark, DB (*cf*. O.P. 498B, 5416); the house mark, a bull, appears inside the base. Half pint (lost lid), sixteenth century; 4½ inches; mark, FE, and rose-and-crown house mark underneath the tapped-up base.

Fig. 9. Baluster measures. Pint ball, c. 1640; height 5¾ inches; mark illegible; North Country. Half-pint hammerhead, c. 1700; 4⅝ inches; mark, RP(?) with anchor. Pint hammerhead, c. 1690; 5⅝ inches; mark illegible.

Fig. 10. Baluster measures in various body styles, c. 1690-c. 1750. Quart, pint, two half pints, gill, half gill, all with bud thumbpieces. The smallest (*left, front*) has a ball thumbpiece; by A. Hincham; stamped *AR* crowned, to show that the capacity was proved in Queen Anne's reign.

Fig. 11. Flat-lid tankards. *Left to right*: Chrysalis thumbpiece, c. 1685; height 4⅝ inches to lip; mark, a male head in profile. Twin cusp, probably c. 1695; 6⅞ inches; no mark. Ram's horn, c. 1690; 5¼ inches; by Henry Seagood, King's Lynn; O.P. 4169; this piece bears also a check for capacity. *AR* crowned.

Church flagons present a sequence of swiftly changing styles (Figs. 13, 14, 15). In 1605 the churches were poor and most of their larger silver had probably been appropriated. At last they were officially allowed to use pewter for flagons, and then followed a stately series with few regional peculiarities. One individual expression is the example (Fig. 13, *second from left*) with cast decoration on thumbpiece and handle. Another (Fig. 13, *right*) is one of a pair by John Emes; about eight specimens by that maker are known, all with different thumbpiece designs. The so-called York acorn (Fig. 14, *right*) is a distinctive North Country type, and the straight-sided "York" flagon beside it, though perhaps made in York, appears to me to be more truly Lancastrian.

Do not always believe dates on pewter pieces. Although their presence, for no valid reason that I can see, enhances the price, they can mean many things—"I was put on last year," for instance. The flat-lid flagon shown in Figure 15 is inscribed *AD/1588*, which is obviously anachronistic; perhaps it marks the centenary of some episode, or it may be the date of donation of a flagon this one replaced. Another (*right*), the small spire top, bears its original inscription, truly dated *1719*, and at the top a much later but equally honest one dated *1833*.

The pieces shown here are only some of the more interesting specimens from a collection that has given me many years of fruitful quest—and is still growing.

Fig. 12. Lidless tavern pot, c. 1690; height 6⅝ inches; by James Donne; O.P. 1415A. The inscription reads *John French, at the Rose and Crown in . . . Streete, Sohofeilds*. The initials *F/IE* appear on the handle.

Fig. 13. Seventeenth-century flagons. *Left to right*: c. 1610; height 8 inches to lip; no mark. Transitional flagon with cast decoration on front and back of thumbpiece and handle terminal, c. 1625; 9¾ inches; mark, RI. "Muffin" flagon, c. 1640; 9¾ inches; mark, CB. "Beefeater" flagon, c. 1670; 8⅝ inches; by Thomas Lupton. Flagon by J. Emes, one of a pair; c. 1690; 7¾ inches; O.P. 3092; Emes alone made this type.

Fig. 14. York flagons. *Left*: Straight sided, c. 1740; height 9¾ inches to lip; mark, IW. *Right:* Acorn, c. 1750; 9½ inches; mark, IH (?) for John Hardman or John Harrison; O.P. 2136 or 2162.

Fig. 15. Flagons with misleading dates. *Left*: Predated flat-lid flagon, c. 1688; height 6¾ inches; mark, IF; inscribed *AD/1588*, probably for some kind of anniversary. *Right*: Post-dated spire-top flagon, c. 1719; 7⅝ inches; mark illegible; inscribed both *1719* and *1833* with the names of churchwardens at both times.

SOME BRITISH PEWTER

By A. SUTHERLAND-GRAEME, F. S. A., A. R. I. B. A.

FIG. 1 — CHARGER, 20¼ inches in diameter, with the wide rim indicative of its seventeenth-century period. The royal arms decorate the well, while the rim is ornamented with a conventional design of roses and thistles between four roundels, those at the sides depicting King Charles II and Queen Catherine and the others the phoenix arising from flames—emblem of the Restoration—and the stork and bambino, expressing, it may be, hopes for the future! Round the booge runs the inscription *Vivat Rex Carolus Secundus. Beati Pacifici, 1662.* There is little doubt that the decoration is commemorative of the marriage of the king, which took place in May 1662. The words *Beati Pacifici* are from the Latin version of the Sermon on the Mount in St. Matthew's Gospel, "Blessed are the peacemakers," an allusion to the probable effect upon Europe of the marriage of the British monarch to a Portuguese princess. There are some eight or ten of these chargers in existence (not counting certain fairly obvious "fakes"), and they appear to have been made only in pewter. The maker of this fine example was probably William Pettiver, who became a master-pewterer in 1655, a date which appears in the touch (another touch used, it is believed, by the same pewterer was dated [16]79); he rose to be upper warden of the Worshipful Company of Pewterers; and died in 1680.

FIG. 2 — COMMUNION FLAGON made for the Church of Dinington. It stands 10¾ inches high, and is inscribed *Dininton Parrish* in Roman capitals, with the first two n's reversed. Its date is about 1650, and it was made by R. B., probably a provincial pewterer. Beside it is a 12-inch PLATE of singularly fine proportion, made by E. E., probably about 1670; the shield of arms and the crest, with Stuart mantling, are those of Jenison.

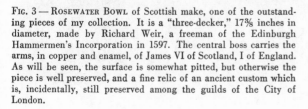

FIG. 3 — ROSEWATER BOWL of Scottish make, one of the outstanding pieces of my collection. It is a "three-decker," 17⅝ inches in diameter, made by Richard Weir, a freeman of the Edinburgh Hammermen's Incorporation in 1597. The central boss carries the arms, in copper and enamel, of James VI of Scotland, I of England. As will be seen, the surface is somewhat pitted, but otherwise the piece is well preserved, and a fine relic of an ancient custom which is, incidentally, still preserved among the guilds of the City of London.

FIG. 4 (*right*) — PART OF THE COMMUNION PLATE of the Associate Congregation of Norham. These congregations no longer exist; they were of Scottish origin, although Norham is actually over the English border. The large FLAGON, to which a latter-day spout has been clumsily added, stands 11 inches high and was made by Archibald Inglis, who obtained his freedom in the Hammermen's Incorporation of Edinburgh in 1732. The wide-bowled CUPS, though unmarked, are doubtless also his work. All three pieces are inscribed *Belonging to the Associate Congregation of Norham. Mr. Jas. Morison Minister 1762.*

IN WRITING of early British pewter—the word "early" usually signifying the seventeenth century—the difficulty is not what to say, but what to omit. There is, in most cases, so much of history, both civil and ecclesiastical, and of usage, bound up with these pieces, that a complete article could be written around most of them—as has, in fact, been done in the case of Figure 1. So in this brief article my subject is not British pewter in general, but a few treasures from my collection in particular, and I shall describe as fully as space permits some pieces of more than usual interest which are illustrated here.

FIG. 6—A MIXED GROUP. On the flanks are two COMMUNION CUPS from the north of Ireland; they are 8½ inches high and unmarked; period, c. 1720. The PLATES are good examples of the late seventeenth-century triple-reeded type; that to the left, 8½ inches in diameter, was made by Thomas Smith, "free" in 1675 and still working in 1703. A rare feature is the complete "hammering" of the surface, an operation intended to strengthen the metal. The other plate is by W. B. In both examples, owners' initials, struck triangle-wise, and the so-called "hall marks," can be seen. In the center of the group is a fine north-country COMMUNION FLAGON, 9½ inches in height, made by Edmund Harvey who was master of the Pewterers' Guild at Wigan in Lancashire in 1676. In front are two SALTS, that to the left being of about 1660, the other about 1680. Neither is marked.

FIG. 7 (below)—AT THE RIGHT is another fine Stuart TANKARD, rather smaller than that of Figure 5. Unfortunately, a large patch of corrosion (the only one) has rendered the touch completely indecipherable. Its height to lid is 4⅞ inches. Beside it is a narrow-rimmed plate bearing a conventional design in wriggle-work, depicting the dove of peace on a tree. These decorated plates are usually known as "marriage plates." It was the custom for young couples, intending to marry and set up house, to lay in a "garnish" of pewter dishes and plates, of which one or more was engraved as a personal gift from one to the other. The maker of this specimen, which is 7½ inches in diameter, was Richard Boyden, probably of Cambridge, whose touch is dated 1699.

FIG. 5 (above)—AT THE RIGHT is an especially fine TANKARD of the Stuart period with its characteristic flat lid, made by Jonathan Ingles (c. 1675). The body and lid are decorated with a wriggle-work motif of flowering shrub on which a bird is perched, and with tulips, to which the photograph scarcely does justice. The height to lid is 5½ inches. The well-proportioned handle is surmounted by a thumbpiece composed of love birds beneath an Ionic volute. Ingles was a member of the Pewterers' Company and was fined for false wares (of which this certainly is not one!) in 1673. He subsequently refused the offices of Steward (1678), Renter Warden (1693), and Upper Warden (1702). To the left is a CANDLESTICK of about the same date. The plate in the rear is one of a set whose maker was Jacques Taudin, descendant of a Huguenot family, as were so many English craftsmen of this period. He became a Liveryman of the Company in 1680 and rose to be its Renter Warden in 1700. In front is a TRENCHER SALT of about 1660.

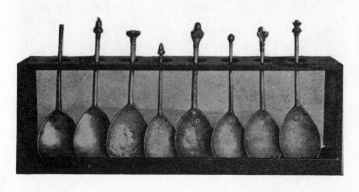

FIG 8 (left)—SOME EARLY PEWTER SPOONS. Left to right: 1. a stump-end, c. 1600; 2. an acorn-knop, c. 1500; 3. a seal-top, c. 1600; 4. a small acorn-knop, c. 1550; 5. a maidenhead, c. 1500; 6. a ball-knop, c. 1500; 7. the only example at present known of Chanticleer, the cock, c. 1550; 8. a baluster-knop, c. 1500. Average length, 6 inches. Nearly all these spoons bear recorded marks, but no records exist of the makers of such early pieces. Most of these spoons were dug up in London.

MORE

BRITISH

PEWTER

By A. SUTHERLAND-GRAEME, F.S.A., A.R.I.B.A

IN ANTIQUES for June 1946, Captain Sutherland-Graeme illustrated a choice group of pieces from his collection of early English pewter. Here he presents another group and discusses them in the following captions. — EDITOR

CONTINUING MY PREVIOUS ARTICLE, I commence with three pieces which will, I believe, be of special interest to American collectors: these are the FLAGON and pair of Two-HANDLED CUPS illustrated in FIGURE 1. These were all made by William Eden, or Eddon, some of whose tankards have, I understand, been found in the United States. All three pieces bear his touch familiar to British collectors, of the hour glass with his initials. Eden was a remarkable craftsman. He was born in Warwickshire and apprenticed to Peter Duffield in 1682. Seven years later he became a Freeman, and "opened shop" in 1690. He filled every office in the Pewterers' Company and was twice its Master, the last time in 1738. He worked in seven reigns from Charles II to George II, and all his work which has come down to us — a considerable amount — is sound, with a leaning toward the severe. The flagon, 8½ inches high, is of typical Scottish design, a circumstance which gives rise to conjectures, especially as some of his products are in Scottish churches despite the fact that very capable craftsmen were working in Scotland at this period. The cups stand 6⅜ inches high and are 4¼ inches in diameter at the lip. The fine broad-rim DISH, 15¼ inches in diameter, is by Robert Mollins who was working in the second half of the 1600's and was also twice Master of the Company (1676 and 1689).

UNLIKE THE OTHER PIECES illustrated, which are all in almost mint state, the remarkable little COMMUNION PATEN seen in FIGURE 2 is much corroded and has evidently been buried in damp soil for many years. It is nevertheless something of a gem, with its ultra-wide rim 2 1/3 inches across in a total diameter of just over 9 inches. These wide rims are, in British pewter, indicative of the mid-seventeenth century, and this piece, by reason of this and other early features, including the type of touch, cannot be much later than 1640. The photograph was taken in a bad light, but close inspection will reveal a finely engraved coat of arms, with widespreading mantling. I regard this as one of the outstanding pieces in the collection.

FIGURE 3 shows a very attractive little "baluster" MEASURE, 4½ inches to the lid, made by Thomas Stone, who was admitted to the livery in 1667, and while serving the office of Upper Warden in 1687, deposed by order of the King (James II). In 1690, however, after that monarch's departure, he was reinstated, and became Master in 1692. These essentially British measures were intended for service in taverns and inns, and were used, as their name implies, for gauging the correct amount of liquids required, and not for drinking purposes. They were in common use for at least three hundred years, from the time of Henry VIII onwards, and were produced in as many as seven capacities, from gallon to ½ gill. Their general shape did not vary much and the four types in which they were made are distinguished by the thumbpiece and lid attachment. The earliest is the "wedge" where these two features are combined; the next is the "hammerhead and bar"; the third the "bud and wedge"; and the fourth the "volute and fleur-de-lis." Certain variants of these types were made in Scotland, and a very few

hybrid types in England. The piece shown belongs to the "bud and wedge" type, and is especially interesting in having belonged to the Customs and Excise department. Around the drum runs the inscription *His Majesty's ware house at Woodbridge,* the word warehouse divided by the *G.R.* cipher of George I beneath an elaborate crown. On the lid is engraved the government sign of the broad arrow. Woodbridge is a charming old town on the river Deben in Suffolk, but all traces of "His Majesty's ware house" have long since disappeared, as, apparently, have the other members of the complete set of measures which must once have existed. It is probable that they were brought into official use some years after their manufacture, as George I's reign did not commence till twenty-two years after Stone was Master.

IN FIGURE 4 appears a CANDLESTICK with octagonal foot, drip shield and nozzle, and fluted pillar (*c. 1675*). Its height is 7⅝ inches; base dimensions, 5¼ inches across the main sides, 5 7/12 inches across the corners. The touch can just be discerned on the top: a fleur-de-lis between two initials, the second of which is B.

FIGURE 5 shows another group, in which are TWO COMMUNION FLAGONS, a broad-rim DISH, and a CANDLESTICK displayed upon a fine old mid-sixteenth-century chest to which age and care have imparted a rich patina. The candlestick is similar in type to that of Figure 4, but differs in minor details, the most noticeable of which is the increased breadth of the lower portion. The touch is beneath the foot and has, for that reason, been so worn as to be largely indecipherable. The broad-rim dish behind it is by W. G., a maker at present unknown (*c. 1675*). The diameter is 18¼ inches. Of interest is the crude shield and equally crude Stuart mantling, evidently carried out by an ignorant amateur, since no armorials appear in the shield but only the owner's initials *R/IH,* the husband's Christian initial to the left, the wife's to the right, and that of the surname above, as always in these triangular sets. The flagon to the left is a sturdy example of the skirt-based type of about 1660, and is 9¾ inches high and 6¾ inches across the base. It is by William Pettiver, free in 1655, died in 1680 while Upper Warden of the Company. The other flagon is of Queen Anne period (*c. 1710*), by John Newham (*1699-1731*); in the latter year he, too, was Upper Warden. Extreme height, 12⅛ inches.

FIGURE 6 shows a COMMUNION FLAGON (*c. 1635*) made by E.G., who is almost certainly Edward Gilbert, first mentioned in 1633 as having refused the office of Steward of the Company. That fact would indicate that he was in business several years earlier, though, apparently, no records remain of this part of his career. He became Master in 1662. The flagon, 10¼ inches high to the top of the finial, is of a type of which many examples have been preserved in ancient churches up and down the land, and which always seem to me to reach the high-water mark of the English craft as regards both design and construction.

THE BEAUTIFUL BOWL shown in FIGURE 7 was made about 1670 by C. T., probably the first Charles Tough (*1667-1680*). There is little doubt that this piece (which has a twin in another collection) was copied from a Continental example, of which several exist; for the handles, griffin-headed, with female torsos, are very rarely seen in England, though the wriggle-work engraving is typically English. 4 inches high to the lip, 5⅜ inches in diameter at that point.

FIGURE 1

FIGURE 2

FIGURE 3

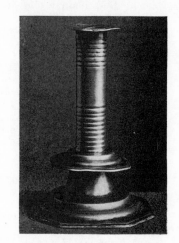

FIGURE 4

FIGURE 5

FIGURE 6

FIGURE 7

THISTLE-SHAPED MEASURES. A rare form and one peculiar to Scotland. *From the collection of the author.*

SOME SCOTTISH PEWTER MEASURES

By LEWIS CLAPPERTON

SCOTTISH PEWTER is much less plentiful than English and, though similar to it in many respects, has an individuality and character of its own. In general, too, it is of high quality in both material and workmanship. Some of its distinctive shapes are found in the vessels made for use as standard measures. These are of various shapes, and are today eagerly sought by collectors of pewter. The types have been classified in collectors' terms according to the shape of the body and also, in the case of covered measures, according to the shape of the thumbpiece — the little projection above the handle that one presses with the thumb in order to raise the lid. The numerous shape and thumbpiece types are illustrated in Howard Herschel Cotterell's *Old Pewter, Its Makers and Marks* (1929), in L. Ingleby Wood's *Scottish Pewterware and Pewterers* (1904), and in Cotterell's *National Types of Old Pewter* (ANTIQUES, April, July, and September 1923). More recently examples in baluster and pear shapes, bearing so-called "embryo-shell" and "double-volute" thumbpieces, were illustrated in ANTIQUES for August 1947 (p. 99).

These latter forms are not peculiar to Scotland and are more common in English pewter. From England they were introduced to America. British measures in these shapes are quite comparable to the so-called barrel-shape and tulip-shape mugs and tankards made by Americans.

Except in the smaller sizes, many of the Scottish measures were used as drinking vessels as well as for measuring and pouring. This was also the case in other countries, particularly in America where apparently the use of standard measures was not enforced even as strictly as in Scotland. According to Ledlie I. Laughlin (*Pewter in America*), sets of liquid measures were made in America in the eighteenth century but no marked examples made before 1820 survive, and even nineteenth-century measures are extremely rare.

Perhaps the rarest, though not the earliest, form of pewter measure peculiar to Scotland is the thistle shape. Individual examples are far from common, and a complete set is rare indeed. Hence the seven examples, in graduated sizes, which are here illustrated are of special interest. They are discussed by their owner, a Scotsman himself and past president of the Society of Pewter Collectors. He also elucidates the relation of the Scots scale of measures to the English, and the regulations governing both. Anyone who wishes to translate the Scots and imperial scale into American terms is welcome to do his own figuring. The Scots pint is equivalent to 3 pints imperial, and to 3.6 pints United States scale. And each of these measures 1.71 liters by the metric scale.

— THE EDITOR

SINCE VERY EARLY in the seventeenth century the citizens of the principal cities and towns in Scotland have appointed an official called the Dean of Guild who, during his period of office, has a seat in the Town Council and has important duties to perform. Among these, until 1835, was examination of the weights and measures in use in his district: those found to be in accordance with the standard measures, he marked, sometimes with his own initials, sometimes with the town's stamp; those that were found to be incorrect he destroyed. The standard measures were established by law and in early days those of Scotland differed in capacity from the English. In 1707, the date of the union of the crowns, the Scots scale was discontinued by the Act of Union, and the English scale was applicable to the whole country. This at least was the legal ruling, but in practice the Scots scale persisted in use in Scotland for over a century longer.

The relation between the two scales was: 1 gill Scots = ¾ gill English; 2 gills Scots (½ pint Scots) = 1½ gills English.

In 1826 an act was passed requiring retailers to conform to the English standard, but this was weakened by permission to continue to use old measures provided they were painted or otherwise marked to show the proportion they bore to the English scale. So this also proved ineffective, and in 1835 a new act was passed, aimed at attaining uniformity of weights and measures throughout the United Kingdom. By this act the Dean of Guild was relieved of his duty of supervision, and inspectors were appointed by the authorities for the purpose of testing weights and measures and stamping them with a crown and the sovereign's initials. However, my fellow countrymen are always averse to change in their customs, and not until the passing of still another law, the Weights and Measures Act of 1878, did the old scale finally disappear. Within living memory in Glasgow, for instance, both the "wee gill" and the "big gill" have been known (the Scots gill equals ¾ of the imperial gill). And even the 1878 ruling, though it definitely stated that the use of local or customary measures was illegal, left some ambiguity in its framing, and to-day by court ruling the imperial measure in the sale of spirits is compulsory only when it is explicitly asked for.

Thistle-shaped measures are peculiar to Scotland, especially to Glasgow and the west; they are found somewhat less in Dundee. They date from the early nineteenth century, and so far as I know no earlier examples are on record. Though measures of this type were made after the act of 1707 presumably abolished the Scots scale, their capacity is usually according to that rather than the English scale. Of the thistle-shaped measures illustrated, starting with the smallest, the first five measure respec-

BALUSTER-SHAPED MEASURE. The actual source of this item is not known; it may well be English rather than Scottish, but it represents a type made frequently in both countries in the eighteenth and early nineteenth centuries and also, with variations and much more rarely, in America.

TAPPIT HEN. The plain lid indicates that this is of the earliest type in this distinctively Scottish form.

tively ⅛ gill, ¼ gill, ½ gill, 1 gill, and ½ pint (2 gills) Scots. Each has its capacity stamped on it, along with a stamp showing that it has been inspected and found to be correct. The ½ pint has the touch mark of Moyes of Edinburgh who carried on business till about 1870; it must have been made when he was a young man. No. 6 is also stamped ½ pint but is larger than No. 5 by half a gill Scots. No. 7 is stamped 1 pint and holds twice as much as No. 6. Thus 1 to 5 are of the Scots scale and 6 and 7, English.

Apparently, when the imperial system was gradually replacing the old Scots system, some makers manufactured measures in the thistle shape according to the imperial scale, but probably these were very few in number. While the various acts enumerated attempted to regulate the capacity of measures, their shape was not restricted until the introduction of the Weights and Measures Regulations in 1907. These made it necessary for measures to empty when tilted to an angle of 120°. Thistle measures could not do this and so were regarded as "facilitating the perpetration of fraud." In the majority of cases, when submitted for verification, they were destroyed by inspectors, which probably accounts for the fact that they are almost impossible to find now. They were made both in brass and copper as well as in pewter.

Another and much better-known type of measure peculiar to Scotland is the tappit hen. This name is properly given to a particular shape only in the size of the Scots pint. Other sizes were made in this shape and they are correctly termed "tappit-hen shaped" measures. The earliest tappit hen I have heard of has a touch dated *1669*. Though *tappit* means crested or tufted, these measures were made in three styles: crested (with a spike or finial on the lid), uncrested (with a plain lid), and unlidded. The uncrested is the earliest, and the unlidded is peculiar to Aberdeenshire. The tappit hen, the mutchkin or half pint, and the chopin or quarter pint are the most frequently found but measures in this shape were also made down to the gill, all of the Scots scale. After the English scale became obligatory a few were made of the English scale but these are not often come by. In Cotterell's *Old Pewter* (plate 48) is illustrated the most complete set known, consisting of ten, of which five are of the English scale.

Another type of measure common in Scotland in the eighteenth century is that known as pot-bellied. They are also illustrated in *Old Pewter* (plate 48), both lidded and unlidded.

I have quoted freely from a statement from the Chief Inspector of the Glasgow district, to whom I am also much indebted for information about the various Acts and Regulations and a demonstration of how liquid measures are tested.

A Note on the Pewter of the Channel Islands

By HOWARD HERSCHEL COTTERELL, F. R. Hist. S.

AS the Channel Islands were attached politically to Great Britain yet by ties of language and geographical position had strong French sympathies, it will at once be surmised that the influences of both countries either worked together or vied with each other over a period of many centuries. What one may almost describe as this "dual allegiance" has found expres-

Fig. 144 — CHANNEL ISLANDS' MEASURES OF THE JERSEY TYPE

Fig. 146 — KNOWN ENGLISH MARKS FOUND ON CHANNEL ISLANDS' MEASURES

sion in the better known of the pewter vessels in use on the islands.

Of plates and the general run of articles, both English and French types were in use; but there are one or two types of measures which seem peculiar to the islands, and which therefore demand special comment here. It cannot be shown that their use extended either to the mainland of France or the British Isles. They have come to be known as the *Jersey* and *Guernsey* types, though instances are on record of both being used in either place. They are illustrated here in Figure 144 (Jersey) and Figure 145 (Guernsey).

The former type has been found in at least six sizes, and the latter in three; but, though I have no note of the smaller sizes in the Guernsey type, it would seem natural to think that such existed originally.

As will be seen, the chief differences between them lie in the more definite foot of the Guernsey type, the addition of bands to the body, and the more gradual tapering from the body to the lip, which, in the larger sizes of the Jersey type, is almost sudden.

The sizes noted of the set range from seven and one half to twenty-five centimeters. The unusual feature of these vessels, however, lies in the fact that, more often than not, this distinctly Continental type of Twin Acorn thumbpiece, with flat heart-shaped lid, is found in conjunction with the marks of known English pewterers, or the *G. R.* Crowned of British Government Inspectors.

No single instance of the use of this type of vessel in England has come to my notice, and yet they were not made in France, though purely French in all their characteristics! Are we then to class them as French or as English?

The answer would seem to be best given by placing them in a class apart, and regarding them — as indeed they are — as a link between the pewter of two great countries.

It would seem but natural to suppose that in the early days the islanders, with their French sympathies, bought their wares from the mainland of Normandy, probably from the pewterers of Caen; and that, in later years, a few enterprising London pewterers made a bid for the island trade, adapting their ideas and patterns to coincide with the local requirements of the people. Hence the impasse in which we find ourselves today — French characteristics with London marks.

The London makers whose marks have been found upon these types are: John de St. Croix, who used the well-known *I.D.S.X.* mark (*Fig. 146 a*), and who was at work from 1729 onwards; A. Carter, *c.* 1750 (*Fig. 146 b*); James Tisoe, 1733 to 1771 (*Fig. 146 c*); and Joseph Wingod, 1721 to 1776 (*Fig. 146 d*). The mark of John de St. Croix, on which his initials *I.D.S.X. appear* within a *divided* circle, is found only on the hinge pins of the lid.

In Figure 147 I give an illustration of three lids. Upon the two right-hand ones appears the mark of Carter and on the left-hand one, the mark of Wingod. In the place of *London,* one often finds the word *Guernsey* stamped on these lids, in a pointed ended label.

Attention must be drawn to the reversed *N* in the word London, both in my sketch and in Figure 147 (left). It is quite a common occurrence on Channel Island pewter, also on some specimens from English provincial towns.

Fig. 145 — CHANNEL ISLANDS' MEASURES OF THE GUERNSEY TYPE

Fig. 147 — LIDS FROM CHANNEL ISLANDS' MEASURES SHOWING ENGLISH MARKS

PEWTER PIECES

In an English Collection

with notes by the owner

ROLAND J. A. SHELLEY

Left, WINE EWER (*English, early nineteenth century*). Probably made by Thomas Alderson of London (*c. 1790–1825*). Height, 20 inches.

BEER JUGS (*English, c. 1790*). The rotund example on the right carries an inscription on the drum *Thomas Moon, Crown Inn, Gloster Road,* referring to a dockside district in Bristol.

Below, FLUTED DISH OR BOWL with plain rim (*English, c. 1720*). Illegible "hall marks" on back. Engraved reverse cipher *EC* on front. Such bowls are sometimes called strawberry bowls and are reputed to have come into fashion after Charles II developed a taste for strawberries while in France. Diameter, 12 inches.

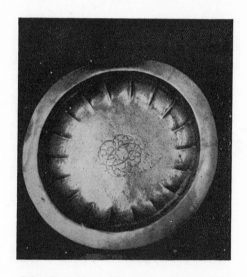

Below, PAIR of late Georgian candlesticks (*English, c. 1775–1820*). Representing one of the numerous baluster-stemmed forms of the period. Height, 8 inches. PLATE (*English, c. 1720*) by James Hitchman of London. Decorated with engraved "wrigglework." Diameter, 8 inches.

BROAD-RIMMED DISH (*English, c. 1657*). A fine example of an early type. The maker's mark with initials *RI,* date *1657,* and crown over crook appear on the London touch plate of the Pewterers' Guild, and is tentatively identified by Cotterell as that of Robert Jones. Other marks, on rim, are indecipherable. Diameter, 18 inches.

Below, PORRINGERS (*English, c. 1680–1720*). All bearing initials of unidentified makers. The two center items, it will be noted, are a pair. Both have crown handles and carry the intitial *D.* Matching examples of this kind are not often found in pewter.

HALF-PINT AND PINT LIDDED MEASURES (*c. 1750–1800*). Called "double-volute" type because of the shape of the thumbpiece. Believed to be Scottish on the basis of the squat shape of the body.

LIDDED MEASURES (*Scottish, early 1800's*). Called "embryo-shell" because of shape of thumbpiece. Quart size and one at far left by Robert Whyte of Edinburgh (*c. 1810*). *Extreme right*, by Adam Ramage, Edinburgh (*c. 1825*).

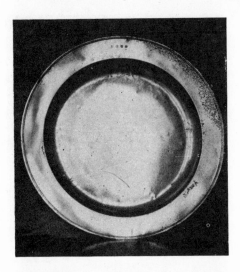

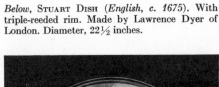

Below, STUART DISH (*English, c. 1675*). With triple-reeded rim. Made by Lawrence Dyer of London. Diameter, 22½ inches.

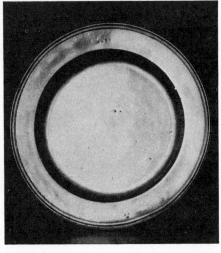

DISH (*English, c. 1690–1710*). Of reeded-edge type, slightly later in date than the example at right. By Richard Webb of London. This dish was lost by enemy action in the war. Diameter, 19 inches.

PINT MEASURE (*English, sixteenth century*). So-called "wedge" type. The excise mark of Henry VIII is struck on the top of the lid, and the "merchant's mark" on the lip. This measure is a very rare early piece.

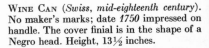

WINE CAN (*Swiss, mid-eighteenth century*). No maker's marks; date *1750* impressed on handle. The cover finial is in the shape of a Negro head. Height, 13½ inches.

Below, CHALICES AND CUP. *Far left and right,* Scottish, engraved *Laigh Kirk/Ayr. 1794. Inner left and right,* Irish, with cylindrical bowls (*c. 1780*). *Center left,* English, inscribed *A gift to the Church of Christ's meeting in Hog Lane, Woolwich, 1758. Center right,* English two-handled cup (*c. 1800*); height, 4¼ inches.

Fig. 1—Two-Handled Porringer (Type I)
This is the bowl to which the lid pictured on the Cover belongs. Diameter, 14 centimeters.

Some Pewter of England

Porringers with Busts of Sovereigns

By Adolphe Riff

Conservator of the Museums of Strasbourg, France

AMONG the pewterware produced by the different countries of Europe, there exists a group which, with good reason, is much sought after by collectors: this group consists of the porringers with decorated lid and handles, dating from the seventeenth and eighteenth centuries.

In France, where this style of receptacle was more particularly developed, the pewterers of Bordeaux, Lyons, Rouen, and Strasbourg produced fine specimens, decorated sometimes with medallions, sometimes with Louis XIV or Louis XV ornamentation.* In Great Britain, also, similar pieces were produced, but they seem to be rather rare; at any rate we do not find any of them reproduced in Howard Herschel Cotterell's fine work, *National Types of Old Pewter*.

In the course of our studies on pewterware in France,† we came across an analogous English bowl as an example for comparison, and since the Editor of Antiques was so kind as to bring to our attention three similar pieces,

we are today in a position to introduce to collectors a little group with decorations in relief, which deserves attention for the quality of its execution. Most of the known items in this group are illustrated here. Reference to two additional porringers is made for the sake of completeness.

For the better comprehension of our brief study, we shall first give a summary description of the characteristics of each porringer type considered.

Type I. (*Cover illustration*) A porringer lid: crowned busts on the right and left. In the centre four shields bearing the arms of England, Scotland, and Ireland, alternating with monograms.* Around these, within the space between two concentric circles, the inscription: *HONI:SOIT:QUI:MAL:Y:PENSE.* Above the whole, a crown held by two angels; beneath, the monogram *W. M. R.*† Three little handles, each in the form of two angels in relief holding a crown.

---

*Adolfe Riff. *Les Étains Strasbourgeois du 16e au 19e Siècle*, 1925.

†Adolphe Riff. *L'Orfèvrerie d'Étain en France* (French Pewter).
   I. *Les Écuelles à Bouillon* (Porringers) 1925.
   II. *Les Aiguières en Casque* (Helmet-shaped ewers) 1926.

---

*These shields are: top and bottom, the three lions passant, and the French fleur-de-lys (the latter added in 1340 in recognition of Edward III's claim to the crown of France) representing England; at the left, the lion rampant of Scotland; at the right, the harp of Ireland.

†The initials have been variously read; as *I. W. M. R.* and as *W. R. M. R.*

Fig. 2 — Two-Handled Porringer and Lid (Type II)
The monarchs represented are King William of England, Prince of Orange, and his wife, Queen Mary. The knob of the lid is in the form of a cock.

In the bottom of the bowl itself (*Fig. 1*): a circular medallion representing the bust of a personage in the wig and costume of the period; on his left the letter *W*, on his right the letter *R* (William Rex). Openwork handles, with beaded edges, representing two dolphins in relief facing each other. Underneath one handle a mark: a rose surmounted by a bishop's mitre and accompanied by the initials *H. S.* (*Collection of Adolphe Riff, Strasbourg.*)

Type Ia. A very similar bowl (Inv. No. 22521) at the Museum of Decorative Art at Dresden. The handle of the lid in the shape of a little cock; same mark.*

Type II. (*Fig. 2*) Lid: busts right and left in an oval. In the centre, a rose surmounted by a crown; beneath, the monogram *W. M. R.*† In the centre of the lid a small upright handle in the shape of a cock.

At the bottom of the bowl, a medallion showing the same busts as the lid; a small rose with foliage. Handles of irregular outline with openwork, but with a smooth surface. Mark: *I. W.* over a pair of scales. (Essex Institute, Salem, Massachusetts.)

Type III. (*Figs. 3, 4, and 5*) Lid (*Fig. 4*): busts to the left and right. In the centre, a rose; around, between two pearled circles, the inscription: *GOD: SAVE: P. GEORGE: AND: QUEEN: ANN.* The whole surmounted by a crown; beneath, the monogram *A. A.*‡ The upright handle, placed in the centre of the rose, is in the form of two little angels holding a crown.

At the bottom of the bowl (*Fig. 5*), a circular relief, a personnage in a flowing cloak, holding in the right hand an olive branch, in the left, a sheet of paper on which appears the following inscription in eight lines: *TO-EUROPE-PEACE-I-GIVE-LET-NATIONS-HAPPY-LIVE.* Above, a monogram giving the word *RYSWICK*.

Horizontal openwork handles in the form of two dolphins in relief. Mark: *A. W.* under a crown. (*Collection of Mrs. A. W. Thayer, Dedham, Massachusetts.*)

Type IV. (*Fig. 6*) Lid similar, but execution not quite so fine, especially the rose. The inscription reads: *GOD: SAVE: PRINC: GEORGE: AND QUEEN: ANN:* (*Collection of The Editor of* Antiques.)*

Type V. Similar bowl, but of clumsier execution, busts and rose, but without inscription. The rose surmounted by a crown. On the lid three small handles in the shape of cocks, which serve as legs when the inverted lid is used as a plate.

At the bottom of the bowl the same relief as that in bowl of type IV, and the same handles. (Reproduced in the magazine *The Connoisseur*, 1909, p. 121, with no indication as to whether the piece has a pewterer's mark.)

These porringers are intended to commemorate — their decoration leaves no doubt on the subject — the reigns of English sovereigns, notably that of Queen Anne and of King William III — whose rule was one of the most glorious for Great Britain.

The inscriptions of two bowls (types III and IV) mention, in fact, Queen Anne (*1702–1714*) and her husband, Prince George of Denmark; while the monograms *W-M* of two other bowls (types I and II) can only refer to William III (*1689–1702*) and to his wife Mary. Two of the bowls have at the bottom a medallion relative to the Peace of Ryswick (*1697*), the most important historical event of the reign of William III. One of the porringers (type V) bears neither inscription nor monogram, but, in its general character and by the medallion at the bottom of the bowl, it is related to the preceding models.

The bowls date, then, from the end of the seventeenth century and the beginning of the eighteenth. From the point of view of artistic execution, they are of unequal quality. Two of them stand out sharply from the others,

---

*Thanks are due to the director of the museum for this information.

†Two *R*'s, one of them reversed may occur here — for *William Rex: Mary Regina.*

‡These initials have also been read as *G. A.*, but really appear to be two *A*'s, one of them reversed, though the loops may form a *G*.

---

*Of this piece only the lid is preserved. It was found in Pennsylvania.

Fig. 3 — TWO-HANDLED PORRINGER (Type III)
Here the lid knob is in the form of two small angels supporting a crown. Width, including handles, 11 inches.

I.W. and H.S., which we have quoted, only the last has been identified by Mr. Howard Herschel Cotterell, the English pewter expert, as that of Henry Smith of London, who obtained his *freedom* in 1724.

Mr. Cotterell, to whom we address our sincere thanks for his kind information, expresses his astonishment that this pewterer should manufacture a bowl with the bust of William III, instead of showing the bust of the reigning sovereign. Sharing his surprise, without being able to explain the fact for the moment, we can do no more than mention that the pewterers were traditionalists, and that they often used, for a long time, the molds of their predecessors. There exist numerous examples of this.

by a more careful decoration, a finer relief, a better general execution. These are: first, model I, with the busts of William and Mary; and, next, model III, with the busts of Prince George and Queen Anne. The other bowls, a little less fine, have the characteristics of copies inspired by the models already cited.

The manner in which the creator of the type succeeded in grouping all the

Fig. 4 — THE LID OF THE PORRINGER OF FIGURE 3
The busts represent Queen Anne and Prince George.

This fact would, perhaps, also explain why the medallion referring to the Peace of Ryswick is found on a porringer (type III) of Queen Anne; whereas this historical incident is connected with the reign of William III. It may, however, be, as is sometimes the case with French porringers, that the lid and the bowl may have been mixed up or replaced in the course of wear, without

ornamentation — the two busts, the crown, the rose, the foliage, the inscription, and the monogram — on a circular surface, denotes a very ingenious decorative sense. It will be noticed that this design type was preserved by the other pewterers, who only modified the details of its arrangement. In this manner, in spite of a certain unity of decoration, the bowls are different from one another, and our five pieces belong to five different types. Even types III and IV, which are fairly similar, possess differences: for instance, in the inscriptions *GOD SAVE* and *GOD SAUE*, *P. GEORGE* and *PRINC GEORGE*, and in the crossed branches under the busts.

The attribution of our porringers to the workshops of pewterers of the period raises serious difficulties, in spite of the numerous recent researches concerning the marks, which have much advanced our knowledge of the subject. Of the three marks, *A.W.*,

Fig. 5 — INTERIOR OF THE PORRINGER OF FIGURE 3

attention being paid to matching the decoration of the two parts.

We have already remarked that these bowls date from the end of the seventeenth century and the beginning of the eighteenth. They thus belong to a relatively limited period, and it is interesting to notice that it is also at this period that the best specimens of decorated porringers were manufactured in France, where, at that time, this style of porringer seems to have been particularly fashionable. Moreover, that moment in France was the apogee of pewterware, for the rapid rise of earthenware and porcelain during the eighteenth century was soon to bring about the decline of pewter. The same was doubtless the case in other countries of Europe. Our English porringers, however, are distinguished from similar French pieces, in which one finds another shape, and, from the point of view of decoration, neither the medallion at the bottom of the bowl nor the busts of sovereigns.

A more thorough study of this group of porringers with busts of sovereigns—naturally other specimens must exist—is called for. Such a study will doubtless permit still more precise conclusions and identifications. For the time being, we simply wish to call the attention of collectors to a few examples of pieces which are among the finest and most interesting specimens of pewterwork in Europe.

Fig. 6 — LID OF PORRINGER (Type IV) Here again the reign of Queen Anne is commemorated.

Note: These curious commemorative porringers, which have no other counterpart in English pewter, present something of a mystery. Aside from their un-English form, their touch-marks seem almost to defy identification. Edwards J. Gale of Boston, a careful student of pewter, thinks that the maker's initials *A. W.*, borne by the example of Type III illustrated, may be those of Abraham Wiggin, *yeoman* of the London Pewters Company in 1707. At the same time he suggests the possibility that this and similar porringers may have been made not in England but on the Continent—perhaps in Holland. Evidence in favor of this suggestion exists in the form of a much damaged remnant of a porringer—now in the office of ANTIQUES. It is here reproduced (*Fig. 7*). The pattern of the bowl of this piece displays a circular portrait medallion, of whose surrounding inscription only the following words are decipherable: *PRINSE VAN ORANIEN ENDE GRAEF VAN. . . .* Clearly this is a Continental specimen. Other reasons for attributing these porringers to some Continental workman might be advanced—the form of certain of the lid knobs, for example; but the subject is sufficiently complex to demand consideration by the experts of many countries. Now that M. Riff has offered so much material on the subject, the task of amplification should prove attractive.— The Editor.

Fig. 7 — BOWL OF PORRINGER WITH BUST OF WILLIAM OF ORANGE

Further Notes on Commemorative Porringers

By Howard Herschel Cotterell, F. R. Hist. S.

In October, 1927, Antiques published an article by Conservator Adolphe Riff of the Museums of Strasbourg, describing several commemorative pewter porringers, and pointing out certain peculiarities in their form and decoration. He likewise raised question as to the identity of the pewterers whose marks appear upon these pieces. An editorial note, further, suggested the possibility that since, in various essentials, these porringers exhibit obvious departures from English practice, they may possibly have originated on the Continent.

Thus the status of a number of interesting considerations relating to these porringers was left somewhat indeterminate. Now, however, Mr. Cotterell offers a wealth of further enlightenment, which enables us to identify the immediate authors of these porringers, their nationality, and the periods of their activity. It is regrettable that an important additional note on this subject from Mr. Cotterell has reached Antiques too late to supplement his original material. It will, however, be found in the Editor's Attic this month.

By way of brief summary of preceding discussions, it may be noted that M. Riff divided these commemorative porringers into four types: Type I, displaying a relief bust of King William in the bottom of the bowl, on the lid portrait medallions of William and Mary, four shields bearing the arms of Great Britain and Ireland, the cypher of William and Mary, and the motto *Honi Soit Qui Mal Y Pense*; Type II, displaying the heads of King William and Queen Mary in the bottom of the bowl, on the lid the portraits of the sovereigns with the cypher *W. M. R.*, and with the mark *I. W.* over a pair of scales; Type III, displaying a mythological figure in the bowl, on the lid the two portrait busts, the cypher and the inscription *God Save P. George and Queen Ann*; Type IV, lid only, without handle, and with the inscription *God Save Princ George and Queen Ann.*

PEWTER enthusiasts the world over will be grateful to Conservator Adolphe Riff for his brave plunge into the complex subject of commemorative porringers*; but he has so established himself as *the écuelle à bouillon* specialist that no one was more likely to take the plunge or so calculated to do it in a masterly way, allowing no conjecture to interfere with establishable fact, a feature which guides all his writings and makes them, therefore, so reliable.

Had I known of M. Riff's intention to write upon this subject I could not only have supplied him with further examples and notes, but also have cleared up the mystery of the mark *I. W.* with scales, which appears on the Essex Institute example, illustrated in M. Riff's article.

I will, therefore, begin these notes with an illustration (*Fig. 1*) of this mark, that of John Waite of London,

*See Antiques, Vol. XII, p. 294.

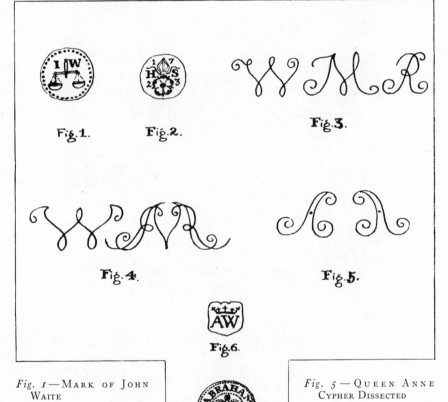

Fig. 1—Mark of John Waite

Fig. 2—Mark of Henry Smith

Fig. 3—William and Mary Cypher Dissected

Fig. 4—William and Mary Cypher

Fig. 5—Queen Anne Cypher Dissected

Fig. 6—Mark on M. Riff's "Type III" Porringer

Fig. 6a—Mark of Abraham Wiggin

which he was given leave to strike on the London touchplate in 1673–4. This gives us the date of 1673–4, *or later*, for the porringer considered under "Type II" of M. Riff's notes and for all other pieces on which this mark appears; for it must be remembered that a touch, once struck upon the touchplates, had to be used throughout a pewterer's career, unless express permission for varying it was given.

In Figure 2 I give an illustration of the mark of Henry Smith, which appears on the porringer considered under M. Riff's "Type I." Henry Smith was made a free pewterer of London in 1724, but was not given leave to strike this touch until March 23, 1726, which gives us the date of 1726, *or later*, for all pieces on which this mark appears.

Now where have we arrived? Well, in the first place, an interval of at least fifty-two years between the striking of the two touches. This leads us to the very natural

tual date of Type III, enough, I trust, has been said to allow this sequence of the types to pass without further question.

We now come to the correct interpretation of the script monograms or cyphers on these pieces. Mr. Riff has interpreted them without fear and without error.

Possibly the simplest way to settle the matter is to resolve these cyphers into their respective letters, which I have done roughly in Figures 3, 4, and 5. If these be traced on tissue paper and set superimposed, one upon the other, they will, when held against the light, display roughly the monograms illustrated on the pieces shown in M. Riff's article.

My Figure 3 shows the cypher which appears on his Types I and Ia; Figure 4, on Type II; and Figure 5, on Types III and IV. The *MR* of my Figure 4 is done in cypher, and, if folded down the centre, it will be found — after making allowances for my faulty penmanship—that the two sides roughly correspond.

There remains for me only to illustrate two further examples of this type of porringer from the fine collec-

conclusion that, in all probability, John Waite was gathered to his fathers before Henry Smith had leave to strike his touch. Thus Type II becomes, beyond any doubt, the earliest of the series. Having thus placed M. Riff's Types I and II in point of age, where does his Type III come in?

The mark on this piece, which I illustrate in Figure 6, tells us nothing. It may possibly be a mark of Abraham Wiggin. If so, it certainly bears no trace of resemblance to the mark which he struck upon the touchplate, and which I illustrate in Figure 6a. It may quite equally well be the mark of Allen Walley or Anthony Warford of London, Arthur Wharton of York, or of half a dozen others, all of about the same period as Wiggin.

But what have we to lead us to some definite conclusions concerning this type? First, the cypher of Queen Anne, the very appearance of which proves the type to be not earlier than 1702. That is one point established; and now comes conjecture: The Peace of Ryswick, which the porringer commemorates, would seem to suggest a still unforgotten gratitude for a recent blessing. One would, therefore, think that it would be placed during the reign of Queen Anne, and probably not long after her accession, let us say 1703 or 1704. We then get our porringers in the chronological order of Type II, Type III, and Type I. Though there may be doubt as to the *ac-*

40

Figs. 8, 8a, 8b — THREE VIEWS OF PORRINGER
   Showing resemblance to those of M. Riff's "Type II,"
   but with a spool-shaped knop replacing the cock
   handle of the Essex Institute example.
   Owned by Alfred B. Yeates.

tion of Alfred B. Yeates, F. S. A., F. R. I. B. A., of London. Figures 7, 7a, and 7b show the porringer, its cover, and the inside respectively. This piece, in many respects, resembles that of M. Riff's Type I; but it also materially differs. First, the Arms of Scotland and Ireland on the lid have, for some reason, changed sides. Second, the three cocks on the cover have been supplanted by three quite delightful *lions sejants*. Other details of the cover offer slight differences. On the inside of the porringer, the monarch's head carries a distinct crown, only part of which appears in M. Riff's example, in which, further, the actual bust of the sovereign occupies more of the field, possibly because the size of the latter is some half inch less than that of Mr. Yeates' example. Finally, the handles have a decidedly more English flavor. The dimensions of this piece are: diameter of bowl, six inches; height of bowl alone, two and one-quarter inches, and with the cover, exclusive of the feet, two and three-quarters inches.

The mark on this piece is very indistinct, the letter

S alone being readable. But it is quite possible that it is the same mark as that on M. Riff's example, in which case Henry Smith must have possessed two molds for the lid, a point worthy of note when one considers the high cost of such molds.

Figures 8, 8a, and 8b show a further example of Type II bearing the mark of John Waite — *I. W.*, with scales (*Fig. 1*). It will be noted that the cover handle which, on the Essex Institute example, is a cock, in this one has been converted into a capstan or spool-shaped knop. In other details the two pieces would seem to be pretty generally alike, and they are probably from the same mold.

The dimensions of Mr. Yeates' piece are: diameter of bowl, six inches; height of bowl alone, two and three-eighths inches, and with cover, exclusive of the feet, three inches. No dimensions of the Essex Institute example are given.

The question of English origin would thus seem to be established beyond peradventure, for, of the few examples before us, we have two by John Waite, two (and possibly three) by Henry Smith. Types IV and V give no marks, and the only one in doubt, therefore, is the *IW* mark on Mrs. Thayer's fine piece. I do not think the question of the English origin of these porringers need keep us awake o' nights.

BY RONALD F. MICHAELIS

Royal portraits and pewter porringers

IT IS NOW ALMOST EXACTLY THIRTY YEARS since the subject of commemorative pewter porringers was first featured in ANTIQUES and, strange to relate, very little has emerged since to shed further light on the origin or purpose of these purely ornamental objects. We have, perhaps, a little more information on the men who made them, and a few more specimens have been traced as a result of a series of articles published in this magazine in the 1920's and thirties. The first of these, by Adolphe Riff, then conservator of the Museums of Strasbourg, appeared in October 1927; others, by Howard H. Cotterell, A. J. Pennypacker, and Harrold E. Gillingham, were published in July 1928, October 1939, and November 1940; Percy E. Raymond discussed individual examples in the Pewter Collectors' Club *Bulletin* for July 1945 and June 1950; and readers who wish to follow the printed history of the form through from the beginning can do no better than refer to these.

In his original article Riff listed and described all the specimens known to him at that time, and he expressed the opinion that, in France, in the late seventeenth and early eighteenth centuries, decorated porringers were particularly fashionable; but he also pointed out that the English porringers of the time differed in shape from the French, and that, in the latter, busts of sovereigns were not known to have appeared.

Certain makers' marks found on the specimens illustrated by Riff were later identified by Howard H. Cotterell (in July 1928) as those of known London pewterers. Cotterell illustrated two further specimens, both undoubtedly English, together with their covers; these pieces were then in the collection of A. B. Yeates, a noted collector of the day, who bequeathed them to the Victoria and Albert Museum in London.

Cotterell was fully satisfied that the type of commemorative porringer now under survey was, in fact, truly English. He pointed out, however, that two very similar, but Continental, porringers, each with two ears but without center medallion in the well and without separate cover, had been brought to his notice by Robert M. Vetter; and details and photographs of these appeared, with editorial comment, in the same issue as his article referred to above. The two Continental examples had ears of the type seen here in my William III porringer, but were marked with the maker's touch of a rose and crown with initials I.H.K. (or T.H.K.) *within the crown* (a Continental feature).

The appearance of these two specimens at this time caused the editor of ANTIQUES to comment ". . . what can these two Dutch porringers . . . mean, except that our presumably English commemorative porringers are essentially Dutch in type? Cast in England, they probably were; dignified with an English touchmark, they undoubtedly were. But whence came the molds?"

English pewterers had long favored cast ornamentation as a means of decorating pewterware, and it is only the rarity of surviving specimens which has led collectors to believe that the practice was uncommon. Finely carved relief decoration was a feature of much

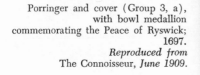

Porringer bowl (Group 2, c) with medallion portrait of William III; c. 1694-1702. *Author's collection.*

Porringer and cover (Group 3, a), with bowl medallion commemorating the Peace of Ryswick; 1697. *Reproduced from* The Connoisseur, *June 1909.*

Details of bowl medallion	Details of cover design	Ear types	Maker's marks	Sizes	Ownership, location, and comments
GROUP 1. 1688/89-1702.					
1(a). Small oval medallions at left and right of center boss, portraying William III and Mary, each facing inwards; Tudor rose in center.	Oval medallion of William III at left; Mary at right; crown above, and monogram *W.M.R.* at foot. Tudor rose in center. Single knob, a cockerel, in center.	1	*I.W.* over a pair of scales. John Waite, London (Cotterell No. 4903a).	Bowl diam. 6″	Essex Institute, Salem, Mass., U.S.A. (Known as the Herrick Porringer.) Illustrated ANTIQUES, October 1927. Written up by P. E. Raymond, in the Pewter Collectors' Club *Bulletin*, No. 14, October 1944.
1(b). Similar to 1(a).	Similar to 1(a). Single knob, spool-shape, in center.	1	*I.W.* and scales. John Waite, above.	Bowl diam. 6″ Bowl depth. 2⅜″	Yeates bequest, Victoria & Albert Museum. Illustrated ANTIQUES, July 1928 and Cotterell's *Old Pewter*, 1929.
1(c). Similar to 1(a).	Similar to 1(a). Single knob, a cockerel, in center.	1	No marks, but probably also by John Waite, above.	No details.	Originally in possession of Harrold family of Pennsylvania. Illustrated ANTIQUES, October 1939.
1(d). Similar to 1(a), but detail shows that a different mold was used for the medallion casting.	Similar to 1(a), but detail shows variations, particularly in the cross-hatching beneath the crown at top. Single knob, a cockerel, in center.	1	*I.W.* and scales. John Waite, above.	Bowl diam. 5¼″ Bowl depth. 1⅞″ Over-all d. 10¼″	Ledlie I. Laughlin. Illustrated herewith.
GROUP 2. 1688/89-1702, but probably 1694-1702.					
2(a). Head and shoulder full-face portrait of William III, crown over his head; crowned *W* at left shoulder; orb over *R* at right.	Small oval medallions, at left of Mary, and at right, of William III. Two angels with crown at top; monogram *W.M.R.* at foot. In the center shields displaying the arms of England, Scotland, Ireland, and France, with encircling band reading: *HONI SOIT QUI MAL Y PENSE*. Three knobs of two angels holding aloft a crown, spaced equally.	2	Bishop's miter, rose and H.S. Henry Smith, London, c. 1727 (Doubtful.)	No details.	Originally in collection of Adolphe Riff, Strasbourg. Illustrated ANTIQUES, October 1927. The porringer is shown in the text, pp. 294/5, and the cover on the magazine cover.
2(b). Similar to 2(a).	No details, but Riff says (ANTIQUES, Oct. 1927) that it (presumably bowl and cover) is very similar to his own porringer above. Single knob, a cockerel, in center.	2?	Stated to be same as above.	No details.	Originally in Museum of Decorative Art at Dresden, Germany (in 1927), but this museum was unable to trace it in 1955.
2(c). Similar to 2(a).	Cover missing.	1	Samuel Lawrence, London and Lynn. (See text.)	Bowl diam. 5⅜″ Bowl depth. 1¾″ Over-all d. 10¼″	Ronald F. Michaelis, London, England. Illustrated herewith.
2(d). Similar to 2(a).	Ovals of Queen Anne and Prince George (named in oval); Anne at left, George at right; at top a horse-mounted figure of Earl of Athlone (Frederick Christian Ginkel, 2nd Earl); at foot of cover a half-length portrait of Prince Eugene. Three knobs, cockerels, spaced equally. (Cover obviously not contemporary with bowl.)	1	Samuel Lawrence (as above).	No details.	Originally owned by Samuel Brown, of Pennsylvania (ownership initials *S.B.* on handle). Illustrated in ANTIQUES, October 1939.
2(e). Similar to 2(a), but detail shows that a different mold was used for the medallion casting.	Similar to 2(a), but detail shows variations, particularly in the reversal of the shields of Scotland and Ireland. Three knobs, of *lions sejant*, spaced equally.	4	Samuel Lawrence (as above).	Bowl diam. 6″ Bowl depth. 2¼″	Yeates bequest, Victoria & Albert Museum, London. Originally illustrated in ANTIQUES, July 1928, and later in Cotterell's *Old Pewter*, 1929.
GROUP 3. TREATY OF RYSWICK, 1697.					
3(a). Standing figure of John Churchill (later Duke of Marlborough), holding in his hand a scroll, reading: *TO EUROPE PEACE I GIVE, LET NATIONS HAPPY LIVE.* In other hand a flail, the seven tails of which spell the word *RYS-WICK*.	Full-face portraits, of William III, at left, and Mary at right; crown at top; orb at foot. As cover depicts William and Mary, at a time when Mary was dead, this may indicate that cover is not contemporary with the bowl. Three knobs, cockerels, spaced equally.	2	No details.	No details.	No details. Illustrated in *Connoisseur*, London, in June 1909, and herewith.
3(b). Similar to 3(a); it is, however, difficult to be certain, as the published photograph (ANTIQUES, Oct. 1927) appears to have been retouched.	Portrait ovals of Queen Anne at left, and Prince George at right; crown at top; *A.R.* at foot. Encircling band of wording in center, reading: *GOD SAVE P. GEORGE AND QUEEN ANN.* Single knob, two angels holding aloft a crown, in center. (This cover is, obviously, not contemporary with bowl.)	2	*A.W.* under a crown, possibly Abraham Wiggin, London. c. 1707, but, if so, it is out of period.	No details.	Mrs. A. W. Thayer, Dedham, Mass. U.S.A. (Known as the "Richards-Thayer" Porringer.) Illustrated ANTIQUES, October 1927. Written up by P. E. Raymond, in the *Bulletin* of the Pewter Collectors' Club, No. 16, July 1945.
GROUP 4. QUEEN ANNE, 1702-1714.					
4(a). Portrait of Queen Anne, facing to left, in center; two angels holding aloft a crown, at top, and *A.R.* at foot.	Portrait ovals of Q. Anne at left, and Pr. George at right; crown at top; *A.R.* at foot. Encircling band of wording in center, reading: *GOD SAUE PRINC GEORGE AND QUEEN ANN.* Three knobs, two angels holding aloft a crown, spaced equally.	2	No marks.	No details.	A. J. Pennypacker, who acquired it from a Pennsylvania family. Illustrated in ANTIQUES, November 1940, p. 230.
4(b). Bowl missing.	Similar to cover of 4(a) with wording reading: *GOD SAUE PRINC GEORGE AND QUEEN ANN.* No knob on cover.	—	—	No details.	Originally owned by Homer Eaton Keyes. Illustrated ANTIQUES, October 1927, p. 297.
GROUP 5. DUKE OF MARLBOROUGH, 1702-d.1722.					
5(a). Head and shoulders of John Churchill, Duke of Marlborough, with tricorn hat, and wording below: *I. D. MARLBOROUGH.* John Churchill was made captain-general of the forces in 1702, and this porringer probably commemorates that event.	Cover with small bust of Queen Anne at top, the cartouche supported by two draped female figures, full length; at the foot the seated figure of Britannia, with scepter and shield, a lion at her feet. To right and left of the cover design, respectively, are the rose of England, and the thistle of Scotland. This combination of national emblems could indicate the Union of England and Scotland, ratified in 1707. Three knobs, which appear to represent doves, spaced equally.	3	No marks.	8 x 25 x 13.5 cms.	Rijksmuseum, Amsterdam. Illustrated herewith.

TYPE 1   TYPE 2   TYPE 3   TYPE 4

Ear types found on English commemorative porringers. Originally published with the author's series of articles on English pewter porringers which appeared in *Apollo* in July, August, September, and October 1949.

Elizabethan and early Stuart furniture, and the same motifs were repeated by potters when making molds for their clay vessels. Such ornamentation originally took the form of running grape-vine or floral banding, and very soon, if not contemporaneously, the pewterers saw the advantages of decorating their own products in a similar manner. In France and Germany men like Briot and Enderlein had displayed unexampled skill in mold cutting, and the English pewterers would not have been left long in the background. It was the pride of English pewterers that their metal was purer and finer than any produced overseas, and one may rest assured that they would not be outdone in other respects.

Some illustrations of examples of early relief casting may be seen in my recent book *Antique Pewter of the British Isles,* and it is precisely this craftsmanship which was revived toward the end of the seventeenth century —probably given a fillip by foreign pewterers who came over in the train of William of Orange and were absorbed into the trade in England. Not only porringers were decorated with cast relief royal portrait medallions, but also spoons, hitherto made in plain forms, were embellished with portrait busts of the reigning sovereigns. The first rulers to be honored in this way appear to have been William III and Mary, his queen. Queen Anne was also a popular figure for portrayal, but the practice seems to have died out with the termination of her reign in 1714.

Thus we have two classes of pewterware—porringers and spoons—both exhibiting unusual and (for that period) un-English features; it is more than probable, therefore, that Dutch influence was the cause. It is also probable that Dutch ear-molds were brought to England, or that molds were made to the Dutch pattern by Dutch craftsmen who had taken up residence in England.

Of the royal commemorative porringers known to exist, the seven which have any maker's mark at all have the touches of known English pewterers, and it must be assumed that the men whose touches appear on these pieces were, in fact, the actual makers and not merely

factors for disposing of pieces made overseas for the English market.

The Pewterers' Company was at this time, as always, very much averse to allowing the importation of foreign wares; nor would it permit foreign craftsmen who had come over as followers of the Dutch king to work in their own right in England. It is quite possible, however, that such men took service with English master pewterers; in that event they would have been required to strike their master's touch upon any wares made by them in his employment. Such wares, however, necessarily rank as the productions of the pewterers whose touches they bear.

For those who have not read the previous writings on the subject, and who cannot easily refer to them today, it may be as well to state that a distinctive feature of all examples in this range is the relief-cast medallion in the center of the porringer bowl, and (in those which still retain their covers) the incidence, on the cover, of still further intricate cast ornamentation bearing some relationship to the bowl design.

It is more than probable that, originally, each known

Porringer and cover (Group 1, d);
1688/9-1702.
Collection of Ledlie I. Laughlin.

specimen had a cover—a practice common on the Continent with the types of porringers, or *écuelles*, in daily use. The covers of French porringers, for instance, frequently had three ornamental appendages standing proud of the lid, and when the lid was reversed and placed upon the table these would act as feet to keep it off the wood, and the cover could be used as a stand for the porringer. The knobs or handles on the covers of most of our English commemorative types are placed so they can be used for this purpose; in only one or two instances is there only one such ornamental knob, placed in the center. These knobs are, themselves, of particular interest, for they vary in design, some being in the form of a cockerel, others of a *lion sejant*, and yet another depicting two cherubs holding aloft a crown, repeated three times—a device also prominently displayed in the bowl of at least one porringer and found at the top of several different castings of Queen Anne spoons.

Some porringers now have covers which seem to be anomalous, such as one bearing portrait busts of Queen Anne (1702-1714) and her husband, Prince George of Denmark (died 1708), upon a bowl which contains a medallion commemorating the Treaty of Ryswick. Since the Treaty of Ryswick was effected in 1697, it is obvious that neither Queen Anne nor her husband could have had much to do with it. It is impossible to illustrate this porringer at this time, as its present location is unknown, but it was shown in Riff's original article in October 1927. He suggested that the lid and bowl might have been "mixed up or replaced in the course of wear, without attention being paid to matching the decoration of the two parts"—a possibility made to seem even more likely by the history of the piece. Mrs. A. W. Thayer, a lady of English ancestry who then owned it, wrote to Professor Raymond: "When I was a child we had eight of these pewter basins. I well remember them being filled with cream—a fine sight. In moving I kept only one." If one considers that these eight porringers were possibly of different designs, commemorating different events, then it is quite conceivable (and, in fact, it seems almost certain) that the covers became interchanged.

The only other known specimen of a Ryswick porringer, in this case with a cover in keeping, is one shown here and illustrated in *The Connoisseur* for June 1909,

page 121. The name of the owner was not given, and the present editor informs me that it is not possible to say now to whom it belonged, as the records of that date have been destroyed. The bowl medallion shows a full-length figure of the Duke of Marlborough, bearing in his hand a banner with the words *To Europe peace I give, Let nations happy live:* a very definite allusion to the Treaty of Ryswick. There is further evidence in the seven tails of a flail carried in Marlborough's other hand, which terminate in a tangled mass of letters forming the name *Ryswick.* The cover shows good full-face portrait busts of William and Mary, the former almost exactly like that in the bowls of the porringers of Group 2. At the top of the design appears a crown, and at the foot an orb. The three knobs on the cover are in the form of cockerels.

To place these porringers in chronological sequence it would seem advisable to take the bowls only as a basis, ignoring (for this purpose) the covers, which may or may not have any definite connection. The covers are, in themselves, of very great interest, especially when associated with bowls of comparable date or related historical significance.

William of Orange, and Mary, daughter of the deposed King James II, were invited to accept the English throne in 1688/89; their joint rule lasted until 1694, when Mary died; thus, any porringer bowl (or cover) depicting both sovereigns probably relates to the period 1688/89-1694, and porringers portraying William III alone, in the center medallion, will almost certainly relate to the period from 1694 to 1702, when William himself died. The treaty of Ryswick automatically falls into position in 1697; thus we can dispose of the first three types in that order.

One porringer shown is of a type of which no other example is known; the bowl displays a bust of Queen Anne, with monogram initials *AR* at the foot, and cherubs holding a crown above her head. This latter device also appears in the knobs on the cover, which incorporates profile busts of Queen Anne and Prince George with a band of wording reading: GOD SAUE PRINC GEORGE AND QUEEN ANN. This piece is in the possession of A. J. Pennypacker, an American collector who acquired it from a Pennsylvania family in whose hands it had remained since its arrival in America.

Porringer and cover (Group 5, a) with medallion portrait of John Churchill, Duke of Marlborough; porringer handle of type discussed by P. E. Raymond in ANTIQUES for January 1948, *Unique Crown-handled Porringers C. 1702-1707. Rijksmuseum, Amsterdam.*

Royal portrait spoons depicting Queen Anne; two cherubs holding a crown above her head; c. 1762. *Author's collection.*

It can be dated in the period 1702-1708, but is most likely to have been made to commemorate the queen's accession in 1702.

Finally, by courtesy of the directors of the Rijksmuseum, Amsterdam, I am permitted to illustrate a superb example in the possession of that museum. The bowl of this porringer contains a good full-face portrait bust of John Churchill, Duke of Marlborough, with legend below I. D. MARLBOROUGH; and the cover displays, at the top, a profile bust of Queen Anne, facing to left; a cartouche supported by two full-length female figures; and at the foot a seated figure with a lion, shield, and scepter (or trident), encircled by the word BRITANNIA. At right and left of the cover, respectively, are representations of the rose of England and the thistle of Scotland. The combination of these emblems seems to indicate that the porringer was made sometime after the Union of England and Scotland, ratified by the Scottish Parliament in 1707. Since Anne is shown alone here, the inference may be drawn that the piece was made after 1708 when Prince George died. This latter date was a significant one for Marlborough, who provided for the defense against the Pretender to the English throne in that year; such an event would have been ample justification for his inclusion so prominently in the porringer bowl. The three upstanding devices on the cover appear to represent doves.

Space does not permit more than the brief mention of the covers given in the Schedule of all known specimens of English commemorative porringers on page 60 of this

writing, but it is necessary to say a further word about makers' marks.

Of our total of thirteen specimens only seven have marks which can be safely attributed to known pewterers. Three of the four in Group 1 are by John Waite, London, who became "free" in 1673; the other is unmarked.

Three of the five porringers in Group 2 are by Samuel Lawrence, London and Lynn, Norfolk, free in 1687; and the other two are said to bear the mark of one Henry Smith, of London.

There is, in my own mind, very definite doubt that the mark on Riff's porringer (and on that recorded by Riff as in possession of the Dresden Museum) can, in fact, be attributed to Henry Smith, a pewterer who did not obtain his freedom to trade until 1724, and was not granted leave to strike his touch until 1726. Riff describes the mark on his own piece as "a rose surmounted by a bishop's mitre and accompanied by the initials H.S." He does not, however, state that it also contained the date 1723, which is an integral part of Henry Smith's touch. I submit, therefore, that the mark was *not* identical with that of Henry Smith (as drawn by Cotterell, and as struck on the London touchplate), but that it belonged to some earlier pewterer who used devices similar to those in Smith's touch. There is, in fact, no other reasonable explanation to account for two only, out of a large total of porringers, being so out of period.

The museum at Dresden was, in 1955, unable to find any trace of the other H.S. porringer its director had described to Riff in the twenties.

When the porringer No. 2 (d) in the Schedule was illustrated by Harrold E. Gillingham (ANTIQUES, October 1939), it was shown together with its mark, misdescribed by Gillingham but now identified as the standing figure of Saint Lawrence, with his gridiron. The initials *S* and *L* denote Samuel Lawrence, who was father of Edward Lawrence (Cotterell, No. 2861); Edward's mark (No. 741 on the London touchplate) also depicts Saint Lawrence with his grid.

It should be recalled that Cotterell himself (ANTIQUES, July 1928) admitted reading the letter *S* only in the mark on the Yeates specimen from Group 2, and he more or less jumped to the conclusion that it stood for the surname initial of the maker, and that Yeates' porringer was, therefore, *probably* by the same maker as the Riff specimen—in other words, also by Henry Smith.

I have now personally examined this porringer, and enough of the mark can be clearly seen to enable me to state emphatically that it is identical with that illustrated by Gillingham, and also identical with the mark which appears on my own William III porringer. These marks are, as stated, now attributed to Samuel Lawrence.

I should like to thank the editor for the loan of all available photographs, used to illustrate past articles, which have been invaluable to me in my researches. I also wish to express my thanks to those private collectors and museum authorities who have so kindly cooperated in this study.   R.F.M.

Mr. Michaelis, honorary librarian of the Society of Pewter Collectors (England) and an honorary member of the Pewter Collectors' Club of America, is author of the recently published *Antique Pewter of the British Isles.* Much of the material in the present study appeared in an article by Mr. Michaelis in the *Antique Collector* for October 1956.

An Old English Provincial Trade Guild

By Howard Herschel Cotterell and Walter Graham Churcher

IN the January, 1926, number,* the Editor, in his *Casual Notes on American Pewter*, gave to us a thrill of the first magnitude in his reproduction of the old painted silken banner of the New York Society of Pewterers, for which, very wisely, he claims no more than that it gives evidence of the existence of such a body, though there is at present no means of knowing whether or not it was of a permanent nature or created for a special purpose — to wit, the great Federal parade of July 23, 1788.

Well, one prefers to be with him on the safe side rather than to allow one's self to be led off into all manner of wildcat conjectures and speculations. But, surely, among our American cousins there is someone who will be willing to seize the baton from the Editor and to do another lap or two in the race for further knowledge; for it is surely to be found, if the search be made in the right channels and with real keenness.

At the time when the January number came to hand, we had but recently completed some notes bearing on two English painted banners, pennants, or streamers, also of silk, with fringed edges, and having reference — *inter alia* — to the pewterers, and displaying the pewterers' arms.

These notes furnish a good example of the regulations which governed, and the bounds which limited the work and the actions of the early pewterer, and open up ground which has hitherto not been cultivated. They cannot be without interest at the present juncture, and one is now

Fig. 1 — The Pewterers' Arms
Enlarged from a part of the banner shown in Figure *2c*.

almost encouraged to hope that something analagous to these regulations may be discovered as governing the operations of American pewterers.

That a more ready comparison may be made with the arms on the American banner, an enlarged illustration is given in Figure 1 of that part of our banners which contains the arms of the London pewterers, though the banners we write about were not of London but of the Hammermen's Guild of Ludlow in the county of Shropshire, England; and the use of the London pewterers' arms by provincial guilds would seem to have been either permitted or winked at.

Ludlow is one of the oldest and most interesting towns in England, with its old and fine feudal castle and wonderful half-timbered houses, and is well worthy a visit by Americans when in the Old Country.

From the most cursory glance, it will at once be seen that the American shield bears but one point of resemblance to that on our banner—the chevron bearing the three slipped roses. In the English example this chevron appears between three "strakes of tin", or ingots, somewhat in the form of a portcullis; whereas the American version appears over the spiral "worm" of a still. Again, the New York crest is *a teapot* in place of our *pewter dish supported by two arms embowed* which rise from a torse resting upon a helmet, which latter feature is absent in the New York banner; and, in place of the sea horses for supporters, that banner has what are described by Sarah H. J. Simpson as "two miners holding burning lamps" (tin

*See Antiques, Vol. IX, p. 19.

miners presumably?). We cannot, at this distance, either prove or disprove this suggestion, since the banner is not before us for examination, but may we put forward as an alternative that these individuals may be pewterers with melting pots full of molten metal?

The only remaining point for comparison is the mottoes: that of New York being *Solid and Pure*, against our *In God is all Our Trust*.

From the above there would seem, at first sight, not much whereupon to base a connection, *but* that chevron with its three slipped roses is sufficient, for it shows that whoever was responsible for the American conception was not without knowledge of, and, who shall say, affection for the old tradition. This is well; it proves that the American interpretation is not chimerical, but that it stands upon a foundation of granite — a conclusion which gives greater force to the hope that something more than an institution for the temporary participation in the Federal Parade was in the mind of the American designer; the hope that, even yet, it may be discovered that the pewterers of the New World were organized and had their ordinances formed on lines similar to those obtaining in the Old Country.

. .

Turning now to the story we have to tell: The Archives of the Ludlow Hammermen's Guild are deposited in the town museum at Ludlow, and it is to the courtesy of John Palmer, one of the joint curators of that institution, that we are indebted for much of the information here given.

Two interesting mementoes of the Guild have found a safe resting place in the museum, in the form of two much frayed silken streamers, or pennants, with fringed edges, each about fifteen feet long, upon one of which appears the date 1734. Each side of these streamers is painted with the arms, helm, crest, supporters, and motto of the various trades constituting the Guild. Illustrations of these are given here from photographs taken by W. E. Harper of Ludlow. These trades and mottoes are as follows, reading from top to bottom in each case:

Figure 2 *a*. Ironmongers . Motto —*In God is all our Strength*
    b. Goldsmiths . " —*In God alone be all Glory*
    c. Pewterers . . " —*In God is all our Trust*
    d. Masons . . " —*In God is all our Trust*

    e. Blacksmiths . " —*By Hammer and Hand all Arts do Stand*
    f. Saddlers . . " —*Our Trust is in God*
    g. Coopers . . " —*Love as Brethren*
    h. Bricklayers . " —*In God is all our Trust*

Figure 3 *a*. Plumbers,
   Motto —*In God is all our Hope*
    b. Glaziers,
   " —*Non sine Lumine*
    c. Tinplate workers
   " —*Unite in Love*
    d. Carpenters,
   " —*Honour God*

    e. Joiners,
   " —*(None)*
    f. Cutlers,
   " —*Pour parvenir au Bon*
    g. Plasterers,
   " —*Let Brotherly Love Continue*
    h. Farriers,
   " —*Honour God*

Figure 1 gives an enlarged view of the pewterers' arms — which are, in every detail, the same as those of the Worshipful Company of Pewterers of London — as well as a better idea of the present frail condition of these banners.

The use of these arms by *local* guilds would seem to suggest some affiliation with or license granted by the parent companies of London.

The streamers were carried by the youngest freemen on all state occasions, at the head of the fraternity when it marched in procession. They were also paraded at the pleasure fair held annually on the first of May.

Figure 4 shows the old membership badge of the Guild, recently acquired by Thomas Warburton of Manchester, by whose courtesy it is here reproduced. This badge is of copper, one and one-half inches in diameter. The reverse side is left blank to receive the name or number of the member; the edge is milled diagonally.

. .

Prior to the reign of Richard I, the smiths, with some sixteen other allied trades, formed themselves into a trading fraternity under the name of *Smiths and Others* for mutual protection, benefit, and support,

Fig. 2 — STREAMER OF THE LUDLOW GUILD OF HAMMERMEN
Obverse and reverse. For a full description of this streamer see accompanying text.

and, in course of time, became a prescriptive corporation.

It is laid down in an ordinance made by Richard, Duke of York, father of Edward IV, whilst Lord of the Castle of Ludlow, and confirmed by the "twelve and twenty-five", the then governing body of the town, that:

No manner craft make no foreign Brother but it be a man of this same town, dwelling and occupye the same craft that he is made brother of, under payne of XLI, so as it playnly apperth under the said Duke's seale and the Comon Seale of the town, to be forfeit as ought times as it may be proved.

King Edward IV, by his Charter dated December 7, 1461, granted to the Burgesses of Ludlow, their heirs and successors forever:

That they have in their Town or Borough aforesaid, the Merchants Guild with a Company and all other customs and liberties to the Guild aforesaid appertaining, and that no one who is not of that Guild shall use any Merchandise in the aforesaid town or suburbs of the same unless by the license and leave of the same Burgesses their heirs and successors.

The Guild or Company, of Smiths, met in the south aisle of the parish church for the transaction of their business, held pews there, and contributed towards the maintenance of the church.

In the year 1511 a charter was granted to the Guild, wherein the following trades would appear to be members: smiths, ironmongers, saddlers, braziers, pewterers, spurriers, bucklemakers, brygand ironsmakers [*sic*], armorers, masons, cardmakers and coopers. Under its Charter, the Guild was ordered to choose from among themselves six of the "most honest and saddest men", to be called by the name of "the six men"; and two stewards, to be called by the name of "stewards"; and the same six men and two stewards to continue in office for two years from the date of their election; and the two stewards yearly to make a true account of all such goods and monies as shall come to their hands, before the said six men.

In the Charter it was provided that any master summoned, and not appearing upon his summons, was to be fined by the stewards in half a pound of wax; and every

Fig. 3 — STREAMER OF THE LUDLOW GUILD OF HAMMERMEN
Obverse and reverse. For a full description of this streamer see accompanying text.

master who was apprenticed, in the town of Ludlow, to any of the occupations "shall have his Freedom in the Guild on payment of 6s 8d and those not apprenticed there on payment of 13s 4d." Any journeyman of any of the said occupations rebuking any master was to forfeit half a pound of wax as often as he offended.

The first record of proceedings is in 1539, when certain alterations were made in the election of stewards and the fees payable by masters on their admission.

Under the new rules, the six men were to choose but one steward, and the body of the fellowship the other. The fees for admission differed according to the different trades — the list of which varied considerably from that of 1511 — and included sixteen trades instead of twelve, the pewterers paying 10s 6d for admission if apprenticed in the town, and 40s 8d if otherwise.

In 1573 a new composition was drawn up under the seal of the fraternity and that of the borough, and approved on the third of April 1576 by the law officers of the Crown at Bridgenorth. This composition is a long document, the chief items of which were much the same as those already in force.

The stewards were each required to give a bond with sureties for £40 on election. Members were forbidden to bring action against fellow-members without the consent of the six men, under pain of forfeiting 3s 4d.

Apprentices could not be found for less than seven years — to end when they attained the age of twenty-four. The apprentice was to be made free of the occupation on payment of the customary fee.

A "foreigner", or one not apprenticed in the town, had to produce testimonials as to where and with whom he had served his apprenticeship and that he had been "of good name and fame" during that time. Should he fail to comply, and set up in business without being made free of the fraternity, he was fined 3s 4d for every day he so offended.

The bailiffs and council of the town were given power to correct, reform, amend, or alter any ambiguity that might arise in any clause.

The charge to masters on their being made free provided for their attendance at meetings when summoned, under pain of a fine of 3s 4d; to pay Hall-money 1s od, yearly; and a fine of 3s 4d, for using "railing words", or commencing a suit against a brother member without leave, or procuring work out of another master's hands.

Finally:

No master of this Fellowship shall suffer his servant or prentyce to come to the occupacons supper, only suche as shall paye their IIIId upon payne of forfeiture of 3s 4d, and lastly, you nor your wief [sic] or other in your behalf shall not use to knele in the Occupacons pewes before you have been Steward.

About the year 1580, there are in the minutes and stewards' accounts many instances of money being spent on the furnishings of soldiers, the stewards also having charge of the fraternity's small armory.

Like other similar fellowships, the Ludlow Guild seems to have had its annual feasts, and the stewards had an annual allowance of "a pottle of sack and a pottle of claret" for their stewards' suppers.

In the year 1600 the fraternity numbered about sixty-five free-masters. After the year 1694, the admission forms bear a one shilling Inland Revenue stamp.

Among the meetings of the fellowship were Election Day, Stewards' Hall, Quarterly Meetings (reduced to two in 1790), with special and private meetings. All these were held in the pews belonging to the fraternity, situate under the east window of the south aisle in the Parish Church, on the spot formerly occupied by the Warwick Chapel, but "an adjournment was frequently made to an neighboring inn".

Members were summoned by notice and by the ringing of a bell. Election Day was formerly held on the Sunday, afterwards altered to the Saturday, after Holy Rood day, and finally to a Tuesday early in May. The fine for refusing to serve as steward, finally fixed at £5, had previously been 13s 4d, and 20s od. The six men were chosen, as a rule, from amongst the latest past stewards, the four key-keepers and box-keeper being chosen next.

Stewards' Hall was generally held on Whit Monday. In later years the audit was transferred from Election Day to this meeting.

Up to 1710 the clerk was chosen from among their own members, but in this year Richard Perks, town clerk of Ludlow, was appointed to the office, about which time also the silversmiths, clockmakers, cabinetmakers, and others were admitted to the fraternity.

In 1792 a motion was set on foot for getting rid of the six men on the ground that they should have no more power than other members, but this came to nothing. Trouble commenced as in other similar guilds early in the nineteenth century, and, from 1815 to 1835, great difficulty was experienced in getting refractory hammermen to take up their freedom. The deathblow came in 1835 in the shape of the Municipal Corporations Act, which enacted that any man might carry on any lawful trade in any borough, whether free of any trade guild or not.

The fraternity drifted on for many years after this, until, one by one, its old members died off and its pews in the parish church were swept away.

Fig. 4 — MEMBERSHIP BADGE OF LUDLOW HAMMERMEN'S COMPANY
Reverse blank to receive name of member.
Diameter 1½".

II American Pewter Before 1800

Pewter was undoubtedly in use in America from the moment the Pilgrim Fathers unpacked the possessions they had brought with them to start life in the new land. Those first pieces were, of course, British-made, and most new pewter for some time after that was imported. Pewter manufacture was undertaken here as early as 1635, using as raw materials the worn and broken pieces that had served out a useful life.

From those meager beginnings, a large and important craft developed in America. In the early years, the men who worked at pewtering here had been trained in England and probably brought moulds and tools with them to establish their shops. By the eighteenth century, they were joined by other pewterers from the continent of Europe who also brought their traditions and tools along with them. Soon the various styles were amalgamated, and some ''American'' forms began to appear which reflected the international composition of our new country. The predominant influence was always British, however, and very nearly every form made in America in the eighteenth century had its precedent in England.

The actual fabrication of pewter objects was accomplished in a similar fashion throughout the world. Charles F. Montgomery, in the first few pages of this section, outlines the making of a pewter plate, and, with the exception of assembly and some hand-smoothing steps, the same procedure would have been followed in all of the forms made by the early pewterers.

In the second part of ''English Influence in American Pewter,'' Percy E. Raymond correctly identifies the major influential forces in pewter made in America and points out the time lag in our adoption of newer styles. The content of the last two brief paragraphs of that article, which deal with britannia metal, are somewhat at odds with the facts, and are best ignored. A discussion of britannia metal is pursued in Part III.

We must judge the pewter made in America before 1750 by a very few examples which have survived to the present. About a dozen known plates and dishes having a multiple reed rim are thought to have been made by the Dolbears and John Baker of Boston. These are well-crafted and based on British designs, as one might expect. In ''The Pewterers of Eighteenth-Century New York,'' Ledlie I. Laughlin illustrates a chalice, dated 1744, that rivals in design and finish any known British example of the period.

From the latter part of the eighteenth century we have rather a large group of forms to study, and it was during that half-century that the creativity and talent of a number of the American

pewterers emerged. Some splendid examples are illustrated in articles by P. G. Platt, Charles F. Montgomery, and Robert Mallory, beginning with the article ''American Pewter as a Collectible.'' The tall coffeepot by William Will of Philadelphia is as fine a piece of pewter as exists anywhere today. Will was an especially creative pewterer, and many examples of his work are illustrated. Four complete articles concentrate on the products of his shop, including the magnificent Aaronsburg, Pennsylvania, communion service discussed in detail by Paul Auman and Ledlie I. Laughlin. Another similar set has been found since that article was written in 1950. Will was a master at ''making-do,'' combining portions of several forms to produce a totally different object. Charles Swain illustrates that element of Will's work in his article entitled ''Interchangeable Parts in Early American Pewter.''

William Will was one of a family of at least five excellent pewterers, the earliest of whom was John Will, Sr., who had come to New York from Germany in 1752. In their earlier work we see the strong influence of the European background. It is particularly evident in the flagons made by John Will and discussed here by Charles Swain. The William Will flagon in the Aaronsburg set also shows the Germanic influence, but by the last decade of the eighteenth century his forms had been almost completely Anglicized.

The work of Johann Christopher Heyne of Lancaster, Pennsylvania, is the subject of articles by Eric de Jonge and John J. Evans and exhibits that maker's Swedish training, de Jonge presenting an excellent study of the early forms which appear quite obviously in Heyne's work in America.

A number of geographic centers of pewter manufacture were established in the eighteenth century. Chief among those areas were Boston, New York, Philadelphia, Providence/Newport, and an area of Connecticut centering around Middletown. These locations had grown rather independently of each other, and the pewter from each area shows some local characteristics. As may be seen in ''American Pewter Tankards'' by Edward E. Minor, those vessels made in Philadelphia were frequently taller and more slender than those made in New York. Pewterers in that latter area seem to have favored tankards having a flat lid, often with a crenate lip, a feature not found on tankards from other locations. The Eastern Seaboard pewterers gave us the so-called ''strap-handled'' mugs shown by Montgomery in fig. 12 of ''Important Early American Pewter.'' The designs of porringer handles also show much regional preference, and flatware often varied in depth and size from one center to another.

In our efforts to discover and identify every early American pewterer we have occasionally included a "wrong-un." The pewterer named Whitehouse, who made the spoon shown in fig. 12 of "American Pewter as a Collectible" was actually an English maker in Birmingham who apparently produced eagle-decorated spoons for export to this country.

Pewter manufacture in America continued at a high level of output during the entire eighteenth century, even in the face of great competition from imports of British pewter, pottery, and porcelain. For the most part, the quality of goods made here was high, and the Wills and Bassetts produced wares that were equal and often superior to those made in England. The spirit, talent, and industry of those early craftsmen must be considered equal to their handsome products as an element of our American heritage.

PEWTER AT THE FORUM

English Influence in American Pewter, I

By CHARLES F. MONTGOMERY

With this summary of the talks by Mr. Montgomery, specialist in pewter, and Mr. Raymond, past president of the Pewter Collectors' Club, we conclude our series of reports on the 1949 Antiques and Decorations Forum in Williamsburg. Other subjects covered were ceramics in April, glass in May, furniture in June, fabrics in July, and silver in August.

WHEN OR WHERE IT WAS DISCOVERED that an alloy of tin and copper could be formed into useful vessels is not known. However, there is every reason to believe that this alloy, called pewter, was known as early as that which gave its name to the Age of Bronze. According to tradition the Chaldeans and Egyptians used the metal, and it has been established that the Chinese were skilled in pewter making more than a thousand years ago. Excavations at the sites of Roman towns in France and England have produced pewter plates and dishes believed to date from the second century A.D. After the Gothic invasion all evidence of pewter disappears, and the next recorded instance of its use occurs in 1076, when the Council of Westminster granted permission for the consecration of pewter chalices for religious services. At that time it must have been a luxury enjoyed only by the nobility and the clergy; as late as the sixteenth century in England woodenware was customarily used in the homes of shopkeepers and peasants. Even in the eighteenth century pewter was considered of sufficient value to be specifically bequeathed.

The earliest pewterers must have worked at their trade almost at will, but as standards of quality were established these craftsmen recognized a need for some governing body for their own protection and that of the public. Out of this need grew the "Craft of Pewterers" in London. As early as 1348 we find the Mayor and Board of Aldermen passing ordinances to regulate the craft, establishing standards of quality, working conditions, and selling restrictions. Wardens were appointed to search out and confiscate pieces made of inferior metal or without proper marks. At the time of the colonization of America this guild had become one of the most powerful trade organizations in the world. Its rules were so exacting and so well enforced that London pewter set the standard of excellence in the western world.

On the Continent, too, pewterers had organized themselves into groups, so that by 1600 there was hardly a center of any importance without its pewter guild. We may therefore be sure that most of the pewterers emigrating to this country were carefully trained, and brought with them not only their molds and their tools but a real tradition of craftsmanship.

In contrast to the production of silver, where each piece was individually fashioned, pewter was first cast in molds and then finished on a lathe or by hand. Complicated forms required a number of molds for each part. These were heavy bronze affairs, difficult to make and expensive to acquire. In fact, they were so expensive that one of the services rendered by the Company of Pewterers in London was the rental of molds to its poorer members. The mold was the all-important factor in the style of a piece of pewter. As tastes changed and the demand arose for new forms, old molds had to be dis-

carded and new ones acquired. In the case of the small pewterer, design changes necessarily occurred slowly. This was true to some degree in England, but far more so in this country, where molds were more expensive and hard to come by. The accepted practice of an apprentice starting in business for himself was to acquire old molds from a pewterer who had gone out of business. Consequently, in 1780 or 1790 pewterers were often turning out pieces in the style of twenty-five or more years before.

In order to acquaint you with the method of actual production, I am going to outline briefly the steps involved in making a plate, which is one of the simplest forms in pewter. The first operation was the preparation of the metal. Pewter is an alloy of about 90% tin with small amounts of antimony or bismuth. Best grades contained as much as 10% copper; poor ones, up to 20% of lead. Contrary to popular belief, fine pewter contains very little or no lead.

In this country the pewterer's raw material consisted chiefly of the metal in worn-out and damaged pieces, which might vary in quality and composition, so that it was first necessary to assay each piece in order to get a uniform batch. This was done by scooping out a chip of metal by means of a hot tool with a diamond-shaped point and testing it for quality—on the basis of its color and the rapidity of its melting and congealing. After sorting out enough pieces of the right quality, the pewterer would melt them in a cauldron, sometimes adding a small amount of bismuth or antimony in ingot form. The molten metal was then poured into the plate mold. If this was not preheated, the first one or two castings, which served to heat the mold, would be defective.

Each casting was quite rough as it came from the mold, with a piece of metal protruding where the pour-hole occurred, and often small icicle-shaped points around the edge of the plate where the two halves of the mold came together. These had to be removed with a pair of nippers and the en-

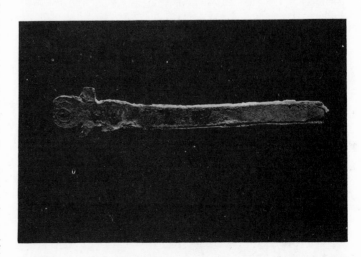

HANDLE OF PEWTER SPOON by Joseph Copeland of Chuckatuck, Virginia (*c. 1675*). The only surviving piece of seventeenth-century American pewter known. *Courtesy of National Park Service.*

In this country during the eighteenth century the production of pewter tableware probably exceeded that of all other materials combined. Wooden plates may have been widely used, but it is unlikely that many were made and sold in shops. The wealthy could and did afford the English pottery and porcelain which were being imported, but the general public continued to use pewter in a great variety of forms until about 1820. Plates and dishes of several sizes, bottles, mugs, measures, sugar bowls, cream jugs, teapots, coffeepots, chamber pots, bedpans, chairpans, candlesticks, great quantities of spoons, and even ice cream molds were among the items listed in the 1799 inventory of Revolutionary Colonel William Will.

When we examine critically the output of his shop and others in the larger cities, we find many pieces worthy of the best English tradition. The tea- and coffeepots of William Will, the tankards of the Bassetts, and the hammered dishes of Simon Edgell have few, if any, English superiors. Although we may find pieces of inferior quality, it is indeed remarkable in the face of the difficulties they encountered that our pewterers maintained such high standards.

PEWTER PLATE WITH SINGLE-REEDED RIM (*late eighteenth century*). By Frederick Bassett of New York (*1740-1800*).

tire surface smoothed down with a file-shaped tool called a float. The casting was then ready to be finished on a wooden chuck in a lathe, usually turned by hand by an apprentice, but occasionally by water power in favorably located shops. As the plate revolved, the pewterer skimmed the surface with a hook, a long-handled wooden tool with a metal cutting face on the end. The next step was polishing with a burnisher, a tool much like the hook but with a smooth face instead of a sharp edge. When the plate was completed on one side, instead of removing it from the lathe, the pewterer used it as a chuck and tacked another plate to it with a few drops of solder. After one side of a stack of plates was finished, he would reverse the pile and finish the backs.

Large amounts of pewter were imported here from England. During the seventeenth century shipments of pewter from London to the Colonies reached an annual figure of more than £4,000. Amazing as it may seem, during the first half of the eighteenth century the value of pewter imports from England was greater than that of household furniture, silver, and tinware combined.

The impact of the English style in the Colonies was so great that Continental pewterers, with definite stylistic traditions of their own, soon anglicized their forms after coming to America, in order to conform to the tastes of their customers. The early work of Johann Christopher Heyne, for instance, who settled in Lancaster, Pennsylvania, in 1742, is as Germanic as any produced in his native Saxony. His early flagons, of which he made many for the Pennsylvania churches, have Teutonic strap handles, ball thumbpieces, and cherub-head or mascaroon feet. As time went by, the strap handle was replaced by a scrolled one, and the flattened dome cover gave way to a double-domed type, the like of which had never been seen in Germany.

AMERICAN PEWTER TABLE SETTING, in the eighteenth-century manner, with blue and white cloth in "furniture checks." Pieces shown include an oval dish holding fruit by William Will of Philadelphia (*1742-1798*), baby's bottle by Thomas Danforth Boardman of Hartford (*1784-1873*), small porringer by Samuel Danforth of Hartford (*1774-1816*), and basin by Gershom Jones of Providence (*c. 1750-1809*). *Metropolitan Museum of Art.*

English Influence in American Pewter, II

By PERCY E. RAYMOND

AMERICAN PEWTER might be called an abridged edition of the English. The American craftsmen followed slavishly the designs of the mother country, for the good reason that their molds were of English design. The early colonists included a number of pewterers, and some of them brought over their molds. Although a good many came to Boston, New York, and presumably to other places, we find no evidence whatever of their work in the seventeenth century. It remained for Virginia to produce the Chuckatuck spoon, the one surviving seventeenth-century American pewter object. The history of pewter-making in this country therefore begins in the eighteenth century.

There were two ways in which England exerted an influence on American pewter. The first was repressive. The Worshipful Company of Pewterers in England was a powerful organization, and naturally tried to prevent the establishment of a competing pewter industry in the Colonies. There was an export duty on British tin, on which the colonial pewterers were dependent, since North America has no raw tin in any quantities. The owners of the mines in Cornwall were always trying to prevent this duty from becoming excessively high, however, so that when they had business enough pewterers in New York and New England were able to import new tin. Contrary to the theory advanced by John W. Poole and Ledlie I. Laughlin, pewterers here were not absolutely dependent on old pewter, though they all bought and used it. That is one of the troubles with American ware: it simply is not made of as good quality metal as English pewter.

The other influence exerted by England on American pewter was one of competition, the effect of which was to keep down the variety of utensils produced here. The American pewterers selected from English forms the simplest ones, and those for which there was the greatest demand, and concentrated on them. In the case of plates, for instance, the English had a dozen different brim styles in the seventeenth and eighteenth centuries, but only two were made over here. Between 1660 and 1700 in England we find plates with a multiple-reeded rim—one of the most decorative types of flatware, or sadware, ever made. So far as I know only one American pewterer ever made a multiple-reeded piece, and that was Joseph Leddell, who was working in New York about 1712.

FLAT-TOP PEWTER TANKARD by Frederick Bassett of New York (1740-1800). *Philadelphia Museum.*

His one example is a baptismal basin. About 1705 or 1710 the single-reeded type came into fashion in England, and was made in America over a long period. Plates were produced wherever pewter was made here, but Boston rather specialized in them. In fact, about all they did make there in the early days were plates and mugs.

American pewter tankards follow English styles, usually with a time lag. From about 1675 to 1690 in England they were making a flat-topped, or flat-crowned, tankard, with a serrated margin on the front called the serrated overhang. This was derived from an early form, which had only a single point in the front, serving instead of a thumbpiece on the old wooden tankards to raise the lid. The other points were added to make it more decorative, and this feature was continued after people had forgotten its original use. The flat-crowned tankard was used in England up to about 1705 or 1710. Already by 1690, however, the domed type had come in. The earliest domed forms also had the serrated overhang, but the later ones were smooth. There are two types, the low double dome and the high double dome. These terms are confusing, since the high double dome is often no higher than the low one, and the low double dome may be higher than the high one. Some other way of distinguishing them is necessary, and a convenient test is the position of the cavetto, or concave area. In the low double dome it occurs just below the upper dome, whereas in the high double dome it is between the lower dome and the brim. The latter type came into fashion about 1725 and continued to be made until about 1780.

New York was the home of the American pewter tankard. The first ones were produced there by a group of four pewterers who began working between 1712 and 1720. This early group made all three types of tankards—the flat-crowned, the low double dome, and the high double dome. Between that early group and another group of four whose work spanned the period of the Revolution, a single pewterer, John Will, came over from Germany and began turning out English-type pewter. He made the low-double-domed tankard, which had

NEW YORK PEWTER TANKARDS (*eighteenth century*). *Left,* with low double dome (note cavetto below upper dome.) *Right,* with high double dome (cavetto below lower dome).

PEWTER TEAPOT by William Will of Philadelphia (1742-1798). *Brooklyn Museum.*

then been out of style in England for some twenty-five or thirty years. His son, Henry Will, belonged to the later group, who began working from about 1760 to 1775. All of them went back to making the old flat-crowned tankard with the overhang, along with the high double dome.

The Philadelphia pewterers were notably up to date. Simon Edgell, an Englishman who had belonged to the Worshipful Company of Pewterers before coming to this country in 1713, made the low-double-domed tankard with serrated margin and also a high double dome without it. Cornelius Bradford, son of the New York pewterer, William Bradford, went to Philadelphia and made the same sort of tankards as those produced by Edgell, as well as mugs in the tulip shape, popular in England from 1750 to 1760. William Will, son of John, made tulip-shaped tankards, with two cavettos—the distinguishing mark of a William Will tankard.

People of Rhode Island, Connecticut, and Massachusetts did not go in much for tankards, but continued to drink out of open mugs. Benjamin Day in Rhode Island, however, made tankards copied from silver, with a finial on the lid, a feature known in England only in ecclesiastical flagons. In Connecticut, tankards did not appear until very late, about 1780 or 1790, and then they were of a common high-double-domed variety. The Hartford men started making these, but then they put on triple domes and coffeepot lids, and tankards ceased to be tankards.

People in America got interested in porringers about the time the English got tired of them. After 1750 not many were made in England, since the increasing quantity of ceramic wares enabled people there to do without pewter. About 1720 or 1730 Joseph Leddell and William Bradford began making porringers in New York, of the so-called crown-handled type, actually derived from a viscount's coronet—a style made in England as early as 1680 or 1690 but never popular there. From New York the idea spread to Rhode Island and then to Connecticut. Finally about 1820 or so the Boston pewterers began making porringers. No one has ever been able to identify the makers of these utensils, since they marked them only with their initials.

The most common English type of porringer handle was

pierced by a median inverted heart, pointed upward. In Rhode Island Melville adapted this design, making it more elaborate. The typical porringer of Rhode Island and Connecticut has what we call the flowered handle.

The solid-handled porringers of Rhode Island are of either French or German design. As a matter of fact, the porringer is really at home in France, where the French used it for everything. Most French and German porringers have two handles, but there is only one American example known in that form. The tab-handled porringers of southeastern Pennsylvania are probably of Germanic origin, though I have never been able to track down a German prototype.

To many pewter collectors even the mention of britannia is anathema. As a champion of lost causes, however, I maintain that britannia metal is the best pewter ever made. The metal itself is much better than that used in the early days when they made what we call real pewter. It is capable of being rolled out into sheets, which cannot be done with old pewter without its cracking. The trouble is that the manufacturers rolled it out so thin that it became tinny.

The only important difference between britannia and pewter is that pewter was cast in a mold, whereas britannia was spun on a lathe, against a wooden chuck turned to the proper form. This matter of spinning versus molding is confusing. On the bottom of a piece of pewter you often see spirally curved lines. These were made in the finishing of the pewter castings, when the piece was taken out of the mold, put on the wheel, and the roughness skimmed off. Such lines are an indication that you have a piece of pewter. If on the other hand you have a piece of britannia—which actually was made by spinning—you won't find those lines, because they were burnished off afterwards. So you find spinning marks on pewter which was molded, not on britannia which was spun!

The britannia maker had more leeway in determining the form of a piece than the maker of pewter, who needed only to know how to fill the mold with metal, how to take the casting out, and how to finish off the roughnesses. A man who was an artist could do a lot better with britannia than could the old-fashioned pewterer. The difficulty was that britannia did not come into use in this country until nearly Victorian times, and suffered from the general deterioration of taste.

BRITANNIA TEAPOT by Roswell Gleason of Dorchester, Massachusetts (1799-1877).

Fig. 1 — CYLINDRICAL TEAPOT BY WILLIAM WILL, PHILADELPHIA, 1795
The eagle touch that appears on the inside of this pot is here reproduced for the first time.
From the collection of the Honorable Richard S. Quigley

American Pewter as a Collectible

By P. G. PLATT

FOR some inconceivable reason, many persons believe that pewter was not made in America before the Federal era, and that, as Colonists, we employed only imported wares. It is now well known that pewtering was practiced in the Colonies at quite as early a date as was any other craft. Unfortunately, however, plentiful though the ware was in its day, virtually no examples antedating 1750 seem to have survived. To be sure, specimens of this date would be difficult to identify as certainly American. In 1750 we were, in effect, English, and touch marks at that time were probably identical with those used in the mother country. It is only when the name of the place of manufacture is included in a touch that positive ascription to a specific source is possible.

Collectors have asked me, in a rather bewildered way, "Why the tremendous value of American pewter, when the English product is so much finer in quality?" The answer should be obvious. The statement as to quality is not founded on fact. Some American pewter compares as favorably with the work of

English pewterers as does our furniture and silver with that of contemporary English craftsmen. Inspection of the superb examples by William Will here illustrated should go far to dispel any doubts regarding the ability of our pewterers, both to produce good metal and to handle it with due regard to design.

It is doubtful that any pewterer in America ever surpassed Colonel Will in versatility. My check list credits him with surviving items of the following kinds: communion flagons; coffeepots; teapots of two types; covered tankards of two types; quart mugs of two types; pint mugs; six-, eight-, and sixteen-inch plates; six-inch basins; tablespoons; and a warming pan. This list might be taken to indicate that William Will pewter is plentiful. On the contrary, though he was extremely versatile, Will's work is sufficiently rare to inspire pride in the hearts of those fortunate enough to own an example from his hand. The Colonel received $150 each for "Tea Potts," $25 for "Basons," and $5 for tablespoons, in 1780. So it would appear that, after all, the values of today are relatively modest, even granting that

Fig. 2 — Bulbous Quart Mug by William Will
The acanthus leaf handle is extremely rare, and is here well executed.
From the collection of Ledlie I. Laughlin

Fig. 4 — Barrel-shaped Quart Mug by Parks Boyd, Philadelphia, 1800
A very pleasing adaptation of this form.
From the author's collection

Fig. 3 — Urn-Shaped Coffeepot by William Will
This pot measures sixteen inches in height, and, by some critics, is considered the finest extant example of American pewter.
From the author's collection

58

Fig. 5 — Rare Porringer by Thomas Danforth the Third, of Philadelphia
From the author's collection

Fig. 6 — Small Beaker by S. Kilbourn, Baltimore (*early nineteenth century*)
From the collection of Ledlie I. Laughlin

Fig. 7 — Provincial Pennsylvania Porringer, Attributed to Samuel Pennock
From the collection of Mrs. J. Insley Blair

Fig. 8 — Teapot by G. Richardson, Boston The exceptionally rare touch is also shown.
From the author's collection

Will's 1780 charges were based on a greatly depreciated currency.

A cylindrical teapot by William Will (*Fig. 1*) is as attractive in design as contemporary silver. Both metal and workmanship are as fine as may be found in any land. An added feature of interest in this specimen is the small eagle head touch, which is unique in my experience. The bulbous quart mug by the same maker (*Fig. 2*) is also a masterpiece of workmanship, and the only American piece of its kind that has come to my attention. The double scrolled handle, with its imposed acanthus leaf, is beautifully designed, and highly successful in every respect. Probably the most superb piece of American pewter that has yet come to light is illustrated in Figure 3. This imposing sixteen-inch coffeepot by William Will seems beyond criticism in design, workmanship, and metal.

Parks Boyd, who worked in Philadelphia a decade later, was another superior craftsman whose product was uniformly excellent in quality. The barrel-shaped mug shown in Figure 4 appears to be a form peculiar to him. It is impressed, on the inside, with the maker's small eagle touch.

Thomas Danforth the third was prolific in flatware; but the porringer shown in Figure 5 seems to be unique in three respects: the shape is Continental in derivation, and boasts a solid handle similar to that employed in Rhode Island; it is, in so far as I know, the only porringer impressed with this touch mark; it also seems to be the only surviving example of a Philadelphia porringer.

Somewhat allied to this interesting piece is the provincial Pennsylvania porringer bearing an initialed touch (*Fig. 7*). Unmarked porringers from this mold are not uncommon in Chester and Delaware counties, but a marked specimen is a distinct rarity. Indications point to the fact that Samuel Pennock of Kennett Square, maker of "Chairs, Reels, and Little Wheels," also made pewter, and the piece in question will be attributed to him until further notice. Students will observe the similarity of the s.p. porringer to that made by Elisha Kirk of York. The molds differ slightly in detail, however.

Unmarked beakers are common; marked specimens by the later makers are not exceptionally rare. That illustrated, by S. Kilbourn of Baltimore, is a splendid and unusual example

of this type of vessel (*Fig. 6*). George Richardson of Cranston, Rhode Island, was a productive worker of late date, and has entered pewterdom's Hall of Fame through the medium of his rather original and very beautiful little sugar bowls. (Some call them butter dishes.) It seems that, before locating in Cranston, Richardson worked for a short period in Boston. The fine teapot shown in Figure 8 bears the Boston touch, and, aside from that, is interesting because of its charming shape and quality. But the specimens thus marked are exceedingly rare.

Connecticut porringers with the initials I. G. cast in the handle appear often, yet the most abstemious pewter collector could not but look with favor upon a tankard so marked. The specimen illustrated in Figure 9 bears these initials, cast in the under side of the handle. Contrary to the conclusions of the late Mr. Kerfoot, I feel confident that they are the initials of the maker. This manner of marking was used occasionally in England; and it is logical to assume that it was continued in America.

That we have not yet reached a complete tabulation even of the later American pewterers is evident in the touch mark of O. Williams of Buffalo, reproduced for the first time in Figure 10. The touch is from the back of an eight-inch plate of fine quality, and is so similar to the small eagle touch of Boardman and Company that we may suspect Mr. Williams of having worked in Hartford before migrating to Buffalo.

The baptismal bowl by Samuel Danforth (*Fig. 11*) is one of the highly prized forms in pewter. This example is most "pewterlike" in shape, and typifies the basic soundness of design that appeals to every collector of the material. The bowl proper was, no doubt, cast in the maker's eight-inch basin mold, the rim partly turned off, and the foot added.

The name of E. Whitehouse, pewterer is shrouded in mystery. Until recently no examples of his work were known to exist. It is with pleasure that I am able to show one of a set of six dessert spoons of patriotic type, carrying the touch mark of this maker (*Fig. 12*). We may fairly credit these spoons to the first decade of the nineteenth century, but the home of Mr. Whitehouse still remains a mystery. That he was a first-rate craftsman is evidenced by the six spoons.

Fig. 9 — AMERICAN DOMED TANKARD, WITH THE INITIALS *I. G.* CAST IN THE HANDLE
From the author's collection

Fig. 10 — TOUCH MARK OF O. WILLIAMS
This mark appears on a nineteenth-century plate, eight inches in diameter.
From the collection of Ledlie I. Laughlin

Fig. 11 — Baptismal Bowl by Samuel Danforth, Hartford
An exceedingly rare and desirable form. For a similar item, see Antiques, January, 1926, page 10. *From the collection of C. F. Hutchins*

I have also seen one plain dessert spoon on which the initial E was included in the touch. Either Whitehouse produced over a very long period, or some britannia manufacturer of the same surname was working in Victorian times; for I recently came across a rather gruesome teapot of the late sixties, marked with an incised WHITEHOUSE touch. Some humor was lent to this inspection, as the owner was sure that the piece had graced the table of one of our early presidents.

No doubt, other provincial pewterers will be discovered in the future, together with a number of pre-Revolutionary workers who plied their trade in the cities before the days of directories. To the collector of American pewter, there is no thrill equal to that accompanying the discovery and identification of an example fashioned by some early craftsman who has hitherto been unknown.

But quite aside from the interest felt in touch marks and the lives of the craftsmen, there are, fortunately, still collectors who acquire pewter through love of its soft sheen and its simple, direct forms. Today, when china and silver or silver plate are omnipresent, it is perhaps difficult to visualize the days when pewter provided almost all domestic tableware. Generations of our ancestors used it extensively, with wooden vessels as a substitute when pewter was unavailable. Only when the manufacture of pottery and porcelain was put on a commercial basis did it fall into disuse. It could not thereafter compete with the far cheaper product of the potters.

Some of the pewterers continued to ply their trade, but the metal, for the most part, had no longer the beautiful quality of the older pieces. Both the alloy and the shapes changed, to keep step with the times and the fashions. For a brief period britannia held sway, only to give way in its turn to white metal, which was used as a base for plating. The era of pewter seemed past.

Hence it is the more pleasing that its day has again dawned among collectors.

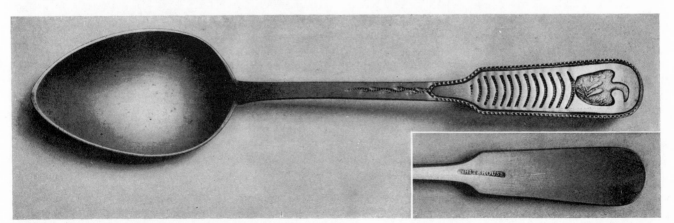

Fig. 12 — One of Six Dessert Spoons by E. Whitehouse
The touch is shown below. *Formerly in the author's collection*

IMPORTANT EARLY AMERICAN PEWTER

By CHARLES F. MONTGOMERY

HAILED as the finest display of American marked pewter ever presented, the Loan Exhibition held at the Metropolitan Museum of Art in March and April of this year constituted a milestone for pewter collectors. Hereafter pewter will be judged according to the standards set by this exhibition.

Pewter selected from the foremost collections in the country, arranged with feeling and taste, and displayed to its best advantage — that is the story of this show. For its excellence every lover of the old alloy is indebted to Joseph Downs, curator of the American Wing. In the Museum *Bulletin*, Mr. Downs wrote: "The exhibition has a two-fold purpose — first to show the diversity of form which the earlier pewterers gave to their work, with attention paid both to the sleekness of the contours and the quiet beauty of the metal, and second to show the widest variety of clear and complete touches, or makers' marks."

Even the most experienced collector came away from the exhibition convinced that he had seen the most complete variety of marks ever assembled. And he had really seen them, for displayed near each piece of pewter was a small plaster cast of its touch mark.

The accompanying photographs bear witness to the accomplishment of the first purpose expressed by Mr. Downs. To illustrate every outstanding piece in the exhibition would be impossible. The examples chosen are not only unusual and of high merit, they are in many instances unique. All are worthy of the attention of every collector.

FIG. 1 (*Continued*) top flight of American pewter. In itself it is a fine example, with tapered sides, rimmed top, and molded base. It is marked *Philadelphia*, but reveals no maker's name or initials. The engraving of the horse and Captain Ickes, who appears to be a Pennsylvania German, compensates in spirit for what it lacks in finesse. The inscription reads *Liberty Or Death / Huzza for Capt. Ickes.*
From the collection of Albert H. Good

FIG. 1 — "LIBERTY OR DEATH" MUG
Legend has it that this quart mug was given to the Revolutionary captain, Peter Ickes, by his townsmen, when he led his company of militia off to fight the British. Be that as it may, feeble indeed is the spark of patriotic fervor in the heart of a collector who would not rank this old mug in the

FIG. 2 (*page 118*) — TINY TEAPOT BY RICHARD LEE

To differentiate between the work of Richard Lee, Junior, and that of Richard Lee, Senior, seems impossible in the light of available information. However, it is a fair guess that this little teapot is the work of the elder Lee (*1747–1823*), who is believed to have made pewter in Lanesborough, Massachusetts, and later in Springfield, Vermont. Much smaller than other known American pewter teapots, it harks back to the days when tea was a luxury, and probably dates from the third quarter of the eighteenth century. It is

FIG. 4 (*preceding page*) — A NEW JOHN WILL TOUCH

This mark occurs on a thirteen-inch plate by John Will. No other instance is known of the use by a New York pewterer of the suspended-sheep type of mark employed by Rhode Island workers and more often incorporated in the touches of English pewterers. Of particular interest is the fact that this is the third primary touch of John Will to be found on the three plates of his making so far discovered. All three are different.
From the collection of Mrs. S. S. Fitzgerald

FIG. 5 — ENGRAVED TANKARD BY JOHN WILL (*New York, 1759–1765*)

Readers of ANTIQUES are already familiar with this rare tankard and its elaborate wrigglework decoration (see issue for January 1926, *p. 21*). It is, however, such a significant piece that any review of the recent exhibition in which it was shown would be incomplete without it. Somewhat over six inches high, it has the double-domed lid with serrated edge and the bulb-finial handle which characterized English tankards in the first quarter of the 1700's and were used throughout the century by American pewterers. The remarkable wrigglework feature consists of scalloped edgings outlining a tree upon a hill, a scroll-framed reserve for monogram or cypher from which spring conventionalized roses, and tulip-like patterns here and there. These engraved scallops evidently derived from the leaf borders with which Dutch silversmiths adorned their tankards. The initials *P H*, crudely engraved on the front, were probably added by a later owner. The maker's mark, *I W* in a circle, is stamped inside the tankard on the bottom.
From the collection of Mrs. J. Insley Blair

FIG. 6 — THE TWO EARLIEST AMERICAN TANKARDS KNOWN

a, quart tankard attributed to Joseph Liddel (*New York, c. 1690–1753*).
From the collection of H. F. du Pont

b, tankard slightly smaller than quart size, attributed to William Bradford Junior (*New York, 1688–1759*).
From the collection of Edward E. Minor

From the collector's standpoint, these two items surpass in quality every American tankard known. Of the earliest Stuart form, they are, in so far as I know, the only two American examples in which is found the combination of short, squat barrel, flat top, serrated lip, and flattened handle with splayed terminal

FIG. 2 (*Continued*) country-made, simple in detail but robust in form. *Height, 5 ¼ inches.*
From the collection of C. K. Davis

FIG. 3 (*page 118*) — WHOSE MARK IS IT?

This combination of touches on an eight-inch plate is puzzling in the light of present attributions. Here we have a rose-and-crown touch long ascribed to Robert Boyle, who worked in New York about the middle of the eighteenth century. Many have questioned this attribution because most of the pieces bearing the touch have turned up in New England. Along with this so-called Boyle touch occurs a *Semper Eadem* touch, such as is generally accompanied by either a London or Boston stamp, the latter identical with that used by Richard Austin and Thomas Badger. To confuse the matter still further, another *Semper Eadem* touch carrying the initials *IS* has been found. This touch occurs on the mug shown in Figure 12, *d*. Every pewter collector looks forward to the day when a piece of pewter will appear that is completely enough marked to clear up the mystery.
From the collection of Mrs. S. S. Fitzgerald

FIG. 7 — WRITING BOX BY HENRY WILL (*New York, 1736–1802*)

While inkstands by English pewterers are not uncommon, this American example, equipped with sand shaker and inkpot, is unique. It is all the more noteworthy for the prominent display of the maker's handsome rose-and-crown name touch and hall marks, so placed as to provide decoration for each of the two hinged lids.
From the collection of John W. Poole

FIG. 8 — PORRINGER BY THOMAS DANFORTH III (*Rocky Hill, Connecticut, and Philadelphia, 1756–1840*)

Porringers by any of the Danforths are scarce, but a Danforth porringer with a Rhode Island handle as handsome as this is a real rarity. This distinctive type of handle has not been found on any other examples made elsewhere than in Providence and Newport, except for a few by Sherman and Thomas D. Boardman. The pewterer's mark is shown in the circle at lower right. Thomas Danforth III combined an eagle touch and a name touch, a habit of Philadelphia pewterers during the final years of pewter-making. He used several variants of the eagle touch; a sketch of one of them appears below, *left*.
From the collection of C. K. Davis

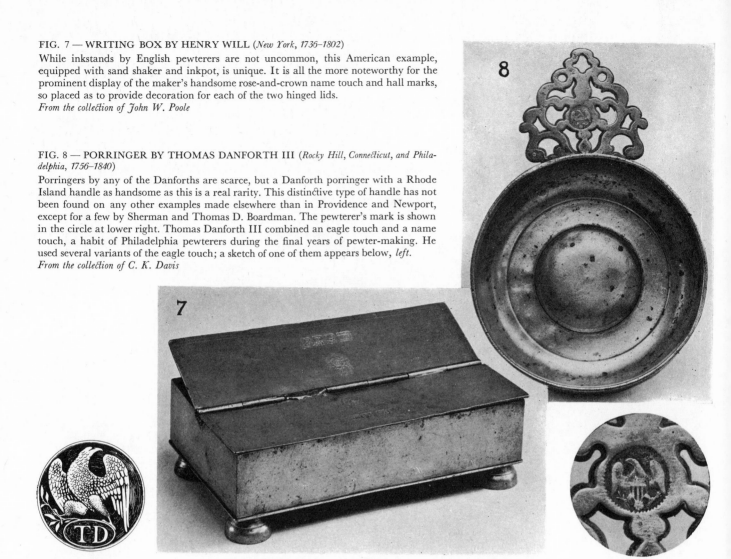

FIG. 9 — EARLY BEAKERS

a, squat beaker by Samuel Pierce (*Greenfield, Massachusetts, 1768–1840*). *From the collection of Edward E. Minor. b*, tall beaker by Edward Danforth (*Hartford, Connecticut, 1765–1832*). *From the collection of Dr. Madelaine R. Brown. c*, tall beaker by Thomas Danforth III (*Rocky Hill and Philadelphia, 1756–1840*). *From the collection of Charles F. Hutchins. d*, tall beaker by Samuel Danforth (*Hartford, Connecticut, 1774–1816*). *From the collection of C. K. Davis. e*, squat footed beaker by Peter Young (*Albany, New York, 1749–1813*). *From the collection of Irving H. Berg.*

Mr. Downs' phrase "sleekness of contours" aptly applies to these large beakers. Nearly all tall beakers seem to be of Connecticut origin; those by the Danforths excel in grace and beauty. In mass and dignity of form, examples such as that of Samuel Pierce (*a*) and the footed example by Peter Young (*e*) are superb. The unique Peter Young beaker is part of a most interesting Communion set from a church in Cheshire, Massachusetts, formerly called Staffordsville. The town was named for an ancestor of Spencer Stafford, who was a partner of Peter Young

FIG. 10 — TWO FORMAL TEAPOTS

a, straight-sided example by William Will (*Philadelphia, 1742–1798*). *From the collection of Joseph France. b*, straight-sided teapot with engraved decoration by Israel Trask (*Beverly, Massachusetts, 1786–1867*). *From the collection of Mrs. S. S. Fitzgerald.*

More formal than almost any other pieces in the exhibition, these two teapots follow contemporary silver styles. In grace and dignity of form as well as in skill of workmanship they compare favorably with related pieces in the finer metal

FIG. 11 — PEWTER PITCHERS

a, tiny lidless pitcher by Timothy Sage (*working in St. Louis, 1848*). This little pitcher has a pert, bird-like appearance, rather pleasing for such a late piece. *From the collection of C. K. Davis. b*, lidless pitcher by Henry Hopper (*New York, 1842–1847*). Apparently Hopper was the only pewterer to copy the design of luster pitchers of the period. *From the collection of Charles F. Hutchins. c*, rare covered pitcher by D. Curtiss (*Albany, 1822–1850*). *From the Mabel Brady Garvan collection at Yale University*

FIG. 12 — EARLY NEW ENGLAND QUART MUGS

a, strap-handled mug by Nathaniel Austin (*Boston, 1741–1816*). *From the collection of John W. Poole. b*, hollow-handled mug by Gershom Jones (*Providence, 1750–1809*). *From the collection of Edward E. Minor. c*, strap-handled mug by David Melvil (*Newport, 1776–1793*). *From the collection of Mary M. Sampson. d*, strap-handled mug marked *Semper Eadem* with initials *IS* above the crown. *From the collection of Edward E. Minor. e*, mug by Benjamin Day (*Newport, 1680–1757*). *From the collection of John W. Poole.* For fine early forms it would be hard to duplicate this group of New England mugs, all unique in some respect. *a* has the maker's name, *N. Austin*, cast on the handle terminal. *b* is the only known Jones tankard of this shape with slender hollow handle. *c, d,* and *e* are the only known mugs of any size by their makers. Noteworthy is *d*, with its unusual mark. One is tempted to credit it to John Skinner, but positive attribution is impossible (see Figure 3). The very early lidless tankard by Benjamin Day is the only known American example of this seventeenth-century English style (see Frontispiece). The slot in the handle where the lid would ordinarily be fastened was cast solid and the lid left off

An American pewter collection

By DR. ROBERT MALLORY III

**35TH
ANNIVERSARY
ARTICLE**

Unmarked chalices, one plain and the other beaded; both almost exactly the same in design and dimensions as the chalice of the Aaronsburg communion service attributed to William Will in ANTIQUES for April 1950 (p. 274). That chalice was 7 15/16 inches in height; here the plain one is 7 13/16 inches tall, the beaded example, 7 15/16, and cup sizes are identical. *Photographs by Taylor and Dull.*

Bowl and chalice by John Harrison Palethorp (Philadelphia, w. 1820-1845). Diameter of bowl, 5 inches; of chalice, 7⅞. Mark on bowl, PALETHORP'S PHILADA; on chalice, . . . ALETHO . . . , in rectangle. Beautifully made pieces by a pewterer of the Britannia period who left few examples of his work.

Hot-water plate with strongly impressed scales-and-name touch (Laughlin 538, 539) of William Will (Philadelphia, w. 1764-1798).

Drum-shape teapot by William Will; not previously recorded. This pot, which came to light recently in the disposition of effects of an old New Jersey family, is almost identical with one by the same maker published in ANTIQUES for January 1928 (p. 28). Only the marks differ; on this, the mark is Laughlin 537, and on the other it is Laughlin 542a. Over-all height, 5⅞ inches.

Five-inch flower-handle porringer of the type described as Rhode Island by Laughlin (ANTIQUES, May 1930, p. 437), with the IK sunburst touch attributed to Josiah Keene (Providence, w. 1801-1817). The handle is apparently from the same mold as that on a 5⅜-inch porringer originally illustrated in L. G. Myers' *Some Notes on American Pewterers*, and very similar to, though not identical with, that on Laughlin's Fig. 349.

MANY LOVERS OF AMERICAN PEWTER seem to feel that marked examples by early makers have all been recorded, exist only in the well-known collections, and can not be acquired today except when such a collection comes on the market. However, in forming our own small collection over the past five years, my wife and I have learned that if one searches diligently and is constantly on the lookout, it is still possible to acquire a group of surprisingly interesting pieces. True, some of these will come from established collections, and many will be examples already reported in the works of Ledlie I. Laughlin, J. B. Kerfoot, L. G. Myers, and Carl Jacobs, or in such publications as ANTIQUES, *The American Collector*, and the *Bulletin* of the Pewter Collectors' Club of America. But occasionally an unrecorded item will be found, or a form new to a particular maker, or it may be possible to associate a recorded maker with an unidentified mark. Instances of such gratifying discoveries are among the pieces I have selected for illustration here.

There are twenty-five pieces with the much discussed Love-bird touch in the collection. I have not included any of these among the items shown because they were described in ANTIQUES for January 1956 (p. 56).

The pewter at the head of the contents page in this issue is making its second appearance in ANTIQUES: it was first published in June 1940 (p. 300). The flat-top tankard and pair of beakers by Peter Young (New York and Albany, w. 1775-1795) originally formed the communion service of the Baptist Church of Cheshire, Massachusetts.

Footed pear-shape teapot by William Will; mark Laughlin 539. One of three such teapots known to be by this maker, it was first recorded in ANTIQUES for June 1940 (p. 300); the other two were published in March 1927 (p. 190) and April 1938 (frontispiece), respectively.

Quart tankards by New York makers, both with crenate lip and ram's-horn thumbpiece. The flat-top tankard with the bud terminal bears the initial mark (Laughlin 499) of William Kirby (w. 1760-1793), and the dome-top with fish-tail terminal that of Frederick Bassett (w. 1761-1780) (Laughlin 465).

Quart mug by Nathaniel Austin (Charlestown, Massachusetts; w. 1763-1807); an excellent example of the work of this maker, with its distinctive handle and touch on the terminal. This type of strap handle, to judge by known marked examples, was used only by the pewterers of New England.

A touch of unusual interest, found on a nine-inch plate in the collection. Crudely cut, it shows a pendent lamb, a fleur-de-lis, and the name Michel, and is believed to be the mark of André Michel, recorded as a tinsmith and pewterer who worked in New York from 1795 to 1797.

Pint and quart cans by Henry Will (New York and Albany, w. 1761-1793); simple in design and without the banding supposed to be typical of New York pewter of the period.

Crown-handle porringers from the same mold but by different makers; two other porringers with handles from this mold, and involving still a third maker (John Danforth, w. 1773-1793), are shown in Jacobs' *Guide to American Pewter* (Figs. 9 and 10). The porringer on the left (5¼ inches in diameter) has the mark attributed to both Joseph Belcher (Newport, w. 1769-1776) and Joseph Belcher, Jr. (Newport and New London, w. 1776-1785); the five-inch specimen on the right is by Josiah Danforth (Middletown, Connecticut, w. 1825-1837). The working dates of these men suggest that the mold was used by Joseph Belcher, Sr., and then passed into the Danforth family, though it could have been transferred when Joseph Jr. left Newport and his first wife about 1784. Crown-handle porringers were discussed by Percy E. Raymond in ANTIQUES for January 1948, p. 60.

Plates by New England pewterers. The largest (7½ inches) bears a double impression of the mark (Laughlin 285) of John Carnes (Boston, w. 1723-1760); the six-inch plate with rounded cavetto (left) has the rose and initial touch of Jacob Whitmore (Middletown, Connecticut, w. 1758-1790); that with the sharp drop is by David Melville (Newport, w. 1776-1793), marked with Laughlin 318 and 322.

FIG. 1—AMERICAN TANKARDS

a, Pewter, attributed to Benjamin Day, Newport, Rhode Island (*c. 1680–1757*). This tankard, found in Providence, is finely hammered over the entire surface of the barrel. The turned finial on the cover resembles those used by the early Rhode Island silversmiths. Compare Figure 1*c*.

b, Pewter, by John Will, New York (*c. 1711–1765*). Mark identical with the double mark accompanied by the full name JOHN WILL appearing on an 8-inch plate formerly in the Calder collection. The engraved initials and date

22 *March 1766* may signify a marriage token. *c* (*below, left*), New England silver tankard by Samuel Casey of Newport (*c. 1724–1770*). Finials on dome-lidded tankards seldom occur outside of New England. *From the Mabel Brady Garvan collection, Gallery of Fine Arts, Yale University*

FIG. 2 (*below, right*) — TANKARD BY JOHN BASSETT, NEW YORK (*1696–1761*)

Dome top; fishtail handle. The IB mark with fleur-de-lis was later changed to FB and used by John's son Frederick

AMERICAN PEWTER TANKARDS

By EDWARD E. MINOR

Except as noted, illustrations from the author's collection

AMERICAN pewter possesses precisely the attributes which Mr. Kerfoot so happily describes in his book as being all-important to the collector. More than that, besides the attribute of what Mr. Kerfoot terms "collectibility," the ware has an inherent beauty of texture and of shape that amply repays the collector for its acquisition and for the labor he may expend in its cleaning and repair. There seems to be an unwritten law that the dealer must never try to change the appearance of a pewter article. Perhaps that is well. The shop example, therefore, is quite likely to discredit those laudations of pewter which refer to the metal's satiny finish and romantic gleam. To one of experience, however, the dirty face is superficial. He knows at once whether or not the true surface lies beneath the outer grime.

Pewter tankards made by early American makers are rare. The acquisition of such a piece is usually regarded by the collector as a special dispensation of providence. Hence it seems worth while to show a group of such pieces, even though in so doing no fresh contribution is made to our knowledge of the early pewterers. Comparing the work of different makers is in itself of interest, and if in the process the reader's interest becomes kindled, he may perhaps ultimately experience those tantalizing pleasures which come to the collector seeking what so often proves to be unattainable. Kipling, in the story of *Kim*, quotes the saying of the ancient Lama,

"All desire is an illusion, and a further binding on the wheel." This is quite true. Yet there comes a time when the devotee is quite reconciled to his binding, confident that in the turning of the wheel pleasure and satisfaction will compensate for disappointments.

The tankard epitomizes the best in craftsmanship and design of the pewterer's work. It is perhaps a country cousin of the more aristocratic silver tankard. Undeniably plain beside the ornate embellishments of the more precious vessel, it still possesses a simple dignity and elegance that entitle it to respect and consideration. In form it may reflect the origin of its maker or the nationality of those for whom it was made. Free from the restrictions and supervision of a pewterers' guild, it may even express the personal art or ingenuity of the maker himself.

Shakespeare, in his play *Henry IV*, refers to pewter. In a scene which occurs in the Boar's Head Tavern, the following conversation between the rollicking Prince Hal and Francis takes place:

Prince Henry: How long hast thou to serve, Francis?
Francis: Forsooth, five years, and as much as to —
Prince Henry: Five years! By'r lady, a long lease for the clinking of pewter.

Now I surmise that the life of tavern tankards must have been hard and strenuous. Presumably they all reached oblivion at an early age. But on the other hand, there is no reason why a tankard dedicated

FIG. 3 — TANKARDS ATTRIBUTED TO WILLIAM BRADFORD JR., NEW YORK
(*1688–1759*)

a, Unusually fine example of the flat-lid Stuart type, solid handle and flat terminal. Mark WB similar to that of *b* but larger.

b, Mark WB with fleur-de-lis similar to that shown in Myers' *Notes on American Pewterers*. A family piece traced through original probate records in the State Library, Hartford, Connecticut, to the estate of Joseph Turner in 1759. This would bring the piece within Bradford's life span

to the more ceremonious libations of domestic hospitality should not have been cherished for an indefinite time, and during its periods of rest have occupied an honored place among the family lares and penates. Thus, in tracing one tankard back through probate records to the distribution of an estate in 1759, I found that the piece passed to the daughter of the house more frequently than to the son. Undoubtedly it was viewed as a symbol of hospitality, and as such was treasured by the housewife. The rifle, symbol of the home's protection, would have been prized by the man of the house and have occupied a place of honor above the fireplace, but still higher, on the shelf above, would have reposed the pewter tankard. And, like the warrior in Homer's *Iliad*, whose bright crest and shield shone with an unwearied fire, so would it gleam in the firelight of some early colonial home.

The design of early American pewter tankards does not closely conform to that current in England during the Stuart and Georgian periods. For this many reasons may be given. The Pewterers' Guild in New York was purely local, and exercised no control or supervision over pewterers in New England or Pennsylvania — probably very little in New York. Different colonies varied in nationality and taste. The attribution of a tankard to a particular maker is often in doubt, for the touches used on tankards rarely carried the full name. Initials, unless confirmed by more extended marks on flatware, are therefore hard to identify. Such difficulties, however, serve only to spur the interest and pleasure found in seeking these rarer forms of the pewterer's work.

The accompanying illustrations, taken from my own collection, are far from inclusive. Many highly interesting and attractive pieces are not

FIG. 4 — TANKARDS BY HENRY WILL, NEW YORK (*c. 1736–1802*)

a, Dome lid. Unusually clear marks.

b, Flat lid; pierced thumbpiece. Marks indistinct

FIG. 5 — THREE TANKARDS BY PEWTERERS OF NEW YORK STATE

a, By Spencer Stafford, Albany (*1770–1844*). A typical Peter Young form with the mark S. STAFFORD.

b, By William Kirby, New York (*c. 1740–1804*). Mark WK attributed to William Kirby. Thumbpiece partially cut away at side; unusually large serrated lip on lid. Letters of the mark are similar to those shown in Myers' *Notes*.

c, Unusually fine flat-lid Bassett tankard, probably Francis, New York (*1729–1800*). The thumbpiece shows evidence of repair

represented. If, however, they serve to awaken or to increase interest in the subject and help bring to light forgotten pieces for someone to enjoy, they will have accomplished their purpose.

A. E. Housman, in his well-known poem *A Shropshire Lad*, writes:

Many a peer of England brews
Livelier liquor than the Muse,
And malt does more than Milton can
To justify God's way to man.
Ale, man, ale's the stuff to drink
For fellows whom it hurts to think:
Look into the pewter pot

FIG. 6 — TANKARDS BY FREDERICK BASSETT, NEW YORK (*1740–1800*)
a, Flat-lid tankard with small lip. Unusually clear mark, FB with fleur-de-lis.
b, Dome-lid tankard, serrated lip. FB with fleur-de-lis mark; at right, illegible mark in serrated circle.
c, Flat-lid tankard with serrated lip. Unusually fine FB mark with stars, in roped circle

To see the world as the world's not.
And faith, 'tis pleasant 'till 'tis past:
The mischief is that 'twill not last.

We may look for the mark on a pewter pot and sigh to find it has lasted not. But the pot is worthy of preservation. Such knowledge of it as we have should be recorded and somehow made available for present and future students. Fulfilment of this duty may yield both justification and commendation to the insatiable yet discriminating collector.

In this connection it is pleasant to note the recent widespread revival of interest in the collecting of early pewter by American makers. The two chief reference books on the subject are *American Pewter*, by J. B. Kerfoot, published in 1924, and *Some Notes on American Pewterers*, by Louis Guerineau Myers, published in 1926. The past twelve years, however, have witnessed further research and discovery, whose results will be embodied in a new and comprehensive treatise on American pewter now being prepared by Ledlie I. Laughlin of Princeton, New Jersey.

FIG. 7 — TANKARD BY WILLIAM WILL, PHILADELPHIA (*1742–1798*)
A fine example of the bulbous form. Similar to William Will tankard illustrated in Myers' *Notes*, but showing pierced thumbpiece, band around the barrel, and a far more crisp and vigorous contour of base and lid

FIG. 8 — PEWTER TANKARDS
a and *b*, By Parks Boyd, Philadelphia (*directories, 1798–1819*). Somewhat similar in form and exhibiting curiously truncated dome lid. The second tankard ornamented with two rows of triple bands above the barrel and beading around lip of lid.
c, Tall tankard by William Will (*1742–1798*). Thumbpiece with heart piercing. Comparison with *a* and *b* is interesting, particularly if Boyd was an apprentice of William Will. General dimensions of all three tankards are similar

Fig. 1 — A Group of English Porringer Handles

a, 1674 to *c.* 1730 or 1735; *b*, 1675 to *c.* 1717; *c*, 1695 to *c.* 1760; *d*, *c.* 1730 in England. This last shape has also been found with the touches of Dutch pewterers. Especially drawn by Howard H. Cotterell, F. R. Hist. S., and printed by his permission.

The American Pewter Porringer

By Ledlie I. Laughlin

Since the late John Barrett Kerfoot, with his monumental volume *American Pewter*, supplied the impulse to further investigation along the lines which he had marked, a great many fresh discoveries have been made. Long-forgotten names of early craftsmen have been retrieved from oblivion; life histories have been reconstructed from scattered and fragmentary documents; and, best of all, out of long obscurity has emerged specimen after specimen to reveal the dignity and beauty of the native pewter of Colonial days. The work begun by Mr. Kerfoot was materially advanced by Louis Guerineau Myers, in his genial *Some Notes on American Pewterers*. From time to time, likewise, ANTIQUES has offered additions to available stores of information. The entire subject of American pewter is now under review by Ledlie I. Laughlin of Princeton, New Jersey, who, in a book to be published in the fall or early winter, will present the results of long delvings into old and new sources of knowledge. ANTIQUES is happy to introduce Mr. Laughlin to its readers through the following article, which, though brief, opens an avenue of approach to pewter collecting, safe even to the beginner's footsteps. — *The Editor.*

SO alluring has the collector of American pewter found the search for rare touch marks that, in many cases, he has failed to make due note of the forms on which these touches are impressed. Some shapes are so definitely American, in fact so definitely the work of specific pewterers, that they may be identified without need for examining the touches upon them. It is merely a matter of comparing their characteristics with those of examples

Fig. 2 — Types of Handle Most Frequent on Surviving American Porringers

Over ninety per cent of marked American porringers fall into one of these three classifications: *a*, Rhode Island handle; only form used by Providence makers; found also on some Newport pieces. Except for one example by the Boardmans of Hartford, never reported on any porringers made outside of Rhode Island. Period, 1771 to *c.* 1825. This specimen by Gershom Jones of Providence (*1774-1809*). *b*, New York and New England (except Rhode Island). Period, 1770, or earlier, to *c.* 1825. This specimen by unidentified maker (*1775-1800*). Initials *W. N.* cast in relief on reverse of handle. *c*, New York and New England (except Rhode Island). Period, 1770, and probably much earlier, to *c.* 1820. Same design in silver of seventeenth and eighteenth centuries. Compare English handle (*Fig. 1b*). This specimen by Thomas Danforth, 3d, of Rocky Hill, Connecticut (*1777-1790*). Some pewterers had molds for both *b* and *c*. *Author's collection*

Fig. 3 (left) — AN EARLY DESIGN
Used in both Great Britain and the Colonies. Period in England, *c.* 1690 to 1720. Probably obsolete in this country before 1770. Rare in both countries. This specimen bears the initials *I. W.* (possibly John Will of New York) on reverse of handle. It is, with little doubt, American, *c.* 1760 or earlier. *Diameter: 5 inches. From the collection of Mrs. J. H. Krom*

Fig. 4 (right) — FOUND IN BOTH AMERICA AND ENGLAND
Exceedingly rare in this country. Period in England, *c.* 1725. This specimen by John Danforth of Norwich, Connecticut (*c. 1772–1792*). *Diameter: 4½ inches.* As Danforth inherited his molds from his father, Thomas, working as early as 1733, we may assume that the mold for this handle dates from *c.* 1733. Probably not used after *c.* 1780. *From the collection of W. C. Staples*

already classified on the basis of their marks. Of all forms made by American pewterers, the porringer, with its exceptional diversity of handle designs, lends itself most readily to such a study, and best repays it.

Porringers were used by the earliest English settlers in America, and were, with little doubt, made by our first pewterers. Although the form became virtually obsolete in England soon after the middle of the eighteenth century — certainly by 1775 — most of the surviving American specimens were produced after 1800. In Philadelphia and the South there was, apparently, little demand for these vessels after the Revolution; and existing New York specimens, all of them made prior to 1800, are rare. But, in New England, porringers were turned out generously until about 1825. For a few years longer

their manufacture continued in Connecticut and Rhode Island, though on a declining scale; and then, about 1830, abruptly ceased, not to be resumed.

The porringer was ordinarily cast in two parts, the bowl and the handle. We shall not tarry long over the former. Its function was purely utilitarian — to hold food — and, after a vessel had been evolved satisfactorily to serve that purpose, succeeding makers deviated but little from a standard form. We find, in general, but two shapes of porringer bowl: first, the normal container with bulging sides, contracted at top and bottom, surmounted by a narrow perpendicular lip, the bottom consisting of a flat circular gutter with domed centre; second, the basin with handle, which is, in reality, not a porringer at all, but a porringer-basin. The latter type of bowl is usually found only in the larger

Fig. 5 — PORRINGER-BASINS
a, Found only with Richard Lee touches. Probable period, 1790–1800 (northwestern New England). No counterpart in English pewter. The elder Lee spent his early years in and near Rhode Island. Hence his reminiscence of the normal Rhode Island handle (*Fig. 2a*). Though handsome in outline, the handle was probably too frail for the hard service to which these vessels were put. Rare. *Diameter: 5⅞ inches. b*, Dolphin handle of John Danforth (Norwich, Connecticut). Cf. Figure 1*d*. Although not so graceful as its English prototype, doubtless more serviceable; much more ambitious in design than any other American handle. Probable date, 1733–1780. See comment in Figure 4. *Diameter: 5⅝ inches. Author's collection*

Fig. 6 (left) — PERHAPS UNIQUE

A four-inch porringer by Joseph Belcher of Newport, Rhode Island (*c. 1780*). Similar in outline to French solid-handle porringers of the same period. During the Revolution a large French expeditionary force was quartered at Newport, and Belcher probably mended foreign examples, which inspired his model. *From the collection of Mrs. J. Insley Blair*

Fig. 7 (right) — TASTER WITH FOUR HANDLES

Single-handle specimens, otherwise identical, also exist. All these pieces bear the name *R. Lee* cast in relief on handle support. Date probably *c. 1790*. Crude and frail. More interesting for oddity than for beauty or usefulness. *Diameter: 4 inches. From the collection of W. C. Staples*

porringers, with a diameter of 5½ to 6 inches, and in diminutive tasters or doll-size basins.

But, whereas the shape of the bowl invited little experimentation, the handle was a feature well adapted to individual decorative treatment. It afforded such endless opportunity for diversification of pattern under favorable circumstances that each pewterer might easily have devised a design peculiar to his own product. Unfortunately, however, molds were very costly in early days. A fledgling pewterer, on completing his apprenticeship, usually started out with an old set of molds, either inherited or purchased, and these in turn he passed on to his successor; so that the same molds were forced to serve one generation after another. And, even when the young pewterer had to buy an entire new equipment, custom and the conservatism of his trade led him to select shapes to which the public was accustomed. Consequently, instead of hundreds of different designs in porringer handles, we have, thus far, found less than two dozen varieties impressed with the touches of American pewterers.

Even at that we may congratulate ourselves, for no such multiplicity is known in England; and it is probably greater than can be matched among surviving porringers of any Continental country. The reason is perhaps discoverable in the fact that our pewterers were men of divers nationalities, catering to buyers who naturally preferred the styles to which they had been accustomed in their respective homelands. Hence the American output embodied English forms, Continental forms, and variations upon, or combinations of, the two.

We may roughly divide all porringer handles into two distinct classes: first, the solid type; and, second, the pierced,

Fig. 8 — AMERICAN TASTERS

Tiny vessels of this type were in use in vine growing countries of Europe, but, it is believed, were never made in England. Except for *b*, which has a slightly domed base, all five are merely diminutive basins with handles. *a* is a form — not a very successful one — used by Thomas D. Boardman of Hartford, *c.* 1810. The apparent intention of the designer to produce a handle resembling a crown in outline suggests that the mold was made for some pewterer first working when the Colonies were still under British dominion. *Diameter: 3¾ inches. b, c,* and *d* (measuring 3¼, 2¾, and 2¼ inches respectively) bear Richard Lee touches (Springfield, Vermont, *c. 1800–1820*). As far as now known, these shapes were used by no other maker. *b* is a very substantial vessel of considerable merit. Others extremely fragile. One can conceive of no use to which they could have been put other than as toys. *e* measures just 2⅛ inches in diameter; the smallest of marked American porringers. The letters *I.C.L. & Co.* are cast in relief on the reverse side of handle; attributed to Isaac C. Lewis of Meriden, Connecticut, in the 1840's. Poorly made; interesting chiefly on account of size. *Author's collection*

or openwork, type. The former was an inheritance from the continent of Europe. Howard H. Cotterell, the foremost authority on British pewter, tells me that he has never seen an English porringer with a solid handle. It is the pierced handle which is characteristic of British porringers. To be sure, this latter form is found also on some Continental pieces; but, generally speaking, the British handle is perforated, the Continental, solid. In this country we find both forms, with the perforated decidedly in the majority and evidently the favorite.

Before taking up the American shapes, it seems wise to call attention to a few of the styles favored by the pewterers of England. Mr. Cotterell has very kindly sketched for me, in silhouette, four generic types of English porringer handle, which I am privileged, through his courtesy, to illustrate in Figure 1. There were, of course, many others, but few of them have survived to the present day.

Contrary to usual opinion, I am satisfied that the earliest form of American handle was pierced rather than solid; for the majority of our early settlers, and the earliest American pewterers on record, were Englishmen, who would naturally have followed English custom. But in the districts where Continental influence was strong we might reasonably expect to encounter solid handles; and in those very sections they come to light.

In the country districts of Pennsylvania, largely settled by Germans and Swiss, solid-handle porringers were the normal form. Likewise the only Philadelphia porringer thus far identified has a solid handle. It is probable, however, that Philadelphia pewterers of English birth or

extraction made porringers with openwork handles. But that matter can be determined only if, and when, other Philadelphia porringers are identified.

In only one other section of the Colonies do we find the solid handle; and there apparently it did not supplant the pierced form, but was manufactured in competition with the latter. Newport, in 1770, was the most cosmopolitan town in New England, with a foreign trade greater than that of New York. It is, therefore, not surprising that the solid handle should have obtained recognition among the pewterers of the Rhode Island city.

In time, we may possibly learn that early pewterers of Dutch lineage in New York or Albany employed the solid handle; but it would be, to say the least, inexplicable were we to find such a form bearing the touch of a pewterer of Massachusetts, Maryland, or any of the southern Colonies, where the great majority of settlers were of English extraction.

An examination of the accompanying illustrations will give an acquaintance with the forms most frequently found in England and America. They will also enable the reader to distinguish between the solid handles of Newport and those of Pennsylvania; the pierced handles of Rhode Island and the shapes made in other Colonies; and, in some instances, to determine, by pattern alone, the handiwork of individual pewterers.

It must not be inferred that this brief survey covers every known variety of American porringer handle. Several designs which differ but slightly from one or another of those illustrated have purposely been omitted. It is, fur-thermore, certain that other patterns are hidden away in collections which I have not had the good fortune to examine. These, we may be sure, will gradually come to light. The interest in pewter awakened by the late Mr. Kerfoot has set many other collectors to studying the craftsmanship of the early pewterers, and to searching for documents concerning these men.

It is to be hoped, however, that the different forms here presented will afford collectors a reasonably comprehensive view of the scope of porringers; and will enable them to determine a little more readily than heretofore the date and source of examples which come under their inspection.

For the embryo collector casting about for some form of his forefathers' handiwork on which he may concentrate his attention with the maximum of interest, I recommend the American pewter porringer. Once a household article on the tables of rich and poor alike, today the vessel is obsolete. The alloy in which it was made has passed from daily use; and the name itself, reminiscent of another age, is meaningless to many of this generation. A perfect symbol of all that we, in this machine-made day, have lost, the porringer has not only beauty, simplicity, and distinction, but the glamour that surrounds any art form of an era that has forever gone.

Note. In reading the proof of these notes, it occurs to me that I should, perhaps, qualify my statement as to the date when porringer-making ceased in England, by observing that, for some time, the manufacture of porringers for export to the American Colonies continued on a limited scale in Bristol. — *L. I. L.*

UNIQUE CROWN-HANDLED PORRINGERS

By PERCY E. RAYMOND

Percy E. Raymond was the first president of the Pewter Collectors' Club of America, in which he has been active ever since. In June 1945 we published his article on pewter teapots and coffee biggins.

COMMONLY ONE SEES as through a glass, darkly. Someone applied the name crown-handled to porringers with a particular type of ear, and as the resemblance to a crown was obvious, the name seemed acceptable. I saw as darkly as others until a friend, C. H. Paige, who is not particularly interested in pewter, pointed out the true significance of this attractive handle (*Figs. 1, 5, 7*).

As he demonstrated, the "crown" is really a viscount's coronet. The band above the shield is the circlet, set with jewels. Each of the little protuberances represents a diamond, ruby, or other precious stone. The bosses in a concentric ring above are the pearls or silver balls which a viscount could display. He was entitled to twelve. Six of these would be on view from one side, and that is the number shown in most small handles. Designers of the larger specimens have taken a liberty with this arrangement, and, to give more prominence to the median axis, have shown only five, the central one larger than the others. Above this ring is the cap, its velvet indicated by raised dots. Topping this is a boss representing the knot of the tassel. Two cords of the latter extend upward, surrounding the opening which enables one to hang the vessel on a hook. Some show a knot above, others lack it. Only the best-preserved specimens show the velvet of the cap; doubtless that is why the true interpretation has been delayed.

The baroque scrolls which embrace the coronet are probably the designer's substitute for the supporters which should uphold the non-existent crest, although it is possible that they represent mantling. Paige has added another charm to these handles, long ignored because they were relatively common, and touchless, or marked with unidentified initials. So have the lowly become exalted!

But porringers of this type are far from being common in England. Roland J. A. Shelley, president of the Society of Pewter Collectors, tells me that he has the only pair he has ever seen in his country. Perhaps this sort was made for export, for rare as they are, we could probably assemble a dozen or more of English origin in our collections. Mr. Shelley's specimens have touches which show that they were made in the latter part of the seventeenth century, but do not lead us back to the original designer, who probably operated under the patronage of a viscount.

The first unique crown-handled specimen to be mentioned be-

FIGS. 1, 2. Front and back views of the David Melville porringer. Note the twists in the cords of the tassel, and the narrow reinforcement plate, with triangular bracket. *Collection of Doctor Madelaine R. Brown.*

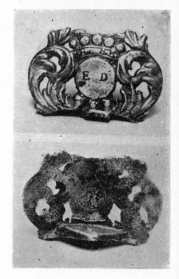

FIGS. 3, 4. Front and back views of the lovebird handle. Note the circle of dots on the bracket. *Collection of John F. Ruckman.*

longs to Doctor Madelaine R. Brown. A rubbing of this appeared in an advertisement by the late George C. Gebelein in the September 1939 number of ANTIQUES. The bowl is 4¼ inches in diameter, the handle 2⅛ inches long and 2¼ inches wide. There really are six pearls above the circlet, although one is definitely larger than the others. In this respect it conforms to the general style for small crown-handled porringers. As can be seen (*Fig. 1*), the velvet is picked out nicely, and the corrugations around the hanger indicate the twists in the cord of the tassel. A unique feature is the narrow, almost parallel-sided plate of reinforcement on the back (*Fig. 2*). One wonders why this porringer is unique. Did Melville make, or have made, a mold in order to cast this one dish? He obviously thought well of it, for he placed his anchor touch, revered by collectors, on the shield. So far as is known, this is the only crown-handled porringer he ever made.

We have thought of crown handles as the products of New England and New York City. It therefore came as a great surprise when John F. Ruckman of Doylestown, Pennsylvania, announced in Bulletin 19 of the Pewter Collectors' Club that he had a crown handle bearing the now familiar "lovebird" touch. Whoever it was who used this mark obviously had headquarters in the general region of Philadelphia, an area in which the native pewterers seem to have completely ignored this sort of handle. A curious

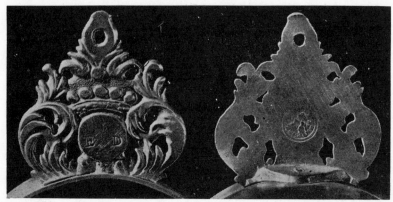

FIGS. 5, 6. Front and back views of the handle of a perfect lovebird porringer. Note the flattening of all bosses and of the tassels, a feature with English implications. *Collection of Joseph France.*

circumstance about the specimen is that the greater part of the body of the porringer is gone, as is the tip of the handle (*Figs. 3, 4*). Someone saved the fragment because it was "pretty" or unusual.

Analysis of the design shows that it is of the English-New York type (see *American Collector*, April 1946, p. 11, fig. 5). It might even have come from the same mold as Joseph France's W B (William Bradford) specimen. The circlet has three conspicuous jewels, bounded on either side by smaller ones arranged in the form of colons. It can easily be transcribed in print, ··:·:·:··, except that the three periods in the middle should be larger than the others. The five pearls above the circlet are flattened, perhaps from constant scouring. More significant is the fact that the circular shield has a narrow median support, on either side of which at the top are two tiny bosses, exactly as in the example by W B. This feature has been seen on no other handle. On each side, beneath the shield, are two large bosses, supported by the innermost of the sprigs belonging to the supporters. This is a general English-New York characteristic. A feature of unknown significance is the presence on the triangular bracket of a circle of seven small raised dots surrounding a boss (*Fig. 4*).

This analysis would lead one to believe that the mold in which this handle was run was made in England early in the eighteenth century. It is impossible to say when the casting was done. If it develops that there was an actual pewterer named Love, he must have had an extraordinary medley of old and new molds. Perhaps he was a collector; perhaps a thrifty purchaser of discarded, outmoded implements. I should think that this mold was contemporaneous with that for his measure, now in the collection of Ledlie I. Laughlin. *Circa* 1725 would be my guess as to their date.

Since the above was written, Joseph France has got a virtually perfect specimen of this same sort of porringer, with, curiously enough, the same owner's initials (*Fig. 5*). All bosses are flattened, but the stem below the shield is exceptionally well preserved, and on it are three little tubercles, in a triangle. The bracket (*Fig. 6*) is exactly like that of Mr. Ruckman's specimen. It is only in the details of the bracket that the lovebird pieces differ from that with the W B touch. It seems probable that all three were poured in the same mold. Did the owner of the lovebird touch buy from William Bradford, or did he buy Bradford's mold?

Another porringer, this one of the Boardman type, 4¼ inches in diameter, presents some unusual features (*Fig. 7*). Joseph France called my attention to this specimen in the collection of Henry B. Reardon, Jr., during the meeting of the Pewter Collectors' Club at the home of the latter at Farmington, Connecticut. As compared with other crown handles, it appears to be simplified. The supporters on all small handles are much less elaborate than those on large ones, both at the base and where they meet the tassel. In this example, the circlet is remarkably plain, there being only a single row of ten jewels, all of the same size. As is usual in handles of this size, there are six pearls. The velvet is smooth, and there is no prolongation above the hanger. The combination of these features makes the whole handle appear short and wide,

and it seems to be rounded rather than triangular.

The bracket, however, (*Fig. 8*) is the feature which makes this porringer unique. A few porringers are known in which the handles are supported by a wedge-shaped downward extension of the metal in the region where they are attached to the basin (*Fig. 9*). This has been called the wedge type of bracket. But the Reardon specimen differs from this in having a triangular projection in the middle of the wedge. To a certain extent, it corresponds to the acro-form type of New England bracket, employed chiefly by the Newport pewterers on their plain-handled porringers. This unique type may be referred to as the wedge-and-triangle bracket. It has been seen on a porringer with the American "old English" type of handle. Although unmarked, there is reason to believe that the latter was made by the Boardmans.

One of the striking features is the clarity with which the jewels in the circlet may be seen. There are other crown-handled specimens that seem to have a row in which all are of uniform size, but in most cases this is because the castings are so poor that it is difficult to count them. Mr. France has an example by R G in which they are fairly well defined, and there appear to be nine, instead of ten.

Melville T. Nichols has a W N porringer of the smaller size (*Figs. 10, 11*) with a broad, elongate, unsymmetrically placed rat-tail, which must have been added after the casting was made, for it obliterates the greater part of the W. Obviously this is no repair job, ancient or modern, for there is no indication of any need for mending. The upper surface is clean-cut, and is especially interesting as showing the jewels, alternating in size, and the velvet. W N appears to have been especially successful with the latter. He must have had a really good bronze mold, and known how to use it. Mr. Nichols' specimen is unique, but, perhaps one might say, secondarily so. I G, R G, and S G had molds which produced small, but real, rat-tails.

JOSEPH COPELAND, 17TH-CENTURY PEWTERER

By WORTH BAILEY

Museum Technician, Jamestown Archeological Project, Colonial National Historical Park

Photographs by courtesy of National Park Service

NOTABLE among the matchless specimens in the Jamestown archeological collection is a bit of pewter more highly prized than might be a jewel from a royal treasure. Its one-time grace of line, refined proportion, and subtle sheen of surface have long since fallen prey to a peculiar pewter malady which accompanies long burial in the soil. As a matter of fact, the object is incomplete, and yet, despite such obvious shortcomings, it is held in the highest regard by those who value an authentic and vital "document" of a past period.

Destined to be the "sesame" to a craft drama enacted in Virginia toward the end of the seventeenth century, this spoon fragment, freshly unearthed from an ancient trash heap, was at first sight scarcely more appealing than thousands of other vestiges of cultural material recovered from Jamestown. However, recognized as an unusual variant of the *trifid, split end,* or *pied-de-biche* type fashionable during the second half of the seventeenth century, it was passed through a strict laboratory routine established to care for all artifacts. This process of watchful observation in turn disclosed the maker's touch impressed in the trefoil finial of the stem, thus rewarding painstaking effort with amazing discovery.

Now entirely decipherable, this mark reveals, in addition to the name of the craftsman, a Virginia place name as his address, and a date which probably refers to the year in which he started business. The form of the mark, which incorporates the heart device, popular at the time, is singularly interesting. The complete legend, framed in concentric circles, proclaims: IOSEPH COPELAND/1675/CHUCKATUCK. In so far as I am aware, this is the sole surviving mark of an American pewterer of the seventeenth century. Quite as important, however, from the standpoint of Jamestown research, is the fact that this mark supplied the clue which led to some hitherto forgotten names and thus to the retrieval of an early craft endeavor from unmerited oblivion.

In the early stages of the investigation, it was established that Copeland, or so-called "Chuckatuck," spoons enjoyed wide usage at Jamestown. No less than six fragments excavated from various portions of the Island were identified as coming from the same mold. Some idea of their original appearance may be gained from the accompanying illustration

showing two views of a composite reconstruction based on several fragments. Conforming agreeably to the outline of the trefoil, the stamp occupied a position noticeably at variance with the usual practice of the period, which placed spoon marks in the bowl or on the back of the stem.

For a report on the composition of the metal I am indebted to Professor Armstrong of the Chemistry Department of the College of William and Mary, Williamsburg, Virginia, who undertook a careful analysis of specimens submitted to him, with the following results:

Tin	85–95 per cent.
Lead	3– 5 " "
Copper	1– 3 " "
Zinc	1– 2 " "
Iron	Trace

This shows that Copeland's pewter formula was substantially the same as that used by English pewterers of his day, and conformed to that for spoons given by Massé (*Pewter Plate*).

The next logical step in the study of the spoon was to follow up the clue afforded by the Chuckatuck address label.

The desperate struggle to obtain a foothold in Virginia, begun by the London Company at Jamestown in 1607, had, by the end of the first quarter of the century, assumed a more hopeful aspect. Virginia as a royal province was prospering. Steadily expanding along her navigable rivers, the settlements by 1634 had been grouped into eight political divisions called "shires" (now counties). Others were created as an influx of population warranted. In 1652 the country "over the water," as the southside region across the James River from Jamestown was then termed, accommodated the counties of Surry, Isle of Wight, and Nansemond. In the northern portion of Nansemond ran Chuckatuck River (later demoted to the status of Creek), which contributed the designation

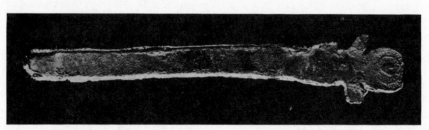

FIG. 1 — HANDLE OF THE COPELAND OR "CHUCKATUCK" SPOON EXCAVATED AT JAMESTOWN
Total length of handle, 5 ½ inches

FIG. 2 — BOWL FRAGMENT OF ONE OF SEVERAL EXAMPLES OF THE SAME TYPE OF SPOON
Diameters of bowls: greater, 2 3/8 inches; smaller, 2 1/8 inches

FIG. 3 — DETAIL OF JOSEPH COPELAND TOUCH
This mark appears on the handle of Figure 1. The type is reminiscent of many employed by English craftsmen of the late seventeenth century. *One and one half times enlarged*

for the parish. Attracting the attention of settlers as early as 1635, the southside counties soon became a haven for dissenters, among them numerous Quakers.

The John Copeland (in the Quaker records variously written Copland or Coplands) listed in Hotten (*Emigrants to America*) as embarking at London for Virginia in 1635 may have been the first bearer of the name to settle at Chuckatuck. He was an ardent Quaker and joined a dauntless group of Friends on a missionary pilgrimage to New England in the hope of converting the inhabitants of that rockbound territory. Instead of being received in a spirit of religious tolerance, the members of the party were dubbed "blasphemous heretics." John Copeland was jailed, and having been deprived of an ear at the hands of the Boston hangman, thought it advisable to transfer his remaining person to a more benign environment. He retired to Chuckatuck, where, by virtue of his mutilation, he thenceforth rated as a hero.

Our theatre of investigation now widens to include London. From that source A. Stanley Grant, of the Worshipful Company of Pewterers, has supplied

FIG. 4 — CHUCKATUCK SPOON AS RECONSTRUCTED BY THE AUTHOR
Based upon fragments recovered at the Jamestown site

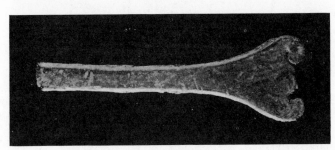

FIG. 5 — FRAGMENT OF A SECOND SPOON ATTRIBUTED TO COPELAND
Another unusual variant of the trifid spoon handle to suggest local origin. These fragments bear no mark and may date from the later, or Jamestown, phase of this pewterer's undertaking

information that places the world of students deeply in his debt. Mr. Grant writes that records, now privately owned by a member of the venerable pewter organization, show one Joseph Copeland to have been the son of Thomas Copeland, a citizen and spectacle-maker of London. The same document further states that the lad was bound apprentice to John Mann, May 17, 1666, for a term of seven years. At that time Joseph must have been approximately in his seventeenth year. Mann's fine professional record is indicated in Cotterell's invaluable work, *Old Pewter, Its Makers and Marks in England, Scotland, and Ireland*. No extant records show that Joseph Copeland took up his freedom in the Pewterers' Company. Not improbably he had early decided on a career in Virginia and considered that the formalities of taking up his freedom in London might hamper rather than help his ambition.

Perhaps it is not wide of the mark to suggest that Joseph was a nephew of the John Copeland already cited and was influenced to settle at Chuckatuck under the patronage of his uncle, who we know was well established as a large landholder and an influential member of a prosperous Quaker community.

We cannot say precisely when Joseph Copeland established himself at Chuckatuck. Since strict regulations prevented his working as a journeyman in England without first taking out freedom in the company, it is probable that he emigrated to Virginia at the expiration of his apprenticeship, and began turning out work in his own name two years later. This hypothesis appears to be confirmed by the date given in his touch. His first mention in the Chuckatuck meeting appears in the following entry in the Quaker records: "Mary Copeland wife of Joseph Copeland departed this Life ye 27th day of the: 3 month 1678."

In due course Joseph remarried, this time espousing a daughter of Major Thomas Taberer of the Virginia Militia, and also a justice and burgess of Isle of Wight County. In the document previously cited will be found frequent reference to meetings at the home of John Copeland and the signatures of John, Joseph, and their wives — both of the latter confusingly bearing the Christian name Elizabeth — as witnesses to marriages performed between members of the congregation.

For the next mention of our pewterer we must look to the *Journals of the Virginia House of Burgesses, 1659/60–1693*. On May 12, 1688, the House agreed that "a careful & trusty person have in his Custody the Severall utensils and Ornaments belonging to this house for their more Safe keeping," and "Resolved that Joseph Copeland have the possession & keeping of the said Ornaments & utensills untill the next Sessions of Assembly & that he have in his Custody the Key of the Assembly room to carefully Keep look after & preserve the same." The colonial authorities appear to have moved at the same dilatory and labyrinthine pace which stamps

officialdom to this day. Three years later, Joseph, still serving as caretaker of the Statehouse, was "praying to be allowed for looking after & keeping cleane the Assembly roome & utensills."

It may have been a desire to be in closer association with the hub of all political affairs and to gain a speaking acquaintance, at least, with the social leaders of the colony that ultimately induced Copeland to acquire property at Jamestown and establish his family there within the shadow of the Statehouse whose properties he had been appointed to supervise.

No documentary reference to Joseph, subsequent to 1691, has been found. Between the date of his last petition for pay due him, 1691, and that of his father-in-law's will, 1692, he evidently passed on to a realm where the cares of a pioneer craftsman were forgotten. In the will referred to, dated January 14, 1692, Justice Taberer provided for a division of his household effects and stock to "dau. Elizabeth Copeland's children." One grandson was noted in particular, Joseph Copeland [Junior], who was to inherit the plantation, known as Basse's Choyce, provision being made to keep him "to school at his own charge till he can write and cypher sufficiently." Taberer's further fondness for young Joseph was shown in bequeathing to him "a feather bed I lie on usually." Under terms of the will Joseph the younger was made the sole executor, with instructions to provide for those on the plantation. Justice Taberer died two years later, leaving Joseph Junior still in his minority.

An inventory of the estate at this time is of particular value in showing what a well-supplied household possessed in the way of pewter. A good assortment follows: "ffour new puter Dishes, one bason: . . . one pewter mustard pot, one pyplate. Eight Deep

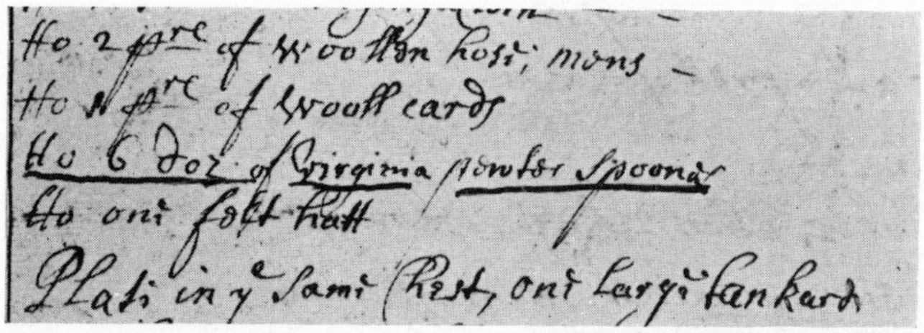

FIG. 6 — PORTION OF THE INVENTORY OF MR. NICHOLAS SMITH'S ESTATE

Taken June 5, 1696, Isle of Wight *Will Book No. II (1661–1719)*, p. 359. The fifteenth entry on the list (underlined in photograph) refers to a group of *"Virginia pewter Spoones."* In view of the Jamestown find, this entry of previously obscure meaning becomes a virtual reference to the work of Copeland

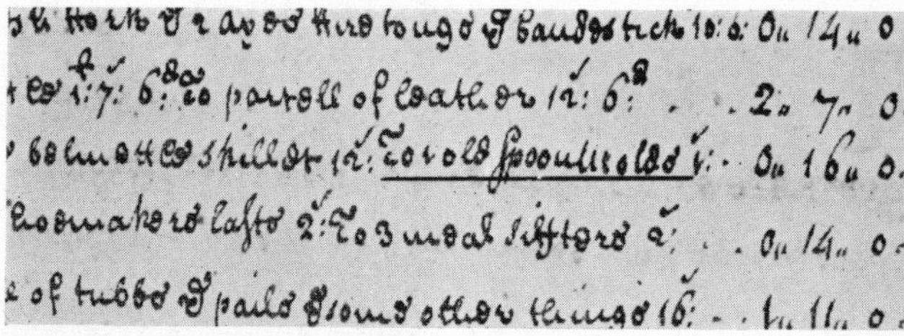

FIG. 7 — SECTION OF THE INVENTORY OF JOSEPH COPELAND [JUNIOR]

Dated August 18, 1726, Isle of Wight *Will Book, No. III (1726–1733)*, p. 10. The passage reading *"2 old Spoonmolds,"* underlined in photograph, not improbably refers to equipment inherited from the elder Copeland. The locating of this interesting document contributes evidence corroborating the spoon discoveries at Jamestown

Dishes, five broad Dishes, Eleven old plates, ffour Peutar Chamber pots, two old sassers, two puter Candlesticks, one barbers bason, two small basons, one skimer, one bed pan, two large fflaggons, two pewter Tankerds, one salt siller." The inventory also listed a good selection of silver items: "one silver heded cane . . . one silver seale, Six silver spoones, one silver sack Cup & one silver Dram Cup, one silver tobacco box."

The archives of the contiguous county of Isle of Wight supply sustaining evidence. Thus, the inventory of the estate of Nicholas Smith, taken June 5, 1696, totaled £338:03:03 ¾ and included 81 ounces of plate at five shillings and sixpence, worth £22:05:06. In addition, the following articles of pewter were listed together: "38 dishes; one doz*n* of New plates, 14 old ditto, one doz*n* old Spoones English, one bason, one Cullender, 1 pye plate, 1 stand, 6 Chamber potts, 2 quart potts, 1 pint pott, one flaggon, 2 Salts, 2 tumblers, 2 dram cups, 3 tankards, one *Pre* Candle Sticks & one od one." However, the most enlightening feature of the inventory concerned a chest of goods in the "Parlour Chamber," containing for the most part English fabrics, but likewise carefully noting pieces of Scotch, French, and Virginia origin. Referring to spoons stored in the same chest, the following designation is carefully made: "6 doz: of *Virginia* [italics mine] pewter Spoones"! We are on safe ground in assuming that these Virginia pewter spoons were the work of Copeland. Their appraisal at one shilling sixpence per dozen was approximately the value placed upon such articles at the time.

In the Court House of Isle of Wight were also filed the will, inventory, and appraisal of the estate of Joseph Copeland, son of the pewterer. Like his father before him, Joseph Junior hardly reached middle age, for he died in 1725. His inventory lists a considerable supply of pewter. More to the point, however, is an impressive entry, all but hidden amongst brass and ironware, listing "2 old Spoonmolds," valued at two shillings. These probably were a remnant of the father's craft equipment.

As for Copeland's products other than spoons, we can only surmise. In this connection it should be remarked that a second type of spoon handle, similar in character to the Chuckatuck specimen but lacking its distinguishing mark, has several times been encountered in the excavations. Other finds worthy of future investigation are the heavy, crude, but extremely decorative dress

FIG. 8 — SECTION OF AUGUSTINE HERRMAN'S MAP (1673) OF VIRGINIA, SHOWING THE SOUTHSIDE COUNTIES IN RELATION TO JAMESTOWN

Chuckatuck lies about 18 miles "as the crow flies" due south of the capital (indicated by circle). Herrman's indifference to the accepted orthography of the time is noticeable in Chuckatuck, which he spells *Chukkotuck*. Nansemond County and River each enjoy different notations. Likewise, Herrman's own name claims two versions

buttons of pewter and lead that from time to time are uncovered. One of these, an imperfect casting obviously discarded, definitely suggests the likelihood of local manufacture. In a country where the raw materials necessary to the practice of the pewter trade were entirely lacking, re-used metal must have supplied the bulk of the deficiency.

Perhaps Copeland's activities in the unfriendly environment of Virginia more closely resembled those of an itinerant tinker than of the traditional English craftsman. Having exhausted the pewter-repairing needs of the Chuckatuck section, he may have been seeking a more lucrative field on the opposite side of the river when he removed to Jamestown about 1688. In any event, the pewterware imported from England must have remained ever a serious threat to his trade. Accumulated evidence, however, in proving Copeland's presence at Jamestown and in uncovering valid examples of his handiwork, as well as specimens that may safely be attributed to him, establishes the point that he persisted in his pewter venture to the end of his comparatively short life.

NOTES

1. Old-style dates have been employed throughout.

2. To those who have generously assisted me in the research essential to the preparation of the foregoing discussion, I take this opportunity to express my very deep sense of gratitude. I am particularly indebted to Messrs. A. Stanley Grant of the Worshipful Company of Pewterers; W. E. MacClenny, who contributed little-known facts in Chuckatuck's early history; Robert H. Land, former historian for the Jamestown project, for miscellaneous historical data; W. L. Guy and A. R. Armstrong, both of the Science Department of the College of William and Mary, for chemical assistance. Special thanks are also due Doctor Earl G. Swem, Librarian of the same institution, for frequent encouragement and advice.

I have likewise had access to the original volumes of Land Patents for the seventeenth century, now deposited in the State Capitol at Richmond, to the court records of the same period in the Clerk's Office in Isle of Wight County, and to the archives of the Williamsburg Restoration. For various favors received at the hands of the custodians of these documents, I offer befitting thanks.

In addition I owe a great obligation to the following staff members of Colonial National Historical Park: J. C. Harrington, for a sustaining interest throughout my investigation; Miss Olive Drinkwine, for able assistance in making complete transcripts of pertinent Isle of Wight records and for attending to the necessary stenographic details incident to publication; also, Thomas O. Fleming, for patient skill in preparing the illustrations.

The pewterers of eighteenth-century New York

BY LEDLIE I. LAUGHLIN

THE PEWTERERS of New York were, as a group, the ablest makers in the Colonies, producing the widest variety in shape and the highest quality in design and finish, if judgment be based upon a survey of their recorded surviving output. Pennsylvania alone may have some right to dispute such a claim, but, after all, two of that colony's finest craftsmen, Colonel William Will and Cornelius Bradford, were born in New York and learned their trade there.

It is a rather amazing coincidence that New York's earliest pewterer of record, Thomas Burroughs Sr. (freeman 1678-d.1703), had been trained in Bristol, England, by Thomas Paschall Sr. (1635-1718), Philadelphia's first pewterer.

Fig. 1. Quart tankard with flat top and crenate lip. Height over all, 7¹¹⁄₁₆ inches. The drum has been tastefully engraved with the cipher of the owners within a floral design. Touch L. 582 (touch numbers throughout refer to illustrations in the author's *Pewter in America, Its Makers and Their Marks;* Barre, Massachusetts, 1969 and 1970), William Bradford Jr. (New York, w. 1719-1758). *Henry Francis du Pont Winterthur Museum.*

Fig. 2. Quart tankard with flat cover and crenate lip.
Height 6⅞₁₆ inches.
Touch L. 483, John Will (New York, w. 1752-c.1774).
Probably unique among American pewter tankards because of the medallion illustrating a Biblical scene let into center of lid. *Collection of Donald Noble.*

Fig. 3. Detail of lid of Figure 2.
The medallion, 1¼ inches in diameter, shows the prophet Elijah being fed by an angel of the Lord and by a raven.

Fig. 4. *Left:* Bellied quart tankard with double-dome cover, chair-back open thumbpiece, and broken double-C handle, atypically marked near handle at rim. Height 7⅛ inches over all. Touch L. 483, John Will. Only known New York tankard of this design. *Right:* Quart pot by the same maker with same touch. Height 6¼ inches. Unusual among New York mugs in that it has no fillet on drum. *Collection of William M. Goss Jr.*

Burroughs seems to have left England a few years before his master, but stopped off at Boston for a time—perhaps several years—before settling in New York.

This newly found maker's story was related recently in Helen Burr Smith's interesting article entitled "A New I. B. Silversmith and Two Unrecorded Pewterers," which appeared in the *New-York Historical Society Quarterly* for January 1968 (pp. 81-85). Although no example of the pewter made by either Paschall or Burroughs is known, the American Wing of the Metropolitan Museum of Art owns an exceedingly handsome lidded porringer in silver, attributed to John Coney of Boston, which is engraved with the initials of Thomas Burroughs and his first wife, Mary, together with the date 1680. It was apparently acquired by Burroughs during his sojourn in Boston, perhaps upon the occasion of his first marriage. By Thomas' will it was specifically bequeathed to his only daughter, Mary, through whose line it descended to Sylvester Dering, a great-great-great-grandson of the immigrant. Mr. Dering presented the porringer to the museum along with its complete pedigree. This magnificent vessel is pictured on page 310 of Francis H. Bigelow's *Historic Silver of the Colonies and Its Makers* (New York, 1917).

In one important field, the manufacture of the lidded tankard, the New York makers were pre-eminent among the pewterers of the Colonies. They have left us a greater number with a wider range in size and a far greater variety in design than the pewterers of all of the other colonies put together. What's more, only in New York was the aristocrat of American tankards made—the flat-lid tankard with a crenate lip, a prize to which every collector aspires. True, the form was made by Cornelius Bradford (w.1752-1785), a pewterer who spent most of his working years in Philadelphia, but Bradford was born in New York and presumably trained in his father's shop there. This handsome design was not only indigenous to New York: it must have been a stock form with every New York shop of any pretensions, at least during the period from 1740 to 1765.

Collections today include tankards with flat lid and crenate lip bearing the touches of not less than nine different New York makers, and the actual number may be even greater. Just such a tankard, handsomely and artistically engraved to include a cipher of the initials of the owner within an elaborate border, is illustrated as Figure 1. Inside, on the bottom, is a touch of William Bradford Jr. (w. 1719-1758). One of Bradford's contemporaries, Joseph Leddell Jr. (w.1740-1754), advertised in the *New-York Gazette* in 1752 that . . . "He [Leddell] also Engraves on Steel, Iron, Gold, Silver, Copper, Brass, Pewter, Ivory or Turtle-Shell in a neat Manner, and reasonably. . ." Leddell may have been the capable decorator of Bradford's fine tankard.

Most unusual of all such tankards was one made by John Will, who worked in New York from 1752 to about 1774. Centered on the flat lid and set in below the surface is a medallion one and one-quarter inches in diameter with a depiction in bas-relief of the prophet Elijah being fed by an angel of the Lord and by a raven. That tankard, shown as Figure 2, is probably unique among American tankards, because of the raised decoration with a Biblical theme. The medallion itself, shown at approximately actual size, appears as Figure 3. One wonders from what old German engraving Will took the design.

John Will, as we now know, was a very religious man. When he first arrived in New York he and his family joined the Reformed Dutch Church, but in 1763 he was apparently the leader of a group that broke away to establish the German Reformed Congregation of New York, and, until his death about 1774, Will appears in the records as that church's senior elder.

Whether the tankard was made for use in that or some other church or as a special order or gift for one of Will's religious friends is not known. Its value and interest would be even greater if it had been inscribed.

In England, tankards with this flat top and crenate lip are termed Stuart tankards. They were in use there during the last half of the seventeenth century, but about 1710 the flat top became obsolete and was replaced by a lid with double dome—a much less imposing design. In New York the Stuart tankard was still being made in 1760 and probably as late as 1775.

Not all New York tankards with flat lids had crenate lips. The plain flat lid without crenation was made contemporaneously with the more elaborate design by such men as John (w.1752-c.1774) and Henry Will (w.1761-1793), Peter Young (w.1775-1795), and William Elsworth (w.1767-1798), to name a few.

Many of the New York pewterers who continued to make the outmoded flat-top tankards were also equipped to make tankards with the double-dome cover currently in vogue in England. This cover is found both on the normal cylindrical, or drum-shape, tankard body and on the bellied, or tulip-shape, body. The latter, however, was not a common form in New York. To date, John Will is the only New York pewterer who is known to have made bellied quart tankards.

An example is illustrated in Figure 4, along with a quart mug by the same maker. The tankard is unusual, too, as far as New York tankards go, for its double-C handle and open thumbpiece; it is the only known New York tankard of this design.

The unusual feature of Will's quart pot is its lack of the heavy rib, or fillet, encircling the drum which appears on practically all New York mugs (or pots, as they were termed in the inventories). This fillet is found on almost all the pots of John and Henry Will, of all of the Bassetts (members of this family were active in New York 1718-1800), and of William Kirby (w.1760-1793), and it is not found on pots of the other colonies.

Figure 5 shows one of the finest of American church flagons, a vessel which only very recently has emerged from its hiding place after perhaps one hundred and fifty years of disuse. It is said to have been part of a service in a small church in western Connecticut. The maker was Philip Will (w.1760-1787), one of John's sons, who moved to Philadelphia in 1763 and spent most of his working years there, but was back in New York in 1766 and probably for a few years thereafter. Prior to the finding of this flagon by Oliver Deming in 1969, we had no certain knowledge that Philip Will had left behind, as testimony to his craftsmanship, any pewter other than a few small plates.

The body of this flagon is very similar in shape to those made by Philip's older brother, Henry. However, the unusual handle, which has no known counterpart in American pewter, is longer and better designed for the use to which it was to be put than Henry's short tankard handle. If one wants to be critical, Philip may be faulted for crowning the lid with a finial that seems too large and overly pretentious: a small classical urn atop the lid would have greatly improved the composition.

Figure 6 illustrates a rare and early form, a fluted presentation dish, said to have been made to hold sweetmeats. It was first illustrated in the January 1949 issue of ANTIQUES (p. 40) and commented upon by its then owner, Oliver Deming. The flutings were formed by hammering a cast circular disk of pewter over a shaped wooden block. Later the face was decorated with a formal border enclosing a floral circlet within which were engraved the initials, *G/Z M,* of the couple to whom the dish was to be given, along with the year of the presentation, *1732.* On its back is a worn but clearly decipherable touch of the first Francis Bassett (w.1718-1758). This is the earliest dated surviving dish of record made in New York, but it is later by perhaps thirty or forty years than the Edmund Dolbeare dishes made in Boston or Salem.

The largest and most imposing American chalice recorded is shown as Figure 7. This magnificent drinking vessel, now in the New Haven Colony Historical Society museum, was once in use by the West Haven Congregational Church. Inside its base is one of the initial touches of the elder Joseph Leddell (w.1711-1753), now confirmed to that maker because with the chalice was found a paten carrying two of Leddell's full-name touches.

Fig. 5. Unusually fine church flagon. Height over all, 12¾ inches. Touch L. 477 and 477a, the "hallmarks" of Philip Will (w.1760-1787); probably made in New York during his early years, c. 1760-1763. Said to have been used in a small church in western Connecticut. *Collection of Mr. and Mrs. Oliver W. Deming.*

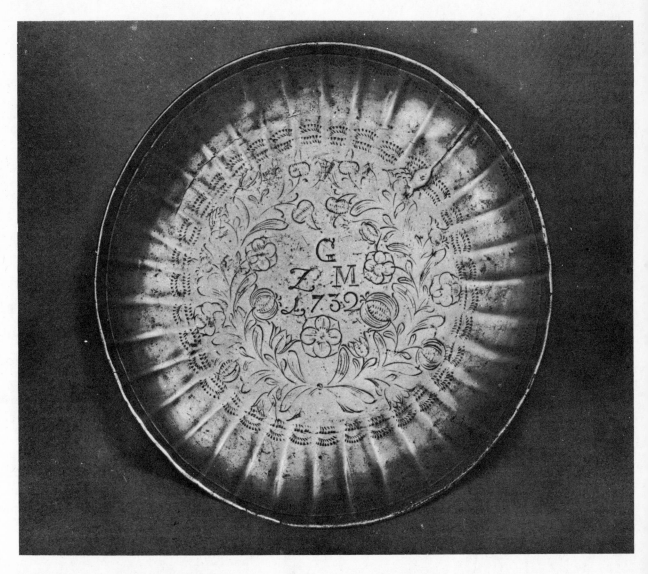

Fig. 6. Extremely rare presentation dish. Inscribed *G/Z M/ 1732*. 8½ inches in diameter, with 33 flutings. Touch L. 461, Francis Bassett I (New York, w.1718-1758). *Collection of Dr. Joseph H. Kler; photograph by courtesy of the Smithsonian Institution.*

Last of the pre-Revolutionary forms to be illustrated (Fig. 8) is a rare early teapot made by Frederick Bassett, whose career began in New York in 1761. The only other marked American teapot of this early form thus far reported is one of slightly simpler design made by one of the Francis Bassetts, either Frederick's older brother (w.1754-1799) or his uncle of the same name. The charm of the teapot's shape is enhanced by the engraving of the bird and floral motif on its body.

The final illustration shows a tea caddy made by that remarkable individualist George Coldwell, whom we can place in New York definitely in 1787, but who may have arrived there a number of years earlier. His known surviving work varies so greatly in form, design, and decoration from that of any of his New York contemporaries and predecessors that it seems all but certain that he did not receive his training in New York. In *Old Pewter* (London, 1929) Howard H. Cotterell lists a George Coldwell as a pewterer in Cork, Ireland, in 1773. It is just possible that the Coldwell of Cork may be the man who turned up in New York some years later.

Although the New York Coldwell advertised the manufacture of the stock pewter forms which every shop made (mugs, measures, commodes, and so forth) and particularly stressed his ability to make candle molds in great variety, he is known to us through his surviving examples as a specialist in the manufacture of small boxes of various shapes and sizes, beakers, and canisters, which were usually neatly and tastefully decorated with graving tools and frequently were japanned. He has also left us spoons with patriotic designs cast in the handle, and lately two or three Federal-period teapots on four feet have come to light. The well-designed caddy in Figure 9 is a very pleasing composition, a typical expression of the feeling that pervades this man's work.

In this brief article it is not possible to do more than show and comment upon a few particularly meritorious examples of New York craftsmanship, but perhaps sufficient evidence has been presented to prove our original premise: the pewterers of no other colony have left us testimony to their abilities as impressive as that of the pewterers of New York.

Mr. Laughlin is the author of the American pewter collector's bible, *Pewter in America, Its Makers and Their Marks,* which was published in two volumes in 1940 by Houghton Mifflin Company and republished in 1969 in one volume, with marginal corrections, by Barre Publishers. A third volume, on which this article is based, is to be published shortly by Barre. Dates and attributions given here are as they will appear in the new volume.

Fig. 7. Chalice of Christ Church Parish, West Haven, Connecticut.
Height 10¼ inches over all.
Touch L. 856, Joseph Leddell Sr. (New York, w.1711-1753).
Largest and one of the finest of surviving American chalices.
New Haven Colony Historical Society.

Fig. 8. Fine early teapot. Height over all, 7 inches.
Touch L. 465, Frederick Bassett (New York, w.1761-1800).
New Haven Colony Historical Society.

Fig. 9. Oval-lid tea caddy decorated with bright-cut engraving. Height with cover, 5½ inches. A handsome caddy embellished at top and bottom with bandings of
classic design. Marked G. COLDWELL, N. YORK. Coldwell
worked in New York from 1787 to 1811. *Photograph by
courtesy of Thomas D. Williams.*

A PEWTER DISCOVERY

By ADELBERT C. ABBOTT

Dr. Abbott, a Syracuse physician, is chiefly interested in early lighting devices, but since he "collects nothing later than the whale oil—camphene period," he writes, "it became a bit discouraging." He has therefore enlarged his field to include American pewter.

HENRY WILL (*c. 1735-1802*) does not appear to have made much ecclesiastical pewter. At any rate, pieces in this category bearing his touch are extremely rare. It was therefore an event of outstanding importance, some years ago, when Louis G. Myers found the magnificent flagon by Henry Will now in the Mabel Brady Garvan Collection at Yale.

I was recently invited to Cambridge, in upper New York, to see the pewter collection at the Historical House. What was my amazement to discover there a second flagon with Henry Will's touch, identical in form and practically so in measurement with the one in the Garvan collection. Even without the touch, one could recognize it because of its unusual design, differing from the flagons of all other American pewterers.

Ledlie I. Laughlin has a theory which might explain this difference in the design of Will's flagons. He suggests that Will probably did not have flagon molds, or molds for flagon handles. These were expensive and not frequently used. To make a flagon, therefore, he may have superimposed one tankard body on another and applied a tankard handle. A study of the design seems to bear out Mr. Laughlin's theory. However they were made, the Will flagons in their sublime dignity are the finest American examples of ecclesiastical pewter.

Accompanying the flagon at Cambridge was an unidentified chalice. The inner base had suffered damage, and a crudely made repair had obliterated whatever mark might have been where the touch is usually found. According to local history, both the flagon and chalice, with a paten of English make, had been in use at the Cambridge United Presbyterian Church in 1791, but there are no records to show when the pieces were bought or from whom.

Judging from the slenderness of the stem, the chalice is American rather than English or Scottish. The double lines of tooling on the cup and stem suggest a possible New York source. It has some resemblance to an unmarked chalice found

HENRY WILL FLAGON; height, 11⅜ inches; base, 5¾ inches. CHALICE accompanying the flagon; height, 7½ inches; base, 4⅛ inches. *Illustrations from Historical House, Cambridge, New York.*

with the Colonel William Will flagon and tentatively attributed to him (Laughlin, Plate XXXVI, fig. 240). The pewter of the brothers Will shows many similarities in design. Since no other chalice by Henry Will is known, this would be a find of considerable antiquarian importance.

Intrigued by the possibility, I sought the advice of Ledlie Laughlin, whose comments I am privileged to quote: "The chalice may very well have been made by Henry Will also. The cup or bowl appears to be of exactly the same shape as those which Peter Young and Timothy Brigden made, and I have always believed that Young served his apprenticeship with Henry Will. . . . It is noteworthy also that the diameter of the top of the cup and the diameter of the bottom of the stand are approximately the same as in Young's chalices. There is a difference in height but this apparently was because the base of the pictured chalice is relatively low whereas Young built up a sort of circular step-pyramid on which the stem rested. . . . It seems to me that a simpler stem and base might be expected on a Henry Will chalice than on that of later makers. . . . He never seems to have used any ornamentation where a plain surface or simple lines would serve. Furthermore, the paired lines of tooling which are found on bowl and stem appear on many pieces of New York hollowware. All in all, I think a good case could be made for the probability that Henry Will was the maker.'"

The pewter collection at Cambridge includes other important pieces. There is a very fine flagon and two chalices by Peter Young (*c. 1749-1813*), once used at the United Presbyterian Church at Coila, a neighboring village. Another flagon, undoubtedly English, was used by one of the early congregations, and there are several pieces of flatware reported to have been buried during the Revolution.

The Historical House was started some twenty years ago by the local chapter of the D. A. R. Their organization is unique. There are no dues, and all the residents of Cambridge are considered to be members. Fine work has been done in preserving the town's historical relics.

FLAGON AND CHALICE BY PETER YOUNG, both with the *PY* touch enclosed in a saw-toothed circle. Height of flagon, 9¼ inches; base, 5 inches. Height of chalice, 8½ inches; base, 4¼ inches.

Three flagons attributed to John Will

BY CHARLES V. SWAIN

IT IS RARE TODAY for an unknown shape in eighteenth-century American pewter to make an appearance, especially since this field of the decorative arts has been so thoroughly documented; it is even more unexpected to find three similar examples of that design within a few weeks, but that is the case with the three bulbous flagons illustrated in Figures 1, 3, and 6. At first glance the shape of these flagons suggests that they are of Dutch or Germanic origin but a closer examination of their thumb-pieces, handles, lids, and spouts identifies them as unmistakably American and, as I will attempt to prove, attributable to John Will.

The flagon and accompanying chalice illustrated in Figure 1, both unmarked, originally belonged to the Round Top Lutheran Church in Bethel, New York, which was founded by German Palatines about 1742. In his *History of Little Nine Partners* (Amenia, New York, 1897) Isaac Huntting wrote that the communion set was purchased for the church in 1760, some fifty or sixty miles away in Albany. The buyer was Alexander McIntosh, husband of Clara Younkhans.

The style of the flagon is consistent with its traditional date of purchase and I feel that the piece itself is attributable to John Will. After emigrating to the American Colonies from Germany in 1752, John Will in all probability continued to make those shapes with which he had become familiar on the Continent. Although the distinctive handle of the bulbous flagon is remarkably like that on the flagon marked by John Will's son Philip (Fig. 2), I do not believe that Philip made them both. In the opinion of Ledlie I. Laughlin (*Pewter in America*, Barre, Massachusetts, 1969, Vol. II, p. 14), Philip "served his apprenticeship in New York [and] moved to Philadelphia in 1763" to set himself up independently three years after the Round Top Lutheran Church had acquired its flagon and chalice. Moreover, in Volume III (Barre, 1971, p. 104) Laughlin has written: "Because Philip Will is believed to have been a journeyman working for his

Fig. 1. Flagon and chalice attributed to John Will (w. New York 1752-1774). *Collection of Deuel Richardson.*

Fig. 2. Flagon by Philip Will
(w. Philadelphia 1763 and later).
Collection of Mr. and Mrs. Oliver Deming.

Fig. 3. Flagon attributed to John Will.
*Art Institute of Chicago;
gift of Mrs. William O. Goodman.*

father, John, for a number of years after completing his apprenticeship, and because it is also thought that Philip may have inherited some of his father's moulds, it seems highly probable that if any of John Will's flagons should have survived and may come to light later, they may be expected to resemble closely Philip Will's masterpiece." Thus, it appears to me reasonable to credit John Will with the flagon illustrated in Figure 1.

Corroborating such an attribution is the pierced chair-back thumbpiece, which is identical to that used on the marked John Will tulip-shape tankard shown in Figures 4 and 5. Moreover, the lid of the flagon of Figure 1 is from the same mold as the lid of the marked John Will cylindrical tankard illustrated in Figure 7. Philip used an identical lid and thumbpiece, with the addition of a foliate finial, on his flagon in Figure 2. (William Will— Philip's brother—also used this foliate finial on the flagon he made for the Oxford Presbyterian Church, and that is pictured in Laughlin, Vol. III, Pl. XCVII, Fig. 792).

The flagon and chalice illustrated in Figure 1 were given to Samuel and Catharine Bockee Deuel, great-grandparents of the present owner, when the Round Top Lutheran Church ceased to exist in 1827. Catharine Bockee's father, Jacob, was a second cousin of Rebecca Bokee who married John Will's son Christian.

The second of the three bulbous flagons under discussion is illustrated in Figure 3. Unfortunately, there are no records to indicate when or from whom it was purchased, but it is known to have been used in the Congregational Church at Farmington, Trumbull County, Ohio. Its most striking feature is the distinctive handle which appears to be from the same mold as that of the marked John Will tulip-shape tankard illustrated in Figures 4 and 5. William Will either copied or inherited this mold from his father, for he also is known to have used it on the Aaronsburg tall pitcher, a pair of two-handled communion cups, and a quart pot, all of which are pictured in Volumes I (1969) and III of *Pewter in America*.

90

The bulbous flagons shown in Figures 1 and 3 not only have the same lid and pierced chair-back thumbpiece but their measurements are almost identical: over-all height, 11¼ inches; height to top of body without lid, 9⅞ inches; widest diameter inside dome of lid, 3¹⁵⁄₁₆ inches; diameter of bottom, 4¾ inches; the diameter of the belly of the first flagon is 6³⁄₁₆ inches, while that of the second is only 6⅛ inches because it has no raised band. Similarly, at its narrowest point the neck of the first flagon is 3⅛ inches in diameter whereas the corresponding measurement on the second is 3 inches because its band is made of thinner metal.

Significantly, the irregular cutout in the thumbpieces of the bulbous flagons matches that in John Will's tulip-shape tankard (Figs. 4, 5). This piercing, usually used by John Will, was never, to my knowledge, used by his son William. I have examined three pear-shape tankards, three cylindrical tankards, and one cylindrical flagon by William Will, and in all cases the piercings in the thumb-pieces were of some shape other than that in the bulbous flagons under examination.

The third of these bulbous flagons (Fig. 6), like its counterparts, looks Flemish or German, except for its typically English bud-terminal handle which was so often used in the American Colonies. The flagon is practically identical to the two previously discussed in the shape of its body and banded decoration. In fact, the height of the body and the diameters of the neck at its narrowest point and the belly at its widest are identical to the corresponding dimensions on the other two flagons. However, over all the flagon in Figure 6 is one inch taller than the other two because of a higher foot and the elaborate, high, dome lid. The handle and solid chair-back thumbpiece of this flagon are exactly like those on the marked John Will tankard in Figure 7.

Another important detail consistent on all three flagons I attribute to John Will is the uniform application of two beads at the base of the spout. William Will, on the other hand, used three beads of graduated sizes on his early cylindrical flagons and one large flat bead on his later, urn-shape examples.

A most interesting feature of the flagon in Figure 6, and one which sets it apart from the other two, is the presence on the inside bottom of an armorial touch which incorporates the initials IW within its design (Fig. 8). John Carl Thomas, past president of the Pewter Collectors Club of America and discoverer of this flagon, feels confident that this touch was used by John Will before those known to have been used by him. Evidence is strongly in favor of this theory, for in all likelihood John Will would have continued to use his German touch immediately after his arrival in the American Colonies. It is possible that the arms in the touch are those of Nieuwied or Herborn, cities in which he worked as a pewterer. Proof, of course, awaits a thorough search of those cities' archives.

There is little doubt that the chalice and flagon shown in Figure 1 were made by the same man. The base of the chalice and the flagon's lid have identical measurements and are interchangeable, as is evident in Figure 9. When this chalice is compared to those known to have been made by the Wills and to one by Peter Young, who is thought to have been associated with Henry Will, it complements an already compatible group (Figure 10). If indeed this chalice was made by John Will, it could very well have been the inspiration for the other four.

Fig. 4. Tankard by John Will. *Author's collection.*

Fig. 5. Another view of Fig. 4 showing the pierced thumbpiece.

Fig. 6. Flagon attributed to John Will.
Collection of Dr. and Mrs. Melvyn D. Wolf.

Fig. 7. Tankard by John Will.
Author's collection.

Fig. 8.   Touch on the flagon
illustrated in Fig. 6.
Attributed to John Will.

Fig. 9. View illustrating the interchangeability of the chalice base and the flagon lid in Fig. 1, which are identical.

Fig. 10. *Left to right*. Chalices attributed to Henry Will, William Will, William Will, John Will; and a marked example by Peter Young. *All from the author's collection except that attributed to John Will.*

Concerning the Pewtering Bassetts

By H. V. Button

The following observations imply some familiarity with the late J. B. Kerfoot's invaluable book *American Pewter*. For the convenience of the reader, however, certain of the *F. B.* touches illustrated in that volume have been here reproduced. For permission to use Mr. Kerfoot's original photographs, ANTIQUES gratefully acknowledges its indebtedness to Mrs. Annie Haight Kerfoot of Freehold, New Jersey. — *The Editor.*

MR. KERFOOT'S volume *American Pewter* mentions two Bassetts, Francis and Frederick, and illustrates their respective marks. The marks which can be attributed to Frederick are fairly numerous, there being, in addition to the touches with the name spelled out and the *New York* touch in a fan-shaped device, four, and possibly five, different *F.B.-in-circle* touches; namely, Kerfoot Figures 45, 45A, 46, 46A and 49, if indeed this last touch be from a different die than 45A. This may or may not be true, since it is hard to be positive on the evidence of the cuts alone, and I have been unable to assemble, for comparison, examples of pewter bearing these several touches. However, the question as to whether there are four or five different *F.B.-in-circle* touches is not important for the purposes of this discussion.

Coming now to the known marks of Francis Bassett, we have only the two touches illustrated by Mr. Kerfoot, in Figure 44. One or two other pewter pieces have come to light bearing the *F.B.-with-passant-lion-in-oval* touch; but examples of Francis' work remain of the first order of rarity.

Mr. Myers, in his book *Some Notes on American Pewterers*, gives us considerable information on the pewtering Bassetts. Briefly summarized, it appears that a Francis and a John Bassett, cousins, were making pewter in New York in the 1720's or 1730's. This John was the father of another Francis, and of Frederick. As to John, Mr. Myers states, "Examples of his work are known to exist, but I have not succeeded in locating any." John's touch is here illustrated; but, before proceeding with comments on the man's work and its relation to that of his sons, it may be well to briefly dwell on the question of the two Francises.

The fact that there was a Francis, cousin of John, making pewter at some

Fig. 1 — PEWTER FUNNEL BY JOHN BASSETT (*1732–1761*)
Marked with the initials *I. B.* in a circle, with fleur-de-lis above and below.
From the collection of Mrs. Richard S. Quigley

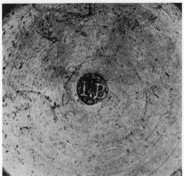

Fig. 2 — THE JOHN BASSETT TOUCH
Photographed from the interior bottom of a pewter beaker.
From the collection of Ledlie I. Laughlin

1930

Fig. 3 (left and right) — VARIANTS OF THE
F.B.-in-circle TOUCH
These circle touches were used by Frederick Bassett, often in conjunction with a rose and crown touch and a fan-shaped device. All of them are shown in Kerfoot's *American Pewter*, Figures 45, 45A, 46, 46A, 48, 49, and 50. Here, only the *F.B.-in-circle* touches are reproduced, for purposes of comparison.

time about 1720, leads us to ask whether the existing Francis Bassett marks may not belong to the earlier holder of the name. At present, the question has only a passing interest, but the discovery of other specimens bearing different Francis Bassett touches would give impor-

Fig. 4 — *I. B.* AND *F. B.* TOUCHES *(enlarged)*
These marks are obviously from the same die. To change the *I. B.* to an *F. B.*, it was a simple matter to enlarge the *I* into an *F*, though the design lost its symmetry.

tance to a consideration of the authorship of the entire group. Yet, before dismissing the question entirely, it is reasonable to suggest that the known Francis Bassett touch — the *F.B.-with-passant-lion* — may well be the mark of Francis I. Its aspect implies relatively great antiquity; the documentary evidence concerning the activities of the various Bassetts shows that Francis I may well have been a more prolific pewterer than his namesake, Francis II; and, in any case, it would not be foolish to assume that the second Francis, for a time, used his predecessor's dies.

Turning now to a consideration of John, cousin of Francis I, we are on surer ground, since the *I. B.* touches here illustrated (*Figs. 1 and 2*) may safely be assigned to him. The mark on the funnel (*Fig. 1*) is not perfectly defined, due to its having been struck on the curved surface near the funnel's rim. But we should be grateful to John for having troubled to strike this touch on so difficult a surface, for the fortunate preservation of this piece adds (so far as the writer knows) a new form to marked American pewter, in addition to giving us a rare new touch. Figure 2 shows the same *I. B.* touch, in legible condition, on the inside bottom of a beaker.

That this *I. B.* touch is attributable to John Bassett is hardly to be doubted on the evidence of the mark itself; but further corroboration of its ownership is found in comparing it with Kerfoot's Figure 46, here illustrated in Figure 3. The same mark appears on the back of an eight-inch plate, credited to John's son, Frederick Bassett. Close scrutiny of Figure 4 will reveal the fact that both the touches there were made from the *same die*, which, for the *F. B.* touch, had been altered to change the *I* into an *F*. There can be no doubt of this when the details of the

two marks are carefully examined. In the first place, it will be noticed that the *F* runs into the "tail" of the upper fleur-de-lis, and that the spacing of the *F* in this touch is faulty, since it is not in the middle of the area which it occupies. In the second place, the vertical members of the *I*, the *F*, and the *B* exhibit, in both touches, the same slightly irregular relation to one another. Finally, these two marks, as they occur on actual pewter pieces, show no variation in any of the measurements carefully taken with micrometer calipers.

It being thus established that these two marks, *I. B.* and *F. B.*, were both struck from the same die (the *F. B.* after alteration), there can be no possible room for doubt that the *I. B.* touch is the mark of the John Bassett who made pewter in New York between 1732 and the year of his death, 1761. The identification of these *I. B.* specimens gives us another name to add to the small group of pre-1750 American pewterers.

The discovery of John's touch and the certainty of its employment, after alteration, by the son Frederick, open a wide field of speculation about all the separate *F. B.* touches, and makes risky their attribution to Frederick alone. The question arises as to whether or not Francis II, or even Francis I, used one or more of the *F. B.* marks. And did the son, or cousin, or both, use the very *F.B. with fleur-de-lis* touch made from John's die? Possibly these queries will be answered with the finding of other specimens of the Bassett family's work; but, until this happens, it is probably safest to leave the ownership of the marks as they are now pretty definitely ascribed. That is to say, we have no known marks of Francis I; we have two or three examples of John's *I. B.* touches; about the same number of Francis II marks. The rest we may allow to the prolific Frederick until additional touches, or combinations of existing touches, appear to puzzle us anew. Though the past few years have added greatly to our pewter knowledge, much remains to be learned.

A BASSETT DISCOVERY

A Unique Piece of American Pewter

By OLIVER WOLCOTT DEMING

A comparative newcomer to the ranks of pewter collectors, Mr. Deming of Westfield, Massachusetts, has nevertheless acquired an extensive knowledge and an unusual collection. He here describes his most exciting find.

JUST WHEN IT APPEARS that there remains little to be found in the way of the unusual in American pewter, it is encouraging to discover such a piece as the dish illustrated, obverse and reverse, on these pages. This is a real find, significant in all the respects that concern collectors — its form, its decoration, its date, and its maker's mark.

Unlike other metal craftsmen, the early pewterers seldom diverged from the customary forms. Their differences lay primarily in the quality of the metal used, the forms of hollow pieces, and the touch marks. The plates, as a rule, were conventional and uniform in design and sizes, and it is therefore surprising to learn that an American pewterer, Francis Bassett of New York, made this unusual dish. On the other hand, it is conceivable that he, as well

as other pewterers of that locality and period, made on special order pieces closely resembling those made by silversmiths.

This dish, shaped somewhat like a shallow saucer, measures eight and one-half inches in diameter and its depth in the center is three-quarters of an inch. In form it is similar to some early pewter dishes made in England and on the Continent. An English pewter dish similarly fluted, but with a rim, was illustrated in ANTIQUES for August 1947 (p. 98). At first glance, one assumes the dish shown here was cast in a mold; however, careful examination suggests that it may have been skillfully hammered into shape, the fluting undoubtedly executed in the same manner as fluting on contemporary silver sweetmeat and fruit dishes. For what purpose this dish was intended is anyone's guess, but to assume that it was made for the serving of small fruit and sweetmeats is not too farfetched.

Much of its appeal lies in the charming floral decoration covering most of its surface. The early manner of presenting tulips and other flowers, accented with elaborate punched work, is typical of the period and locality. This type of decoration, made by using a punch with a V-shaped end, was a common practice in England around 1700. It was also employed on the Continent during the seventeenth and early eighteenth centuries, but was rarely used on pewter in America. That this was a presentation piece is borne out by the triad of initials G/Z M and the date *1732* below. Certainly no skilled artisan did this engraving, but the very lack of finesse contributes to its appearance. Ledlie I. Laughlin, author of *Pewter In America*, ventured the opinion that the engraving may have been done by Joseph Leddell of New York City, a pewterer and engraver at that time. It is also very possible that Francis Bassett himself did this sort of work.

The reverse side of the dish shows two identical oval touches, faint but identifiable, of the lion passant with fleur-de-lis and initials *F.B.* (L. 461), attributed heretofore to one or the other of the two Francis Bassetts.

The history of the Bassett family still lacks many pertinent facts, yet enough is known to have established a foundation for further research. Mr. Laughlin's book tells us that the first John Bassett had at least two sons, Francis and Michael, both of whom followed the sea for their livelihood and both of whom had sons who worked in pewter. Laughlin says:

"Francis, son of Francis and Marie Magdalen (Vincent) Bassett, was born in New York in 1690, according to the records of the French Church, and in 1707, with the consent of his widowed mother, was apprenticed to William Horsewell, pewterer. In 1718 he became a freeman of the city. Nothing else is known of his history except that he served as constable for the East Ward in 1732 and died in New York in 1758, leaving his estate to his wife, Elizabeth Mary.

"His first cousin, John Bassett, son of Michael," became a freeman in 1732. "Of his seven children, the oldest and youngest, Francis and Frederick, were to carry on the family trade. John died in 1761, leaving to his son Frederick his pewter-making tools. . . ."

This Francis, son of John, was born in 1729. In 1758, when the elder Francis, his uncle, died without issue, "it is not unlikely that his kinsman and namesake acquired his tools and touches." At the time Mr. Laughlin's book was published (1940), there were no means of determining which touches, if any, were used by the elder and which by the namesake. To date, four different touches have been recorded, all of which could be attributed to either Francis.

Hence the date 1732 engraved on this piece of pewter is significant, because it necessarily follows that the dish could only have been made by the elder Francis, and also assures us that this touch mark was definitely used by him. Attention is called to

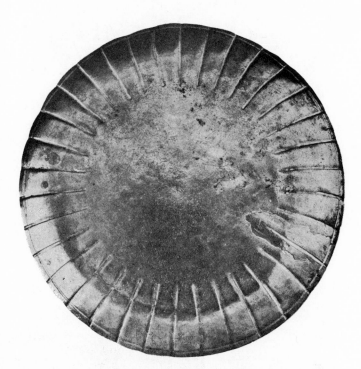

Photographs by Edward W. Doyle

the fact that the marks in this instance are not accompanied by the *Frans. Bassett/ in New York* touch (L. 460a). On the pieces where the combination occurs, could this second touch have been added by the second pewtering Francis, or could it have been an additional touch used by the elder Francis on his later pieces? Study of the touches of other New York pewterers, working at the same time as the younger Francis, reveals that several used similar New York touches. Included in this list are Henry Will, Robert Boyle, and Frederick Bassett.

After having the dish for some time and realizing its importance to pewter history, I finally was successful in tracing it back to a former owner. From her I learned that it was a family piece, prized and handed down to each succeeding generation, possibly prized less and less as the years passed; for the last member cared very little for it, and after several fruitless attempts to clean it, decided to dispose of it along with other family possessions. The crude repair is of long standing, made any time prior to the life of this descendant. Before coming into my possession the dish had been carefully cleaned with Bon Ami, restoring the pewter's original color and the appearance that only age and use impart. With this cleaning, the marks came to light.

Research to establish the early, original owners, while promising, is still incomplete. The date 1732 and the uncommon initial Z of the husband's Christian name may make possible the identification of the first owners. Whether the piece was a wedding present or a presentation gift for some other occasion, Francis Bassett was inspired to attempt the unusual and produced a work of beauty and fine craftsmanship. Possibly one of many such individual items, produced on special order by early pewterers, this dish fortunately escaped the fate of most pre-Revolutionary pewter.

Thus summarizing all the known facts, it is safe to state that the form is unique in American pewter flatware. The dish is also endowed with that unusual combination of beauty and rarity. In so far as can be ascertained, this dish is the earliest known engraved piece of American pewter, as well as the earliest dated piece of American pewter, excepting the fragments of the Jamestown spoon (1690). By the same token it is the only piece of pewter that can definitely be assigned to Francis Bassett I.

AN AMERICAN SILVERSMITH
AND HIS PEWTER

By JOHN W. POOLE

THE frequent practice of attributing unidentified initial touches on pewter to some American pewterer whose initials chance to coincide with those of the mark is quite unjustified. Nevertheless, those in the know have long conceded that a certain TB touch must be that of some man working in or near Albany, whose pewtering activities lay within the first quarter of the nineteenth century. To make a long story short, there seems reason to believe that this TB touch, illustrated in Figure 3, could belong to no one other than the Albany silversmith Timothy Brigdon.

Peter Young and this TB are tied together at every conceivable point. Their wares are discovered in localities circumscribed by identical limits. Furthermore, these limits are such as would represent normal distribution from Albany as a centre. Young, we of course know, was an Albany pewterer. Frequently, his pieces and those of TB are found together. A communion set that I recently acquired consists of three pieces by TB and a fourth by Young (*Fig. 2*).

In another set, of which I was able to secure the chalices only, PY and TB are most astonishingly commingled. The bowl of one chalice bears the circular PY touch; on its base appears TB. The base of the second chalice is marked TB. Certain repairs suggest that the respective bowls and bases may at some time have been switched; but how, when, or why remains a mystery. Enquiry, however, has uncovered convincing evidence that, while in the present condition, the pair was used for communion services.

In at least two other instances, TB pieces have been found in communion sets to which Spencer Stafford also contributed his wares. Since

we know of many pieces which bear the marks of both Stafford and Young, the two sets cited fit neatly into the picture.

But it is in the character of their products that I find most conclusive evidence of some close relationship between Young and TB. All but one piece of twenty or so by TB exhibit features exactly duplicated in Young's work. Most of these items are chalices. The TB examples average slightly taller than Young's chalices; but except when placed side by side, the work of the two men appears to be identical. The cast bases *are* identical, and the differences in the bowls of the two men are no greater than those in different bowls by one man. The type of chalice referred to appears to have been made only by Young and by TB.

Besides chalices I have seen only three pieces by TB — two flagons and a teapot. Since I know of no teapots by either Young or his satellite, Stafford, TB's example does nothing for the argument either *pro* or *con*. On the other hand, comparing TB's flagons with one by Stafford yields evidence quite to the point. While I have not placed these pieces side by side, they appear to be much alike save in a few minor details. All their handles have the same peculiar wiggle (see illustration), which ensures a firm grasp. This handle — with its wiggle — is distinctive and has no counterpart within my ken. The bodies similarly correspond, and are noticeably more sharply tapered than any to be found in the most closely approximating piece by any English or American maker. They are more like certain Dutch designs. The cover of the Stafford flagon, being domed, differs from the TB covers, which are of "flat," or plateau form. On the other hand, the TB covers so resemble

FIG. 1 — TANKARD AND CHALICE BY PETER YOUNG; TEAPOT ASCRIBED TO TIMOTHY BRIGDON

Beading around the chalice stem is unusual. This piece and its companion tankard are the work of an artisan living 1748–1815?

FIG. 2 — COMMUNION SET FROM MADISON, NEW YORK

The chalices and flagon carry the TB mark as illustrated. The 13-inch dish is by Young

193

the very distinctive lids on Peter Young's tankards that they might have come from the same mold.

The most striking thing about the similarity between Young's wares and those of TB is that they are so distinctly apart from the products of all other Anglo-Saxon makers. Whether or not the chalices by these men, like their flagons, are reminiscent of the Dutch manner, I am not qualified to judge.

In light of these considerations, plus the research of Ledlie Laughlin, who has found Brigdon listed for a few years as a pewterer, it seems beyond reasonable doubt that Timothy Brigdon and TB are one and the same person. Before Young's death, about 1815, Brigdon makes no claim to pewtering. But shortly thereafter he does appear in the pewterer's rôle and apparently sustains it for three or four years.

The character of his pewter is fairly consistent with silversmithing. I have found no heavy pewter plates, basins, mugs, porringers, with the TB touch, although such forms were the principal reasons for a pewterer's existence. On the other hand, the chalices, flagons, and teapots made by Young and Brigdon are not very unlike equivalent items in silver. It may be fair to guess that Brigdon added a cheap line to his silverware, but limited it to such pieces as required some of the silversmith's skill. The *average* pewterer was probably more a metal dealer than anything else.

In so far as I can determine, a rather notable fraction of the more or less liquid assets of colonial America consisted of pewter as metal. To maintain the value of this asset it was essential only to keep it in usable condition. Since junk pewter could not supply

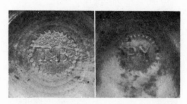

FIG. 3 — MARKS OF "TB" AND OF PETER YOUNG

Both from chalices. The Young mark appears to be in a circle with serrated rim instead of with a beaded rim such as Myers illustrates. Both marks occur. The TB mark is likewise within a circle with serrated rim

the entire demand and some metal had to be imported, no necessity existed for many pewterers of the calibre of the Wills and Bassetts. The economic demand could be satisfied by the exercise of skill no greater than that required to produce plates, basins, mugs, and the like. This meant merely casting, finishing on a lathe, and a little soldering or welding. In a week one man could turn out hundreds or even thousands of pounds of finished wares. For such pieces the metal represented much greater value than did the labor and profit.

The silversmith, on the other hand, sold his *craftsmanship*. Frequently he had no cash investment in his product. Possibly Brigdon took over some of the more refined angles of pewtering just to keep himself occupied. It would be safe to say that the cost of the materials in a pair of his pewter chalices was much less than the charge for his professional services. Brigdon's pewter added to Stafford's output seems just about to duplicate Young's line. What more logical than to believe that the two men portioned Young's molds and his artisan-metal business to give Brigdon the artisan part and Stafford the metal part?

In any event, it seems safe to say that our fine TB pieces represent the one *proved* instance in which an American silversmith "made pewter." Incidentally, it is of interest to note that the flat-topped TB flagons are probably the earliest in type, although not in date, of all known American flagons. They are also significant as affording another example of Continental European influence on American styles. Many TB pieces, especially the flagons, are quite Dutch in appearance.

Cornelius Bradford, Pewterer

By Ledlie I. Laughlin

LOUIS G. MYERS, in a delightful paragraph about Malcolm McEuen in *Some Notes on American Pewterers*, writes:

There were three Malcolms in all. The first was a bookbinder; then came Malcolm, the pewterer, and finally Malcolm, the plumber. Thus, in father, son, and grandson, we see a typical case of American evolution, with the grandson landing at the top.

As a companion picture, let me recite the story of the Bradfords — father, son, and grandson. First came William, printer and newspaper publisher; second, William, Jr., a printer who turned pewterer; and, finally, Cornelius, brother of William, 3rd, who, beginning as a pewterer, realized, no doubt, that he was not fulfilling his destiny, and added plumbing to his previous occupation. And perhaps it was just to give me the pleasure of linking my story more closely with that of Mr. Myers that Cornelius obligingly chose Malcolm McEuen as his partner.

In 1682, William Bradford, a printer of Leicestershire, England, emigrated with William Penn to Philadelphia, where, in 1685, he set up the first printing press in the Middle Colonies. Not long afterwards he moved to New York, was appointed royal printer for that Colony, and, in 1725, published New York's first newspaper.

A son, William Bradford, Jr., born in Philadelphia, in 1688, is said to have learned the printing trade in New York. But, as his health proved too poor for such confining work, he turned to the sea for a livelihood. Just when he abandoned a sailor's life we do not know; in 1719, however, he became a freeman of New York, his occupation appearing on the records as that of pewterer. And a pewterer he remains in all subsequent documents where his name is found. His will was probated in 1759.

William Bradford, 3rd, a son of the pewterer, returned to the family trade of printing, became a newspaper publisher in Philadelphia, and eclipsed even the reputation of his famous grandfather. During the trying days that preceded the Revolution, his newspaper admonished the Colonies to "Unite or Die"; and his tavern, the London Coffee House, became Philadelphia's hotbed of patriotism. When the war came, he received a commission; served under General Washington at Trenton, Princeton, and elsewhere; and rose to the rank of Colonel.

It is little wonder, therefore, that Cornelius Bradford, last of the tribe, has remained in the background, his story untold. But he, too, played a man's part in the events of his time, and deserves at least brief recognition for his various achievements.

Cornelius, fifth and youngest child of the pewterer, William Bradford, Jr., was born in New York, October 18, 1729. Unquestionably he served his apprenticeship in his father's shop. In 1752, he was married to Esther Creighton, and, soon thereafter, moved to his father's birthplace, Philadelphia, where he had inherited a home and shop from an uncle, Andrew Bradford. In the issue of the *Pennsylvania Gazette* for May 3, 1753, he advertised the manufacture of pewter in his shop on Second Street. In the same journal, the following notice appeared, October 14, 1756:

To be sold by Cornelius Bradford, Pewterer,
At the sign of the Dish in Second St. opposite the sign of the George wholesale or retail at the most reasonable rates all sorts of pewter ware, viz:
Dishes and plates of all sizes, basons, tankards, quart and pint mugs, porringers, tea pots, sugar pots, cullanders, bed pans, stool-pans, half pint and gill tumblers, wine measures, salt-sellers, spoons, milk pots, pint and half-pint dram bottles, slop bowls and all sorts of other pewter.
Said Bradford makes the best of pewter or block-tin worms, of all sizes, for distilling, as shall be ordered, as also cranes for hogsheads or bottles, candle molds of different sizes. All persons may have pewter mended at a reasonable price, and ready money given for old pewter, or exchanged for new.

A similar advertisement, in 1758, exhibited but one change, the addition of "ink pots" to the announced stock in trade. From later notices, we gain the impression that Bradford became a general merchant; and, in 1769, when he is taxed for property in High Street Ward, his name occurs for the last time as a resident of Philadelphia.

The records of Christ Church show that, between the years 1754 and 1759, four children were born to Cornelius and Esther Bradford. In 1765 the wife died. About five years later the widower, with his children, returned to New York where, in the following year, he was married again — this time to Catherine, widow of Captain Dennis Candy. Whatever had been his position in Philadelphia, Cornelius became one of the prominent New York figures of his day. If the city had required a Paul Revere, no doubt Bradford would have filled the rôle. In the years just before the war, he was the trusted dispatch bearer between the Committees of Correspondence in New York and Boston, and in New York and Philadelphia.

We have already told how the brother William, at his inn, the London Coffee House in Philadelphia, became a central figure in the city's patriotic councils. Cornelius Bradford was to play a similar

Fig. *1* — Touches of Cornelius Bradford (*1753–1786*)
From an 8⅜ inch plate in the author's collection

Fig. *2* — Touches of Cornelius Bradford (*actual size*)
From an 8⅜ inch plate in the collection of Francis Mason

Fig. *3* — Another Impression of the Upper Touch in Figure 2 (*enlarged*)
From a quart tankard in the author's collection

part in New York. The Merchants' Coffee House, at the corner of Wall and Water Streets, had long been the business rendezvous of the merchants of the locality. Early in 1776, Bradford purchased the establishment and the property on which it stood. Almost immediately it became headquarters for those ardent spirits who brooked no temporizing with the British Government; and we are told that Bradford proved himself an energetic and enterprising host.

But his tenure was brief. War had come in earnest. The British fleet arrived at New York; the landing of troops necessitated the withdrawal of the Continental forces. Bradford might have remained to enjoy a thriving business in catering to His Majesty's soldiers and to Tory citizens. Instead, when Washington's soldiers marched out, Bradford deserted his inn and shop and went with them. For seven years thereafter, he and his family lived at Rhinebeck, some distance up the Hudson.

Fig. 4 — Quart Tankard by Cornelius Bradford (1753–1786)
Height: 6¾ inches; top diameter: 4⁵⁄₁₆ inches.
From the author's collection

In 1783, the war over, Cornelius returned to New York and again assumed charge of his famous hostelry. To W. Harrison Bayles' interesting *Old Taverns of New York*, I am indebted for much of the subject matter of this sketch. He tells us that Bradford

prepared a book, in which he proposed to enter the names of vessels on their arrival, the ports from which they came, and any particular occurrences of their voyages, so that merchants and travellers might obtain the earliest intelligence. Bradford's *Marine List* appears in the newspapers of that period. He also opened a register of merchants and others, in which they were requested to enter their names and residences, the nearest approach to a city directory that had yet been made. Bradford, by his energy and intelligence, revived the good name of the house . . .

We now return to the starting point of our story. In New York's earliest directory, that of 1786, Bradford and McEuen are listed as plumbers, at 147 Water Street. This McEuen was the second Malcolm, who spent most of his days as a pewterer. The two men were working together at least as early as 1774, as evidenced by the

Fig. 5 — Pint Mug by Cornelius Bradford (1753–1786)
Height: 4½ inches; top diameter: 3½ inches.
From the author's collection

recorded approval of a bill presented by the firm in that year for deliveries made to the New York Almshouse. I doubt, however, that Bradford took any active part in either pewtermaking or plumbing after 1775. The shop was closed during the War, and his duties as host of the Coffee House would have required most of his energies after the return of peace. It is, therefore, my belief that any examples of Bradford's pewter that come to light may be identified, with reasonable assurance, as preRevolutionary.

Although, until very recent years, the existence of any such examples was unknown, there is now record of at least seven objects of his handicraft — three quart tankards, a pint mug, a ten-inch smoothrim plate, and two plates with normal rim, measuring eight and nine-sixteenths inches and eight and seven-eighths inches, respectively. All three plates have hammer marks on the bouge.

Francis Mason made the first Bradford discovery; and to him we are indebted, not only for a new touch, but also for a brand-new mystery. Examine the marks reproduced from the Mason plate (*Fig. 2*). Why should the initials in the hall marks (so-called) be *D.S.* instead of *C.B.*? Possibly English precedent affords the answer. In England, when a pewterer succeeded to another man's business, he frequently applied for and received permission from the Pewterers' Company to adopt the touches used by his predecessor — to capitalize, as it were, the good will of a going establishment. It seems not improbable therefore that *D.S.* was an earlier Philadelphia maker whom Bradford succeeded; but thus far I have been unable to find trace of such a man. The other Bradford touch (*Fig. 1*), found, as yet, on but the one plate, could have been used only in Philadelphia. Hence it unquestionably antedates the Revolution.

Cornelius Bradford died November 9, 1786. His work ranks with that of the New York makers — the Wills, the Bassetts, and the rest.

PEWTER COMMUNION SERVICE of the Salem Lutheran Church, Aaronsburg, Pennsylvania *(1789-1794).* Made by William Will of Philadelphia and presented by Aaron Levy. All engraved *Das Geschenke zu denen Deutschen Gemeinden in Arensburg von Aron Levy.* Bowl only is marked *(see detail).* Height of chalice, 7¹⁵⁄₁₆ inches; diameter, 3⁹⁄₁₆ inches. Height of pitcher, 10¾ inches; diameter, 5 inches. Height of flagon, 13¹¹⁄₁₆ inches; diameter, 5⁹⁄₁₆ inches. Diameter of bowl, 10⁵⁄₁₆ inches; depth, 1⁹⁄₁₆ inches. *Photographs by Nittany Studio.*

NEW FINDS IN OLD PEWTER BY WILLIAM WILL

The Aaronsburg Communion Service

By PAUL M. AUMAN

Even after all the fruitful study that has been made of American pewter, new discoveries are still being made. Though the communion service discussed here was illustrated in the popular press at the time of Aaronsburg's celebration last fall, its importance as an addition to the known work of William Will has not before been emphasized. Mr. Auman, a Pennsylvanian, here gives its historical background, and Mr. Laughlin, author of Pewter in America, *offers his specialized comment on the set, which he says seems the most noteworthy "find" in American pewter in the past ten years.*

ON OCTOBER 23, 1949, the little village of Aaronsburg, in Centre County, Pennsylvania, was the scene of a special observance "to focus national attention on this outstanding, historical example of the interdependence of all races and creeds." Aaronsburg, near the geographical center of Pennsylvania, was founded in 1786 by Aaron Levy, who had hoped to see it become the capital of the Commonwealth. The recent celebration centered in the Salem Lutheran Church, built on land deeded to its members by Aaron Levy, com-

pleting 150 years of continuous worship. The "Aaronsburg story" was widely publicized at the time, with emphasis, appropriately, on its religious and humanitarian significance. It has a sidelight, however, of distinctly antiquarian importance.

Besides providing land for a church building, Levy commissioned the Philadelphia pewterer, Colonel William Will, to make a communion service for what was to be a united church of the Lutheran and Reformed congregations. Plans for this Union Church failed, but the Lutherans erected the Salem Lutheran Church. The pewter communion service was given to them.

In 1852 the original Salem Lutheran Church was torn down and replaced by the present building. Between 1869 and 1873 the latter was remodeled and, perhaps accidentally, the communion service was enclosed within a platform on which the pulpit stood. There it remained until 1917, when the church was again remodeled and workmen, tearing out the platform, found the forgotten pewter.

The set consists of four pieces, chalice, pitcher or ewer,

flagon, and bowl. Each is engraved *Das Geschenke zu denen Deutschen Gemeinden in Arensburg von Aron Levy* (the gift of Aaron Levy to the German congregations in Aaronsburg). On the bottom of the bowl Will's eagle touch is struck twice, and once his touch *Wm. WILL/PHILADELPHIA* in scroll. Though this is the only piece of the set that is marked, there seems little doubt that all four were made by William Will. Their date can be set between 1789, when Levy granted the ground to the Lutheran congregation (the date of the Union Church agreement is unknown), and 1794, when the Union Church plan had been abandoned and the cornerstone of the Salem Lutheran Church was laid.

Comment on the Communion Service by Ledlie I. Laughlin

I had not heard of this communion set previously and hope that there may be other equally interesting sets hidden away in other country churches. As far as can be discovered from the photograph there seems to be no reason at all for questioning the Church's ascription of this set to the shop of Colonel William Will, Philadelphia, for the period from 1789-1794. I presume that this cannot be confirmed by a surviving bill of sale or other church record.

We might wish that the maker had seen fit to mark all four pieces, instead of the basin alone, but there can be no doubt that Will made the flagon and pitcher and we need not hesitate greatly about attributing the chalice to him also.

At that same period Peter Young, who probably had been an apprentice of Henry Will, William's older brother, was making, in Albany, chalices with bases of similar design, but with a cup of greater flare and a stem of less accentuated outline. To my mind what strengthens the attribution of this unmarked chalice to William Will is the shape of the bowl, which is simply a reproduction, reduced in scale, of the bowl of its companion flagon. Some may feel, as I do, that had the bowl been placed upon a plainer stem, one of more gently modulated contours, the composition as a whole would have been simpler and more dignified. It furnishes, however, another American pewter chalice variant and nothing in the design is foreign to what might have been looked for from William Will.

The flagon and pitcher need no maker's touches to identify the shop from which they came. Unique though each may be in American pewter, both express the individuality of, and, exhibit the characteristics which have always been associated with, William Will's work. On each we find the beaded decoration of the knurling tool on rims or joints, just as it appears on Will's teapots and coffeepots.

The design of the flagon is directly traceable to the coffeepot design—or vice versa. Several of the same molds were apparently used for both. Subject to confirmation by actual measurement, the foot of the flagon appears to be interchangeable with the coffeepot

base and the same can be said of the necks of both vessels. Again, the lids, or covers, are from one mold but the graceful finial of the coffeepot has not been added on the flagon, an omission that is, perhaps, regrettable.

The spout was made from a mold designed for the spout of Will's earlier straight-sided flagons, one of which appears as figure 218, plate XXXI in *Pewter in America*. In the design of the later flagon the Colonel unfortunately added a button-like ornament at the base of the spout, a decoration which seems too large and too heavy and breaks the curving lines of the spout, instead of carrying the eye down to the less prominent and more pleasing tear-drop terminal of the earlier composition.

Whether it be fair to criticize at all Will's design of chalice or flagon, it is difficult to pick a flaw in the beautiful Aaronsburg pitcher, a shape which has no counterpart and bears no close resemblance to anything else in American pewter, yet is so exactly what we might have expected of Colonel Will at his best.

Here again we see the base that was used so satisfyingly on Will's coffeepots and with it he uses the acanthus-leaf handle that adorned his tulip-shaped quart mugs. No doubt if one such mug were placed alongside the pitcher it could be immediately proved that both handles were from the same mold.

For the belly of the pitcher a new mold was probably required, but even of this we cannot be certain. Although no William Will teapot of early design has been reported that would have had a bowl as large as the bowl of the pitcher appears to be, he may have made such a form and may have been able thus to convert it for other uses. In any event, he used just one mold, old or new, for the belly. Without sacrificing charm in the final composition Will made a design requiring the minimum of outlay in new molds. On his coffeepot base he placed a globe, truncated at top and bottom. The globe was formed by taking two castings from the same mold, upending one and soldering them together at their greatest diameter.

The neck, spout, and handle-strut definitely called for new molds. These were so nicely designed that the resulting pitcher is one of the finest tributes to the art and craftsmanship of the American pewterer. The graceful sweeping curve of the top rim, from handle to tip of spout, recalls the tiny creamers of the Queen Anne period; and the proportions and shape of the spout furnish just the proper balance to the opposing handle. Not only is the pitcher a work of art but it is a magnificent demonstration of what a real artist can do with a few simple forms and a knowledge of how to use them.

It would be interesting to know whether there is any surviving Philadelphia pitcher in silver which might have served as Will's model or whether the design was original with him. Whatever his inspiration, Will fashioned a pitcher of beauty and dignity. We can be very grateful to the little Lutheran Church at Aaronsburg for having preserved to this day this masterpiece of American pewter.

MARKS BY WILLIAM WILL, punched on bottom of bowl of Aaronsburg communion service.

PEWTER PITCHER OR EWER of Aaronsburg Communion Service.

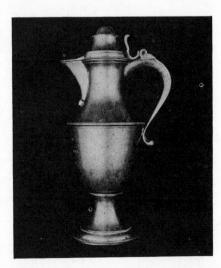

PEWTER FLAGON of Aaronsburg Communion Service.

Three Pieces by William Will of Philadelphia (*1742-1798*). The pitcher or ewer and the bowl are without counterpart in American pewter. The footed Queen Anne teapot is both fine and a rarity. *Illustrations from the Hershey Museum, Hershey, Pennsylvania.*

Some Pewter by William Will

BY JOHN J. EVANS, JR.

IT WAS EARLY Saturday afternoon and I was faced with the problem of entertaining an almost teen-age boy. In search of diversion, we drove to Hershey, Pennsylvania, famous among other things for its recreational facilities. It turned out to be an "off-day;" nothing seemed to be open for business. We were about to give up when we came upon a sign to the Hershey Museum, of which I had not previously known. It offered a ray of hope and we grabbed it.

The Museum had its beginning with the acquisition in 1936 of the George H. Danner collection, which two years later was placed on exhibition. Mr. Danner, a resident of the little town of Manheim, Pennsylvania—home of Baron Stiegel, glassmaker—was among the earliest in this area to collect on a large scale the his-

torical items which many of his contemporaries rated as second-hand stuff, He was collecting Stiegel glass well before the turn of the century.

The purpose of the Museum is to preserve for posterity those things which are known to have played an important part in the everyday lives of Americans more than a hundred years ago, with particular emphasis on the so-called Pennsylvania Dutch country. A series of rooms is furnished as one would have found them in the home of an Amish, Mennonite, or "Plain" family of the eighteenth century; the family itself is present, in wax, even to the family dog. Other exhibits include an array of Pennsylvania rifles, a magnificent display of Stiegel glass, and a large collection of Indian artifacts.

Nearing the end of our tour, my friend and I came

William Will's earliest touch, impressed in the well of the bowl, is believed to be pre-Revolutionary.

Will's Touch—WM WILL in serrated rectangle—in the inside bottom of the pitcher or ewer.

to a display of pewter pieces in a glass case. They were unidentified and so placed that the makers' marks were concealed. Inquiry disclosed that the attendant on duty had no knowledge of their identity and the display case could only be opened by the curator who at that time was serving with the U. S. Navy.

Conforming to the proverbial practice of "home-towners" who travel great distances to visit points of interest and overlook those right around the corner—Hershey is a thirty-mile drive over excellent highway from my front door—I did not make a return trip for six years. When I did, Mr. Richard Light, curator, opened the long-closed display case, and I found that during all that time a discovery of real importance in the field of American pewter had been waiting to be made.

The first piece in the case to catch the eye is the Queen Anne teapot standing on three feet, a little gem in excellent condition. It is a product of William Will's shop in Philadelphia, identified by his name touch on the inside bottom of the teapot. In size (height, 7 inches) and appearance, it matches the teapot by the same maker illustrated by Laughlin in *Pewter in America (Fig. 190)*. The sole difference seems to be the use on this piece of the more slender finial shown on Will's footless teapot (Laughlin, Fig. 189).

Directly below this teapot stands a handsome footed baptismal (?) bowl—unique in American pewter. In size and form it is more nearly comparable to the modern pewter and silver "Revere" bowls than to the product of an eighteenth-century American pewterer. Perhaps this bowl served as part of a baptismal service, together with the third piece illustrated here. The height of the bowl is 4⅛ inches; its diameter, 8¾ inches, including the lip which extends approximately ½ inch; the base is one inch high. The piece is solid, heavy, and in mint condition, and stamped boldly on the inside bottom is a clear impression of Colonel Will's early lamb-and-dove touch (Laughlin, Figs. 534, 535a).

The next item is a pewter pitcher or ewer and this, like the other two pieces described, was made by William Will. I have never seen anything of similar design or "feel" previously illustrated as the work of Will or any other American pewterer. The overall height of the piece is 9⅞ inches. The base, 1¼ inches in height, was cast from one mold. The section above it, to the middle of the bowl, resembles closely the body of the sugar bowl illustrated in Laughlin's Figure 198. The height of that section is 2¼ inches and quite probably the same mold was used to produce the section above it, bringing the height of the piece to 4⅞ inches

before the top section, including the neck of the vessel, was placed. The handle differs in contour from that of the ewer in the Aaronsburg communion service (Antiques, April 1950) or that of the Will quart pot (Laughlin, Fig. 127), and its acanthus-leaf decoration is somewhat more pronounced and ornate. The mark, although a bit smeared, appears quite legibly on the inside bottom of the pitcher—WM WILL in rectangle with serrated edge, as shown in Laughlin, Figure 539.

Other rare pieces in the collection include two covered chalices. One of these, though unmarked, appears identical with the one by Johann C. Heyne of Lancaster, Pennsylvania (Laughlin, Fig. 239), and matches a lidless unmarked one in my collection which was acquired with a marked Heyne flagon. The second bears Heyne's *ICH* stamp inside the lid (Laughlin, Fig. 533). There are slight but important differences between the two chalices, in size, contour, finials, and decoration. The marked example is approximately ½ inch shorter, simpler, and without banding on the cup. Engraved on the upper surface of the base are a date and two sets of initials, presumably those of donor and recipient, R K-1753- J E M.

Completing the list of American pewter pieces in the display are a creamer, apparently a duplicate of that shown in Laughlin, Figure 210; three basins in prime condition by B. Barnes (7⅞ inches), Harbeson (8 inches), and "Love" (10 inches); a late six-piece tea set by Reed and Barton; and a covered sugar bowl by Smith and Feltman of Albany. The collection, though heterogeneous, includes rarities of interest to any collector of American pewter.

Heyne's framed *ICH* touch as it appears on the under side of lid of the marked covered chalice.

Two rare covered chalices by Johann Christoph Heyne of Lancaster (1715-1781). The one on the left bears his touch, and an inscription on the base indicating its purchase in 1753. Chalice at right is unmarked but is almost a duplicate of an existing marked specimen.

Interchangeable parts
in early American pewter

BY CHARLES V. SWAIN

Fig. 1. Pewter creamer, two salts, and a chalice; unmarked and here attributed to William Will (Philadelphia, 1764-1798). *Creamer, from the collection of Mr. and Mrs. John H. McMurray; beaded salt and chalice, from the collection of John F. Ruckman; plain-edged salt, shown reversed, from the collection of Mr. and Mrs. David W. Gordon.*

ENGLAND'S POLICY IN THE EIGHTEENTH CENTURY was to discourage in every possible way the manufacture of most types of wares in the Colonies. From the very beginning the American pewterer was hampered by the restrictions placed on the importation not only of tin, the principal ingredient of his metal, but also of the brass and iron required for the fabrication of his molds. A number of makers overcame this difficulty by using one mold in combination with various others in order to create new shapes without additional expense. Many such composites have been found without touches, and it is interesting to attempt attributions by comparing such pieces with marked ones.

The pieces here attributed to William Will of Philadelphia are excellent examples of the ingenious use of a

limited number of molds. Will not only overcame the shortage of materials, he produced forms of beauty and originality which are much sought after today.

Figure 1 illustrates how the bases for a chalice and a creamer appear to have been made from the same mold as that used for two salts. The stem of the chalice could have been formed by placing two of the salts end to end, after removing about a quarter of an inch from the base of each in order to form the knop. The salt forming the upper part of the stem, above the knop, was also trimmed considerably at the top as well before the cup was added. The lower portion of the stem, however, is apparently composed of an almost complete salt, while the base on which it is mounted seems to have been cast in the mold used for a Will tankard cover (Fig. 3). This chalice is

Fig. 2. Pewter sugar bowl and chalice, unmarked and here attributed to William Will. *Ruckman collection.*

identical to one made by Will for the Aaronsburg communion service (ANTIQUES, April 1950, p. 274).

It is obvious that the upper body of the creamer was simply superimposed on a salt to form a most pleasing shape. The spout is reminiscent of Will's large ewer in the Aaronsburg service.

Figure 2 offers another instance of various forms from one mold in the unmarked sugar bowl and the Aaronsburg-type chalice attributed to William Will. The cover of the bowl is the same as the foot of the chalice; the flange around the latter fits as snugly on the sugar bowl as does the bowl's own cover. This sugar bowl is identical to one which was attributed to Will by John J. Evans Jr. in ANTIQUES for April 1950 (p. 276). Its relationship to the chalice shown with it offers further evidence in support of that attribution. Eighteenth-century covered sugar bowls are extremely rare and were apparently made only in America; this one is particularly handsome. Incidentally, the beading on the creamer, salt, sugar bowl, and chalice is typical of Philadelphia.

Figure 3 offers another parallel: the base of the chalice is identical with the cover of the marked William Will tankard shown with it. There is therefore a strong probability that the chalice was also made by William Will. Moreover, it is similar to a chalice illustrated by Ledlie I. Laughlin in his *Pewter in America* (Plate XXXVI, 240) which was found with a marked Will flagon. He describes it as "A chalice of dignified simplicity . . . Contemporaneous even if not made by Will."

Recognizing interchangeable parts in early American pewter not only demonstrates the ingenuity of the early craftsman; it can also be helpful in making attributions.

Fig. 3. Marked pewter tankard by William Will, and unmarked chalice here attributed to this maker. *Ruckman collection.*

107

A Flat-Top Tankard

By J. J. EVANS, JR.

A good many years ago Mr. Evans bought a pair of small pewter basins at an auction. Then he began to study the subject of American pewter, and today has a splendid collection and a wide knowledge. His article in ANTIQUES *in September 1931, I.C.H., Lancaster Pewterer, contributed to the identification of Johann Christopher Heyne.*

RECENTLY A LOVELY flat-top tankard made by pewterer William Will of Philadelphia emerged from the obscurity of the years. This rare piece adds one more proof to the claim that Colonel Will, soldier-patriot, public official, and craftsman, was top artisan among early American workers in pewter. The acquisition of a covered tankard is a bright spot in the life of any pewter collector and the "finding" of this particular piece is surrounded with additional highlights. Since it is a flat-top tankard, it is earlier than those which followed the changing mode in favor of the rounded dome lid. Then, too, it brings into Pennsylvania a form which previously was felt to be primarily a product of New York pewterers—Frederick Bassett of New York City, Peter Young of Albany, William Kirby of New York City, Henry Will of New York City and Albany, and so on. Finally, the fact that this magnificent piece was fashioned by the renowned Colonel Will adds extra luster to the occasion.

It is not surprising that a tankard with a flat cover should have been produced by William Will in view of his background, early training, and source or at least inspiration for his original molds. William was born in Nieuweid on the Rhine, January 27, 1742. When his pewterer father, John Will, brought his family to this country from Germany, he settled in New York. William received his early training in the shop of his older brother, Henry, in New York, and it has been known for years that flat-top tankards were made there, in all probability were the standard style there and in other New York pewter shops at the time of young William Will's apprenticeship. It is natural then that Will, who in his early twenties struck out for himself and started to ply his trade in Philadelphia, should offer tankards of the style in which he was schooled. Differences in measurement and ornamentation of the tankard here illustrated indicate the use of new molds rather than the acquisition or alteration of any previously used by Henry Will or any other New York pewterer, samples of whose tankards are known to exist.

Cylindrical flat-top tankards of New York fall into two general classifications—quart and three pints. The height of the "quart" group approximates 5 inches with a base diameter of about $4\frac{1}{2}$ inches. The three-pint giant size—little wonder that tavern chairs were strongly reinforced—exceeds 7 inches from bottom to top. By contrast, William Will, perhaps after a comparative study of Philadelphia Quaker capacity with that of the New York Dutch, decided one size would suffice and chose an in-between point. Brimful, the tankard pictured here holds two and three quarter pints. Comfortably filled it will dispense a full quart and a dividend. Its height is $6\frac{5}{16}$ inches, above which the thumbpiece extends an additional $1\frac{5}{16}$ inches.

Will, unlike his contemporary Pennsylvania pewterer Johann Christopher Heyne, departed almost completely from the style influences characteristic of the land of his birth. Heyne turned out pewter for approximately a quarter century prior to 1781, the year of his death in Lancaster. This thriving community, the country's "oldest inland city," was some sixty-five miles from Philadelphia on the highway leading to the vast western frontier. Like Will, Heyne came from Germany, having been born in Saxony in 1715. The work of Heyne, who is best known for his ecclesiastical pewter pieces, continued throughout his lifetime to have the Germanic "feel" and appearance. Perhaps the Pennsylvania German customers of his natural market preferred the Germanic styles—it was good, solid stuff—and large investment in new molds would not have increased customer satisfaction.

On the other hand, Will's existing examples are almost devoid of any Germanic association, unless the decorative beading motif which appears frequently and to good advantage in his work is so catalogued. The only recorded instance of Will's use of a German form is a spout on a flagon which in all other respects is English, as cited by Ledlie I. Laughlin in *Pewter in America*. He seemed never to hesitate to try what was new and good, borrowing ideas wherever he found interesting ones, from English pewterers and

FIG. 1—PEWTER. Flat-top tankard, tulip-shaped tankard, tulip-shaped mug, teapot, and ladle made by William Will, Philadelphia (1742-1798). Covered sugar bowl, unmarked, probably of Philadelphia origin. Fake William Will porringer. *From the author's collection.*

from both American and English silversmiths. In fact, Will produced a broader line of products and attempted a greater variation of design and ornamentation than any other American pewterer.

In Figure 1 are shown a ladle, a teapot, a quart tulip-shaped mug, and the double-dome and flat-top tankards. All were made by Colonel Will and each bears one of his touchmarks. A covered sugar bowl, although unmarked, is included in the group since it is believed, if not actually by Will, certainly of the type he did make. Sugar bowls are among the items listed in his inventory.

And to complete this particular collection of pewter pieces bearing the name of William Will, a porringer plainly marked with a Will touch is shown. But here all connection ends. Will himself neither saw nor made a porringer like this one and never owned a die like the one from which this impression came. How the dealer who sold it for a fair sum must have smiled as its excited purchaser hurried home to remove the heavy, opaque, greasy coating which allowed only a *W* to be seen! Both ardor and grease disappeared together as a most amateurish counterfeit of Will's touch appeared.

Attention is called to the attractive use of beading, previously referred to, around the lip of the ladle and on the body and base of the covered sugar bowl. In spite of the fact that beading appears on pieces made by later pewterers Samuel Danforth and Thomas Boardman, who worked in Hartford, Connecticut, this treatment seems

Fig. 2—Will's Touch, appearing on inside bottom of flat-top tankard. Same touch is used in teapot.

Fig. 3—Flat-top Tankard. *Right,* Side view showing concealed pin in hinge construction. *Below,* Front of tankard showing engraving added later and detail of thumb-piece.

to have been pretty well confined to the pewterers of Philadelphia, and it may well be that credit for its introduction to American pewter belongs to Will.

The touchmark used by Will to identify the flat-top tankard as his product is *Wm. WILL (Fig. 2)*. This same touch appears in his Queen Anne-style teapot and is pictured in Mr. Laughlin's *Pewter in America* (figure 539) and in J. B. Kerfoot's *American Pewter* (figure 74). Both the tulip-shaped tankard and the mug are marked with the familiar crossing *WW's* in concentric circles (Laughlin, figures 541 and 541A, and Kerfoot, figure 78). In all four of these pieces the dies were struck on the bottoms inside the vessels. On the back of the ladle handle appears the touchmark *W. WILL/ PHILA/DELPHIA* in oblong frame with serrated edge.

Though these two tankards and the mug are products of the same pewter shops, no two handles are alike. Each differs from the other in convolution, gripping thickness, raised ornamentation at the top, and in design of terminals.

Another most interesting departure in construction detail is in the seating of the hinge pin in the flat-top tankard. Contrary to customary practice of having the pin extend completely through the hinge, it is visible only on the side of entry. The opposite stationary component attached to the handle has been only partially bored and one end of the pin fits into this cup as a candle into a candle holder. The swinging portion of the hinge attached to the lid is a single tab fitting accurately between the two end pieces affixed to the handle. In the case of the later tulip-shaped tankard there are three immobile hinge components as part of the handle, to receive the two intermediate ones forming part of the lid *(Fig. 3)*.

Figure 3 *(below)* shows the ram's-head style of solid thumb-piece and the concentric circles centered on the top surface of the lid. The circles became the base of a petal design, and the initials of the later owner *D K* together with *1815* were engraved on the tankard's front surrounded by a delicate sunburst framing.

BY ERIC DE JONGE

Swedish influence on American pewter

Flagons right and left by Johann Christoph Heyne; center flagon, by H. Müller of Rothenburg, Germany, served as model. *Photograph by courtesy of John J. Evans, Jr.*

ON ITS FRONTISPIECE IN February 1928 ANTIQUES showed a Pennsylvania pewter communion flagon, then in the Reifsnyder collection, which immediately attracted widespread attention. The piece bore an inscription indicating that it had been presented to St. Peter's Church in Mount Joy Township by one John Dirr in 1771; it also bore the previously unrecorded touch of I C H LANCASTER, surmounted by a crown. At that time the maker was unknown and interest centered about certain stylistic peculiarities of the piece, which seemed to indicate a Continental source modified by English influences. It was concluded that the maker was of German or Alsatian extraction.

A few years later an important article (ANTIQUES, September 1931) by John J. Evans, Jr., identified I C H as Johann Christoph Heyne, tinsmith and pewterer of Lancaster, and showed some other examples of his work—among them a pair of church flagons made in 1771 for the Trinity Lutheran Church of Lancaster to match a German communion flagon of about 1725 then in possession of the church. An unusual editorial postscript to

this article suggested additional possibilities as to Heyne's birthplace and apprenticeship, and identified the maker of the original German flagon as Heinrich Müller of Rothenburg ob der Tauber, Bavaria.

Heyne was an able and gifted craftsman and his copies compared well with the original, but he departed in several instances from its features: he adopted a hollow cast bud-end handle instead of the strap-handle, and he arranged the thumbpiece in a very curious manner. These deviations were attributed partly to certain changes in style which had taken place in the intervening years, and partly to lack of molds and to limited shop equipment. Great importance was attached to them, and they were assumed to be proof of a conscious or unconscious absorption of English ideas and styles then prevalent in the Colonies.

This assimilation of current local fashion is an important factor in the work of any creative craftsman, and our colonial artisans must have been as subject to such influences as anyone. To attribute any significant change of style or form entirely to a surrender to new habits and surroundings, however, diverts attention from the importance of the original training of the craftsman.

To comprehend fully the forces which were responsible for the training and development of our foreign-born American craftsmen of the seventeenth and eighteenth centuries one needs an understanding of the intricate web of rules and regulations in which English and Continental craftsmen of these periods were enmeshed. Neither English nor Continental craftsmen were free agents; their lives were circumscribed by the rules of their particular craft guilds, which the guilds enforced with astounding authority.

Of major importance for our purpose are the rules which governed the life of the apprentice and his subsequent life as a journeyman. Upon graduation from his apprenticeship, the young journeyman was compelled by guild rules to go on a long journey. He had to travel from town to town, from master to master, always looking for an opportunity to ply his trade. Depending on the craft, this was a five- to ten-year extension of his apprenticeship. When finally the journeyman could apply for his master's certificate, his work in other towns and foreign lands and his adoption of varied working methods under many masters had broadened his horizon.

With the American phase of Heyne's life rather well established by Mr. Evans, his unknown years as a journeyman became of utmost interest. Where had he worked, what countries had he visited, and what forms and designs had impressed themselves upon his mind?

The tracing of Heyne's peregrinations was facilitated when it was established that his road had led him to Stettin. This northern German city is separated from Sweden by the Baltic Sea, not a great obstacle. Pewterers of Sweden and northern Germany, and their journeymen, had intimate working agreements, and their guilds were often united in regional groups. Having worked in northern Germany, Heyne was acquainted with the closely related styles of that area and of Sweden; and the record shows that after finishing his Saxonian apprenticeship in 1733 and arriving in Stettin in 1734, he was registered in Stockholm in 1735. He made his mark there in 1736, when he was elected "Ortsgeselle," or executive officer, of his journeyman's guild. His duties were manifold, and only the highly qualified and respected journeyman could aspire to such an exalted position. Heyne's name appears again in the Stockholm records of 1737, and we do not hear of him after that until 1742, when he arrived in Philadelphia from England. However, it seems improbable that he worked in England as a journeyman pewterer in the intervening five years, since English guilds were strongly opposed to the employment of foreign craftsmen.

The records show that Heyne worked for a period of years in Sweden and that upon leaving the Continent he was familiar not only with the forms of middle and southern Germany, but with those of northern Germany and Sweden as well. And an evaluation of his work as an American pewterer strongly suggests an even longer sojourn in Sweden than can be documented at present.

When Heyne's copies of the old German flagon were recognized for what they were, the significant deviations from the original drew attention to the so-called "English" hollow cast bud-end handle, then in style in colonial America, and to the typically Teutonic thumbpiece. Had Heyne worked only in southern Germany he would have known only the conventional German strap-

Tankard of a seventeenth-century type by Petter Noren, Hedemora; 1765. *Except as noted, illustrations are by courtesy of Nordiska Museet, Stockholm.*

Wine pitcher by Heinrich Gottfried Pschorn (master 1715-1743), Stockholm; datemark 1738.

111

handle, and his task of copying it from the original flagon would have been easy. Heyne's application of the hollow cast handle was interpreted as proof of his rapid Americanization; and it was suggested that the peculiarities of his thumbpiece were necessitated by the sweep of the handle. Had these surmises been correct, the craftsman could have solved the difficulty by adopting the contemporary erect thumbpiece. He did not adopt this thumbpiece until later, and we must attribute these deviations to lessons learned long ago but readily recalled.

These two apparently unrelated features, the hollow cast handle and the elevated thumbpiece, were in style in Sweden as an entity for about two hundred years—long before and long after Heyne. Distinct attributes of Swedish hollow ware, they are not found in any other country except northern Germany. The hollow cast handle was known in Sweden from about the middle of the seventeenth century on; an example is the seventeenth-century tankard by Petter Noren, which incidentally has the same type of handle Heyne used on his Lancaster flagons, the "English" bud-end. The elevated thumbpiece, an outstanding feature of Heyne's flagons, was a functional and ornamental part of Swedish hollow ware even in conjunction with the strap-handle, as the wine pitcher by Heinrich Gottfried Pschorn of Stockholm demonstrates. A flagon by Erik Hindersson and a tankard by Carl Saur show that even the erect thumbpiece and the double dome found on Heyne's later flagons were used in Sweden.

Written and visual records show conclusively that Heyne worked in Sweden for a number of years. There have been many indications of Swedish influence in American pewter, but these features of the vessels Heyne fashioned in Lancaster are the first definite proof of this influence. Transcending the scope of this article, we are reminded that Continental life, mannerisms, and habits so strongly helped to mold the craftsmanship of the immigrant artisan that an intimate acquaintance with these forces is a must for the student of American crafts.

Flagon by Erik Hindersson, Stockholm; dated 1650.

Tankard by Carl Saur I (master 1735-1781), Stockholm; datemark 1775.

This flagon by Samuel Marnell (master 1748-1775) of Stockholm shows the principal features of Heyne's church flagons; datemark 1749.

112

I. C. H., Lancaster Pewterer

By John J. Evans, Jr.

WE MUST never for a moment forget that the roots of the early American arts and crafts must be sought both in England and on the continent of Europe, and that, unless we have some understanding of these roots, we are in no position to offer critical judgment upon the various flowerings that succeeded their transplantation to a new soil overseas and the cross-fertilization that inevitably occurred where varied national strains were brought into intimate association in a new environment.

No doubt the dominant tradition under which the arts of early Colonial days developed was derived from England. In the long run, English-born prejudices and English-born tastes forced American craftsmen of Continental descent and upbringing to adapt themselves to English conceptions of style. But the process of subjugation was by no means rapid. In some instances, it was so slow as to be long unrecognizable. And, even when and where it seemed to have been triumphantly completed, the conquering mode still found itself unmistakably marked with traits of that which it had supposedly vanquished.

One of the most impressive illustrations of the intermingling of English and German tradition on the neutral ground of Pennsylvania is the pewter Communion flagon published in ANTIQUES for February, 1928, and at the time included in the Reifsnyder collection (*Fig. 4*). Inscribed as a gift from John Dirr to Saint Peter's Church, Mount Joy Township, 1771, this flagon bore the touchmark "I. C. H., Lancaster." As to the identity of this I. C. H. no statement was made, for the honest reason that nothing was certainly known about him. Recently, however, with the assistance and moral support of Ledlie I. Laughlin, I have been able to fill that gap in American pewter history, and, in so doing, to satisfy my desire to win for Lancaster, Pennsylvania, its rightful place in the sun.

The cataloguers of Mr. Reifsnyder's collection were distinctly unkind to Lancaster when they credited its splendid flagon, even with reservations, to J. C.

Hera, the only pewterer listed in Mr. Kerfoot's volume whose initials satisfied the hazard of an attribution. There was no other ground for the guess. Subsequently, the discovery of a dram bottle bearing the I. C. H. of our elusive friend naturally whetted my desire to learn more about this mysterious individual (*Fig. 5*). A visit with Mr. Laughlin gave me my first view of the initials in combination with the crown and Lancaster touch.

Later, a member of Saint John's Church at Compassville, Pennsylvania, showed me a duplicate of the familiar flagon, and added the information that the piece was presented to the church in 1766. Still another trip, this time to Trinity Lutheran Church in Lancaster, rewarded me with the opportunity to study two examples by the same craftsman. I have also heard of other I. C. H. pieces, bringing the total list of known items bearing this mark to four flagons, two chalices, a sugar bowl, an eight-inch plate, a six-inch plate, a dram bottle, and a porringer. I have recently seen a duplicate of the dram bottle, evidently cast in the same mold, but unmarked.

Trinity Lutheran Church was established in Lancaster in 1729. On September 30, 1733, "John Martin Weybrecht [said to have been a blacksmith residing in the vicinity of Manheim, Pennsylvania] presented a pewter flagon, having a lid and a wreath on it. It rests on three feet of angel-heads, and holds about two quarts. There is a lamb, with a banner and a cross engraved upon it; also the three letters I. c. s."

This flagon has always been highly prized by the Church. In every detail it corresponds to the above description taken from the Church records. Its touch, however, is not that of I. C. H. Stamped on the handle occurs an evidently foreign design, a shield with two turrets, between which the numerals 71 and 9 are decipherable below the initials H. M. On the bottom, within, appears a rose, stamped in the metal. Though the touch is by no means his, the design of the flagon is strikingly similar to that which I. C. H. employed. For that we shall shortly discover the reason.

Fig. 1 — THE PROTOTYPE OF THE I. C. H. FLAGONS (*3 views*)
Given in 1733 to Trinity Lutheran Church, Lancaster, Pennsylvania. Identified as the work of Heinrich Müller of Rothenburg. View at the right shows rosette inside the flagon

Fig. 2 — THE THREE TRINITY FLAGONS
The flagons right and left were made by I. C. H. in 1766 to match the original that stands between them

Fig. 3 — BOTTOMS OF THE THREE TRINITY FLAGONS
Early form in the middle. The later bottoms are six-inch plates

In passing, it will be sufficient to examine the different views of the flagon in Figure 1, and to note its major features.

In 1757 a treaty was made with the Indians in Lancaster that encouraged the members of Trinity Church to purchase ground and begin the construction of a new building. In spite of violations of this treaty, the new edifice was ready for dedication May 4, 1766. In the meantime, while preparations for a larger and finer building to house the growing congregation were progressing, it was appropriate, perhaps even necessary, that additions be made to the Communion service. In any event, we read in the records that, on the day of consecration, "at ten o'clock the schoolmaster with the children, then the deacons solemnly bearing the sacred vessels, next the invited ministers, followed by the elders and trustees of the congregation, and last the deputies of the united congregations, marched to the Church."

To whom did the deacons entrust the order for producing the two new flagons? At that time I. C. H., the Lancaster maker, had been established in the town for several years, and must have enjoyed at least a local reputation. He was the logical man for the work. Is it not natural to assume that the flagon already owned by Trinity served him as a model for the two that he was to produce? In executing this commission, our craftsman departed slightly, yet significantly, from the design of the original, a procedure that may be attributed in part to changes in style that had occurred during the preceding third of a century, in part, to his limited equipment, and, in part, perhaps, to his own conscious or unconscious absorption of English ideas.

Except for the addition of banding around the middle of the 1766 vessels, the body of each is practically identical with that of the prototype. The lid almost duplicates that of the older flagon,

though its rim is less rounded and its dome proportionately higher. However, when we examine the bottoms of the later flagons, we discover that I. C. H., instead of casting them in a conventional bottom mold, employed the easier method of substituting a pair of six-inch plates, for which he had a mold.

The most radical differences between the early flagon and its younger mates lie in the design of handles and lid-hinges. At this point the Lancaster maker succumbed to the trend of the times and the dominant style of his environment. For the somewhat weak German strap handle of the 1733 flagon he substituted the sturdy hollow-cast English form. His moving the hinge back was also a concession to English custom.

Nevertheless, despite the latter change, he still clung to a ball thumbpiece conforming to the German mode. In so doing, he found himself in the midst of structural difficulties that necessitated the building of a bridge between handle and lid upon which to impose his ball. He evidently appreciated the awkwardness of this arrangement; for on the later flagons of Saint John of the Compass and of the Mount Joy congregation he abandoned the ball in favor of a thumbpiece of a more practical English type. It is unfortunate that we have no flagon dating from the maker's closing years. Perhaps in such an example we should discover still further evidence of departures from European tradition.

The first clue to the identity of the producer of these remarkable flagons I found in the tax list of the Borough of Lancaster for 1779. "Christph Heyne, tinman," is among those listed; but, as if consciously dodging future fame in pewter history, that individual failed to claim closer association with its manufacture. But to him, a German, *Zinn* and pewter were one and the same. Further to complicate search, Heyne apparently died intestate;

at least no record of any will has so far come to light. As a final means of escaping detection, he emulated Shakespeare by varying the spelling of his name with nearly every recording. It remained for Mr. Laughlin's discovery of a record for the sale of property to "Christopher Heyne, Tinsmith and Pewterer," to prove that the original clue had actual possibilities.

Working on the assumption that, at length, we had our man, and with the aid of not a small amount of luck, we discovered the meagre skeleton at first unearthed beginning to fill out into the substance of the following chronologically arranged facts. For the various spellings, and for the probable incorrectness of some of the foreign names, the records alone must bear the responsibility. These are the facts:

December 3, 1715 — John Christoph Hayne was born in the village of Feuntschen, Bohra, in Saxony. (See editorial postscript.)

June 27, 1746 — He was married to Maria Margr. Schiefeun.

April 11, 1761 — Jno. Christ Hayne of Lancaster appeared before a "Supream Court" in Philadelphia and transferred his allegiance to King George.

1764 — Maria Margr. Schiefeun [wife of Hayne] died.

July 27, 1764 — He married "the widow Steinman."

June 22, 1767 — Joseph Simons, merchant, and Rose, his wife, of Lancaster, for £600 paid by Christopher Heyne, Tinsmith and Pewterer, sold a piece of ground and "Brick Messuage or Tenement" thereon to Christopher Heyne, his heirs and assigns. The property was on King Street, Lancaster.

Tax list of 1771 — Lists him for a tax of 10 shillings.

Tax list of 1772 — Does the same.

Tax list of 1773 — Increases his tax to 12 shillings.

November 30, 1773 — 100 acres owned by Christopher Heyne in the county of Cumberland were surveyed.

The Census of 1779 — Reveals that Christph Heyne possessed no acres, horses, cattle, sheep, or negroes.

January 11, 1781 — He died, and was buried in the Moravian Churchyard, Lancaster.

January 13, 1781 — Frederick Stoneman and Anna Rosey Hiney (wife of the deceased) appeared and gave bond for administration of the estate.

January 30, 1781 — The inventory of Christopher Hiney was recorded. There were goods, etc., appraised

Fig. 4 — THE SAINT PETER'S CHURCH FLAGON (*1771*)
Lid more domical than that of *1766* flagons. English type thumbpiece. The I. C. H. mark, also on the two flagons of Fig. 2, is shown at the right.
Formerly in the Reifsnyder collection

at £182 8s. 2d., also bills against the State of Pennsylvania, running from 1777 to 1780 for $6,500.

Included in the inventory were:

	£	s	d
6½ Doz. of pewter spoons	1	2	6
15 " " " "	0	4	0
17 lbs. old pewter	0	14	2
4 Pewter Pints	0	10	0
16 do Plates	1	2	6
8 do Basons	0	13	4
7 Salt Sellers & two plates	0	8	0
2 Chamber pots	0	10	0
1 Quart and 3 Church Cups	1	10	0
5 Bottles	0	5	0
Sundry tools	25	0	0
" moulds	8	0	0
" "	30	0	0

May 13, 1783 — "Anna Regina Hayn, born Robin (widowed Steinman) November 24, 1717, at Eifurt, in Germany; baptized and brought up in the Lutheran religion, died and was also buried in the Moravian Churchyard, Lancaster. In 1736 she entered the state of matrimony with her first husband, Christian Frederic Steinman, with whom she had four children, of whom two survive, namely George Michael, who is in Sarepta, Asia, and Frederic Steinman here in Lancaster. Anno 1760 on the 17th of December her first husband departed at Lititz. In 1764, July 27th, she was married to the widower, Christoph Hayne, in Lancaster, who departed Jan. 11, 1781. In 1748 she came to Herrnhut with her first husband and was there admitted to the congregation. In 1739, in March, they came to Pennsylvania."

Apparently Heyne had no children of his own. Under the act of Parliament that governed the procedure of naturalization through which Heyne passed in 1761, he had to show proof of residence in the Colonies for seven years and membership in a Protestant or Reformed congregation; consequently, if the act was rigorously administered, he arrived in America in 1754 or earlier, which gave him twenty-six years or more of pewtermaking in this country.

The excellence of his workmanship and the variety of articles that he made establish Johann Christoph Heyne as a prolific artisan of the first order. His addition to the family of American pewterers is an event of high importance.

An Editorial Postscript

THE information acquired during the long and careful research of Mr. Evans and Mr. Laughlin so clearly justified an attempt to discover the original source of inspiration for the extraordinary series of Heyne flagons

Fig. 5 — DRAM BOTTLE BY I. C. H.   *Author's collection*

that correspondence with European authorities was undertaken. As usual in such cases, R. M. Vetter of Amsterdam was first consulted. Quite according to expectation, that broad-minded student and connoisseur was deeply interested, declaring in a letter of some length that the process by which "in these flagons the purely German idea is gradually over-ridden by English influences, first by the adoption of the English handle, and finally by the acceptance of an English thumbpiece type, deserves the attention not only of the pewter collector but of historians in general. There will be few instances where the merging of one civilization with another is more clearly demonstrated than in this case." Further he observes, "The use of small plates for the bottoms of the later flagons is a delightful and original feature.

Fig. 6 (above) — Sugar Bowl by i. c. h.
The inverted pear shape recalls forms current previous to the Revolution. One of the finest surviving examples of American pewter

Fig. 7 (right) — Chalice or Covered Cup by i. c. h.
Perhaps the unique example of its kind in eighteenth-century American pewter. The shape suggests the period *1765-1785.*
Both from the collection of Ledlie I. Laughlin

Christoph Heyne had become a practical Yankee workman who knew how to make the most of a restricted stock of molds. It is delightful to think of this German thus adapting himself to his new surroundings, showing how we are all creatures of circumstances, and how time-honored traditions are subject to adaptation. In Europe plates so used would not have passed!"

For a consideration of some of the purely historical questions raised by the flagons, Mr. Vetter advised consultation with Professor Doctor Erwin Hintze, Director of the Schlossmuseum, Breslau, Germany, and the foremost authority on German and Germanic pewter. Professor Hintze's reply to a lengthy letter of enquiry brought the following lucid answer:

"I have the happy opportunity to name the master of the flagon of German origin, dated 1733. The touch is that of a pewterer Heinrich Müller of Rothenburg ob der Tauber, Bavaria. On January 16, 1721, the said Müller became a citizen of that town. The touch shows two turrets, and between them the figures 71, and apparently 9 — that is to say, the year 1719. This would mean that Heinrich Müller established his business as a pewterer at Rothenburg ob der Tauber in the year 1719.

"The shape of the flagon, with its slender body growing wider in its lower parts, the three angel heads supporting the base, and, further, the strap handle, all are characteristic of southern Germany. The thumbpiece appears there as well as in the northern parts of our country. My identification of the origin of this flagon is authentic, and you may fully rely on it.

"The note in ANTIQUES for February, 1928, page 112, by Mr. Vetter of Amsterdam, can, in certain points, be rectified by the above explanation. The said flagon, brought from Germany to America, did *not* originate in Alsace, but in Rothenburg ob der Tauber, Bavaria.

"I am sorry not to have been in a position to find out the exact dates of the pewterer Johann Christoph Heyne, who emigrated

from Germany, and later settled in Lancaster. There are several villages named Bora or Bohra. One village is near Nossen in Saxony; there are even two with the same name Bora. Another Bohra is situated near Altenburg (Saxony-Altenburg). Though I have at my disposal rich documentary material regarding the Saxon pewterers I could not trace in them the name of Johann Christoph Heyne. If he was born December 3, 1715, he must have been serving his apprenticeship from 1729 to 1733. I have examined the lists of pewterer-apprentices of Dresden, Altenburg, and Leipzig, in which are contained the names of the apprentices of the entire country, but I could nowhere find one Johann Christoph Heyne. But two other pewterers of the name Heyne apparently are near relations of Johann Christoph:

"(1) the pewterer Tobias Heyne, son of the carrier Michael Heyne of Grumbach. He was serving his apprenticeship in Rochlitz from 1698 to 1702, and 1709 he got his freedom as pewterer in Leisnig. His son Gotthelf Heyne served in the capacity of his apprentice from 1740;

"(2) the pewterer Johan Christian Heyne, apprentice of his cousin Tobias Heyne, became a master at Rochlitz, March 27, 1733. There he was still known as pewterer in 1755."

So much for that. We must return for a moment to the original flagon of Trinity Church. It is now certain that the piece is of Bavarian origin — not Alsatian. We even know who made it. Precisely how it came into the possession of the smith John Martin Weybrecht, who presented it to his church, is beyond telling. Evidently, at the time, the Saxon Heyne had not yet appeared upon the scene. In that case, where did he procure the molds from which to cast the angel heads and the spouts of his later flagons; and whence came his ball thumbpieces? Can he for the purpose of duplication have made plaster molds from the original Bavarian flagon, and can he further have wrested his thumbpieces from some old tankards found in the possession of his German neighbors? Those which he used are not quite identical in shape, and both differ materially from the ball on the prototypal vessel.

It would, of course, be pleasant to assume that Heyne came to America in 1733 fresh from his apprenticeship in Germany, and armed with the Rothenburg flagon and some, at least, of the essential molds for reproducing it. Unfortunately, such an hypothesis will hardly stand the strain of analysis. The theory advanced by Mr. Evans and Mr. Laughlin that our craftsman was set to the task of copying a venerated piece and did the best he could under the circumstances is probably the only tenable one. To spin a number of fine fancies would be easy enough — but far from profitable. It is sufficient that we have a sequence of flagons, one of them a pure German piece; the others modeled after it by a German-American pewterer whose successive and ingenious copies of the original show progressively wider departures from the authentic German form with which he began.

Fig. 1 — Lee Pewter Porringers
The first is marked *R. Lee;* the second, *Richard Lee;* the third, *Richard Lee;* the fourth with a *fleur-de-lis* and the initials *R. L.* Approximate diameters, from 2 to 6 inches.
Owned by Albert C. Bowman

Richard Lee, Pewterer

By Harold G. Rugg and the Editor*

IN his invaluable work on American pewter, J. B. Kerfoot states that Richard Lee, the pewterer, was probably born in England and lived in Taunton, Massachusetts. Recently however, it was my good fortune to discover that this same Lee was American born, and that his places of abode were many. Some of the facts of his varied life may be of sufficient interest for recital here. Lee was a man of multitudinous sorrows and of much grief, but, if the frequency with which he sought to heal the wounds of marital bereavement by fresh adventurings in matrimony may be accepted as a criterion of character, he remained, to the last, essentially an optimist.

Fortunately Lee has left us an autobiographical record of part of his life; and, though this record deals primarily with the author's religious experiences and his sundry mundane misfortunes and gives little information concerning his pewter making, sections of it are of sufficient moment to be worth reprinting here.

The autobiography in question is entitled: *A Short Narrative of the Life of Mr. Richard Lee; containing a brief account of his Nativity, Conviction and Conversion . . . Printed for the author, 1821.* A copy of this 1821 edition, a pamphlet of eighty-three pages, is to be found in the

*For all the investigation upon which these notes are based credit belongs to Mr. Rugg. It has been the function of his collaborator only to give sequence to the material which, owing to pressure upon his time, Mr. Rugg was obliged to submit more or less in the rough.

library of the Vermont Historical Society at Montpelier. There were, however, two earlier editions: the first, a pamphlet of over twenty-four pages, printed at Kennebunk, Maine, in 1804; and the second, a pamphlet of seventeen pages, printed at Burlington, Vermont, in 1808. The third edition, naturally, offers more details of the life of Lee than the others.

From this autobiography, it would appear that Lee, himself, made pewter in Lanesboro, Massachusetts, and that, later, when in Springfield, Vermont, he *sold* pewter for his son. We may surmise, therefore, that there were two Lees who made pewter.

Descendents of Richard Lee, still living in the town of Springfield, maintain among them a tradition that both Richard Lee and his son of the same name made pewter in Vermont. Pewter porringers and basins marked *R. Lee* have been picked up in the neighborhood of Springfield. I have in my own collection a brass skimmer and a brass ladle both similarly imprinted. It is possible that *R. Lee* is the mark of the son, while the father used his full name. To date I have located pewter plates, spoons, ladles, porringers, and basins bearing the Lee mark. An unusual four handled porringer with the *R. Lee* mark is owned by William C. Staples of Springfield, Vermont (*Fig. 2*).

At this point it may be well to let Richard Lee,

Fig. 2 — Four Handled Pewter Porringer
An unique piece. The mark *R. Lee* appears on the underbracket of each handle. Diameter of bowl, 2½ inches. A detail of one handle appears at the right.
Owned by William C. Staples

Sr., speak for himself. As we are interested in his physical career, and, only incidentally, in the soul wrestlings which accompanied the process of his conviction of sin and subsequent conversion, I shall offer only such excerpts from his autobiography as deal with the former. Unfortunately Lee gives us few dates; but he is specific as to that of his birth, and, despite the impairments to his health which were induced by brief service in the Continental army, he lived to a ripe old age — until March 26, 1823. He is buried in the cemetery at North Springfield, Vermont. His son, who survived him by some thirty-five years, rests close by.

Here then is Richard Lee's narrative:

I was born in Situate, Providence Plantations, January 27, 1747 . . . Not long after . . . my father moved to Swansey Massachusetts, his native place, where I was brought up . . . I will here reprint a little pamphlet for my reader, which briefly shows a scene of disappointment and a world of trouble which I passed through chiefly in the space of 7 years. In the year of our Lord A.D. 1773, I assisted the removal of a family to Lanesborough. I liked the land so well that I bought 50 acres . . . and before I returned home I cleared two acres and sowed it with wheat. . . . And so cleared up the largest part of seven acres and partly built me a log house, and paid eleven silver dollars interest money for the land, and had hired the greatest part of my household goods moved up there, and expected to go with my family every week for several weeks. I was, however, disappointed; the unhappy war broke out in this country . . . I enlisted myself for eight months in the service and went to Roxbury; I had served about two months and a half and my brother came down to take my place . . . I have never been well a day since, which is more than twenty two years and one month . . . So the doctors advised me to take to riding for my health so I did a while, and traded a little, having a family to take care of, and then I moved back into the country, about forty miles and set up keeping a small shop of goods, which I purchased on credit. . . . I used to make it my rule to go to Providence once in three weeks. . . . In the above actions they tore Mr. Lee's clothes considerably and injured his body so much that he was ill for some days, and then he returned home to Gloucester in the County of Providence. . . . In the first place when I married my second wife I sought to extricate myself from debt; and for this end I set up tanning in Gloucester (Providence) and hired a man for one year. This was at the close of the British war with America. . . From thence I moved to Springfield, Vermont where I retained fourteen acres of land, and built an house and cleared ten acres, and sold it towards paying my debts. Then took a lease lot and after clearing four acres and building another house sold that for the same purpose. From thence I moved to Grafton in New Hampshire, where I set up storekeeping. . . . I traded in wild land and helped others to farms. . . . I bought me a farm, built me a house and store. . . My next object was pewtering with my son and making hardware but-

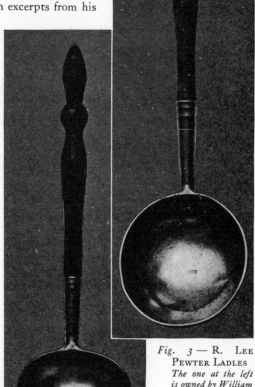

Fig. 3 — R. Lee
Pewter Ladles
The one at the left is owned by William C. Staples; the one at the right, by Albert C. Bowman

tons, but the cost of tools was great and we were obliged to purchase them by labor, which caused us to be gone from home eleven months, in which time we both were sick but through the goodness of God we recovered, and then removed to Ashfield, Massachusetts where we lived one year; . . . from thence we removed to Lanesborough, in Massachusetts where we lived two years and a half. Here to augment our debts and sorrows we all had the smallpox. But after recovering I set out with my two sons on a long journey to collect debts, and sell wild land, and make payment as fast as possible. We purposed to return in two months, but I met with a hurt in one of my eyes, and outstaid the time and here the advantage was taken by three men. The two first proceeded in a legal way, and took twenty two and a half dollars. Here I object not but for the needless cost; but the other a Mr. Hoit I had settled with to a trifle, before I went from home. If my family had lived in his house till spring, I should have owed him fifty shillings only. He laid violent hands on my tools and clothes and household furniture and sold them . . . a quart bason mould was sold for two dollars twenty five cents; which to buy new would cost me thirty dollars. Two other moulds were sold for two shillings and sixpence which cost me five dollars each;* and other things in like manner. . . . Now I was poorer than before I set out on my journey. I must begin to obtain my tools again. But the reasons why I did not return to Lanesborough were these . . . In the year of our Lord 1802 on the twelfth day of May the Lord took my second wife out of this transitory world but I hope to a better one; after which I returned to Springfield, in Vermont, where I had formerly lived about three years, in order to reside with my children who lived there. And being poor and in debt I undertook to carry out pewter and brassware to sell, for my oldest son, for a while . . . Now I would note that in the year 1805 November 14th I was married to the widow Hannah Starr, of Guilford, Vermont, and I removed her and two of her children to Springfield, Vermont† . . . and I went to live with my son and sell pewter and brassware for him again, and I lived with him for the next summer when I bought a small piece of land; then I went to clearing up my land and built me a small house on it . . . and the next June 18th day 1807 I moved into my house. . . . On the 5th of September 1809 I undertook a long journey, to Swanzey, Rehoboth, Dighton, Taunton, and Dartmouth, to see all my brothers and sisters living in these places these being the places of my nativity and where I had formerly lived.

Lee appears to have been one of those restless universal geniuses, not uncommon in the New England of his day. We have seen that he was something of a speculator in real estate, a dealer in wild lands, a storekeeper, a pewterer on his own account, and later a peddler of brass and pewter for his son. From two histories of the town of Springfield we learn, further, that he preached in the Baptist church in the village of North Springfield, where, in spite of the deference due to his

Fig. 4 — RICHARD LEE PLATE
Shown in obverse and reverse. Marked *Richard Lee*. 8 inches in diameter.
Owned by William C. Staples

*It would be interesting to know where and how he acquired his molds.

†Lee was then 58 years of age.

clerical calling, the children called him Grandpa Lee.

Not content with looking after the spiritual welfare of the community, Lee also tinkered with distillates of herbs, which he prescribed for bodily ailments. The village children gathered wintergreen for him, and he repaid them with picture books of his own making. A copy of one of his books, which may have been given in exchange for a load of wintergreen, is an eight-page chapbook, preserved in the Library of Congress. It bears the cheery entitlement *The Melancholy End of Ungrateful Children*, and the imprint *Rutland, Richard Lee 1795*. The Library of the *American Antiquarian Society* at Worcester possesses another of Lee's entertainments for children in the form of an eight-page work, likewise printed in Rutland. It offers incitement to wintergreen picking under the alluring title of *Several Facts of Scripture Adduced in Support of Adult Baptism*. Whether these chapbooks are by Richard Lee the elder, or by his son, I cannot state with assurance. But their contents suggest the work of the former. In the second edition of this work may be found the following irresistible appeal to the infant mind. The acrostic is obvious.

> Riches of a glorious kind,
> In Christ Jesus we may find;
> Come poor sinners take a share
> Here's a plenty and to spare;
> All is glorious and divine,
> Richer than the burning mine
> Dost delay the precious call,
> Leave your toys and troubles all,
> Each soul who lives must learn to die
> Ere it can dwell with God on high.

To return for a moment to the various wares turned out by Lee and his son. While the father speaks of producing pewter on his own account, he makes no mention of brassware except to state that he made some attempt to sell the latter on behalf of his son. From this fact we may, perhaps, conclude that all brassware bearing the Lee mark should be at-

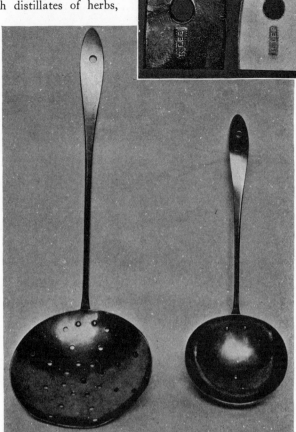

Fig. 5 — Lee Brassware
The illustration shows a skimmer and a ladle and the backs of their handles, each of which is marked *R. Lee*. The skimmer is a fine specimen of brass, 15 inches long. The ladle, almost equally impressive, is 11¼ inches long.
Owned by Albert C. Bowman

Fig. 6 — R. Lee Pewter Basin and Porringer
Evidently made from the same mold. Size 6 inches. The handle of the porringer bears the *fleur-de-lys* touch and the initials *R. L.*, as well as the name *R. Lee. Owned by Albert C. Bowman*

tributed to the son. This mark, where it occurs on brass, is, in so far as known, invariably *R. Lee*. Pewter objects, however, sometimes bear the mark *R. Lee*; sometimes, *Richard Lee*. If it is true that only the younger man made articles in brass, there seems reason for attributing to him the pewter pieces bearing the abbreviated touch, and to his father those bearing the name in full. There is no other means of distinguishing between the products of the two men.

Whatever difficulties beset their path, and whatever obstruction to their enterprise they encountered as a result of constantly strained credit, the Lees, father and son, turned out a good deal of pewter of high quality and of considerable diversity of form. Particularly notable is the variety of patterns displayed by their porringer handles (*Fig. 1*).

Seldom, or never, it should be remarked, do their porringers conform in shape to the standard, slightly bulbous New England type. All the Lee porringers appear, indeed, to have been formed from basin molds. Some, however, show a slightly rounded lip, some a well defined overhanging rim. In all cases, as may be judged from Figure 6, the addition or omission of a handle was a matter of choice.

On the *R. Lee* brass (*Fig. 5*), which apparently occurs in the form of skimmers and ladles, little need be said except that the pieces are well made, of a pleasing quality of metal, and that the handles, which recall those current in late eighteenth and early nineteenth-century silverware, are exceptionally graceful.

The Lee marks appear in Roman capitals, usually in a rectangle, as *R. LEE* or *RICHARD LEE*. A *fleur-de-lys*, flanked by the Roman initials *R. L.*, in addition to the *R. Lee* touch, appears on the handles of two small porringers.

III American Pewter After 1800

At about the beginning of the nineteenth century a new generation of pewterers began to replace the Bassetts and Wills who had led the trade during our early years as an independent nation.

The change was not dramatic at first, and some forms, such as porringers, continued to be made in the old styles and in increasing numbers. However, the hollow-cast pewter handle began to replace wooden ones on teapots, and Samuel Danforth initiated the first of the tall teapots of the new century. The lidded tankard had nearly disappeared completely by 1815-1820, and the new "britannia" alloy was rapidly replacing pewter.

Britannia had been developed in England late in the eighteenth century. It was really not a new metal as such, but merely an improvement on the alloy that had served so faithfully for centuries. Tin was still the principal element in the alloy, usually over ninety percent of the total content. Antimony and copper made up the balance of the mix in about a three to one ratio respectively. The addition of antimony gave the metal a very lustrous quality as well as greater hardness and strength. It was possible, using the "new," stronger metal to make the ware a bit thinner, thus saving on cost, and the less expensive, gleaming objects gave a great boost to the trade.

The britannia formula was kept a close secret in England, and the exports to America enjoyed a competitive edge over our "old-fashioned" local products.

Thomas D. Boardman of Hartford is credited with the development of britannia on his own in about 1806. The wares he produced received an immediate and high acclaim, and within two decades many makers had switched to the new formula. Israel Trask and Roswell Gleason in northern Massachusetts and William Calder in Providence were among the early manufacturers, and great centers for britannia production were found in Taunton, Massachusetts, and in the Connecticut River valley.

At first, britannia ware was cast in moulds as pewter had been. The difference was only in the strength and shine of the pieces produced. Casting remained the principal method of forming britannia ware in America until at least the 1830s when the techniques of spinning and stamping were introduced. The spinning process employed sheets of britannia which were formed into shape over a wooden block on a lathe. The stamping process was a drop-forge system much the same as is in use today in factories making automobile parts.

Those last two processes were used exclusively in a few shops after 1840, but most continued to cast britannia and to use the casting and spinning methods together. Some shops, like the Boardmans of Hartford, also continued to produce pewter along with their britannia ware.

In addition to the new metal formula, the nineteenth century workers had the advantage of better lathes, some operated by water or steam power. The combination of improvements made the mass production of attractive, cheaper wares possible, and with the expanding marketplace the industry fared exceedingly well for a few decades.

Today we observe the later period with some sadness. The craftsmen who labored to assemble a handsome tankard were replaced by a machine-operator who perhaps made only a single part of a teapot, passing the part along for further processing and assembly. The soft curves and subtle decoration of the pewter era were replaced by sharp corners and machine-turned ornamentation. But we forget that all of that was merely a reflection of changing style and technology, just as it was when the pewter plate replaced the wooden trencher.

Even the marks used by the men of the britannia period indicate the "hurry-up" fashion of the day. The early lions and roses had given way to eagles in the late eighteenth century and early nineteenth, and now the national bird was replaced in many shops by a simple one-or two-line statement of the maker's name and address.

Many new forms were introduced in the 1800s. Lamps for burning whale oil, camphene, and lard were new fashions in lighting, and from the late 1820s to the Civil War era they were produced by the pewter and britannia makers in ever-increasing numbers. Many late firms seem to have made nothing but lamps and candlesticks. Water and cider pitchers, with and without lids, were made in capacities from a pint to over a gallon. Teapots were produced in a vast array of shapes and sizes, as were the attendant sugar bowls and cream pots.

Ecclesiastical wares were made by many of the nineteenth century firms, and, although they do not have the massive importance of the earlier styles, such items were among the most handsome of all products of the period. It was a segment of the trade that T. D. Boardman and other Connecticut workers seem to have dominated, although excellent examples also were made in Providence, Rhode Island, and in Massachusetts.

The coexistence of pewterers and britannia makers is shown

by examination of the articles concerning Samuel Pierce by Julia Snow and Marion and Oliver Deming and the article "A Massachusetts Pewterer," by J. W. Webber, which describes the career of Israel Trask, a britannia maker.

Excellent representations of nineteenth century forms are included in nearly all of the articles in Part III and should provide a fair notion of what was made here from about 1810 onwards. The "creamer" shown as fig. 5 in Percy E. Raymond's "Some Pewter of Little Importance" appears actually to be a syrup pitcher with its lid and hinge removed. Syrup jugs were a popular form and many Boardman examples are known in this shape. In the article entitled "Three Maine Pewterers," the statement is made that Allen Porter's output is represented only by lamps. Since publication of that article a number of tall and short teapots have come to light and further indicate a high degree of ability in Porter's work.

As our Western frontiers were pushed further and further back, the production of pewter and britannia followed. The largest of the Western shops was located in Cincinnati, Ohio, and its history, along with that of other firms located in St. Louis, is related in "Ohio and Missouri Pewter Data" by J. G. Braecklein.

The era of our unfortunate Civil War is also that of the final years of the pewter and britannia industry in America. By 1860-70 only a few large firms were still manufacturing britannia teapots, lamps, and candlesticks. A few highly mechanized shops were producing literally millions of britannia spoons during the same decade, but even they would soon lose out to the makers of silver plate.

The era of steam-powered machinery and mass production had finally edged the pewterer completely out by about 1880, and a generation or so later, when reproduction was begun, it was necessary to stamp "PEWTER" on the bottom of the object so that the customer would know what it was. Perhaps a few remembered and retained the "old family mug"—for our enjoyment today.

Marked American Pewter

By Charles L. Woodside

IT seems almost incredible that any of our American pewterers — especially those of the nineteenth century, whose work may be known to all lovers of the metal and whose names are impressed upon thousands of specimens of their handicraft — should, in the passage of time, drift into such obscurity as to render many things about them uncertain or unknown. Yet such is the case; and Mr. Kerfoot, in his admirable book *American Pewter*, has cited many instances of the kind.

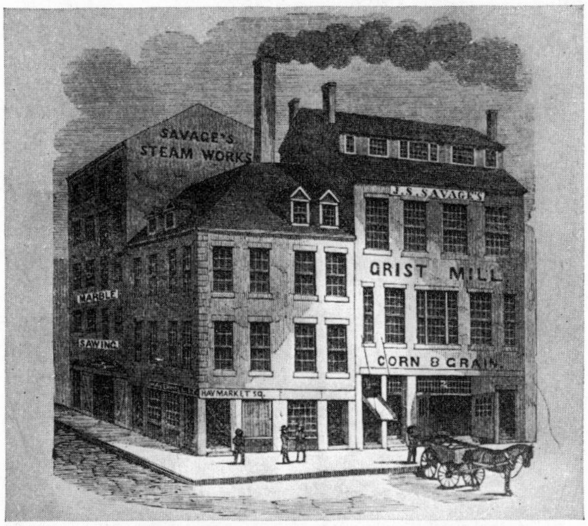

That which follows treats of two pewterers whose history has hitherto been either unknown or forgotten. One of them is Smith & Company; the other Bailey & Putnam.

Both concerns were engaged in the manufacture of pewter during the middle period of the nineteenth century, and nearly all of their members lived in the immediate neighborhood of my own home in Malden, Massachusetts. They were industrious men, lived honorable lives, made good pewter, prospered and eventually passed on, leaving many evidences of their integrity and ability.

Smith & Company: Predecessors and Successors

This firm, which has been ascribed both to Connecticut and to Philadelphia,* was located in Boston. The name here given is one of several of a partnership that was founded in 1841 by Thomas Smith and David B. Morey under the firm name of Smith & Morey. These men began business in a shop at 4 Market Street, corner of Merrimack Street in Boston, as manufacturers of block tin and pewter ware. Both men resided in Malden, and there is evidence to support the suggestion that for several years prior to the opening of the shop in Boston they were at work in their home town. This evidence, however, is not conclusive, and it is mentioned here as a subject for further investigation.

Thomas Smith was born in England in July, 1791, the son of Thomas and (?) Smith. It is not known when he came to Malden; but the records show that he was living there in 1834, on June 24 of which year he married Sarah

*J. B. Kerfoot, *American Pewter*, Boston and New York, 1924, p. 180.

Fig. 2 — Advertisement of Smith & Company
From the Boston *Directory* of 1848.

Fig. 3 — Mark of Smith & Morey (1841-1842)

Upham. Both he and his bride were residents of the town at that time. It is quite probable that Thomas Smith followed the trade of his father, as was commonly the custom in those days; and it is interesting to note that he, in turn, was followed by a son, Thomas Jr., who lived in Chelsea, Massachusetts, and who made britannia ware there and in Boston during the 1860's.

Thomas Smith, Sr., lived on Main Street south of Madison Street, Malden, in a house, still standing, in that part of the town then known as Bailey's Hill. He was a member of the firm during most of its many changes, and retired from it in 1864. In 1870 he is recorded as being engaged in the manufacture of britannia ware on Causeway Street, opposite the Eastern Railroad station, and in 1872 he was in the employ of his son, Thomas Smith, Jr., as a britannia worker in the latter's shop at 81 Second Street, Chelsea. He died in Malden on November 2, 1876, at the ripe age of eighty-five years and four months.

David B. Morey, the other founder of the firm, was born in Malden, May 6, 1807. He married Almira Bailey, a daughter of Timothy and Eunice Sweetser Bailey of Malden, May 9, 1842. The couple lived in a house still occupied by their descendants on Hillside Avenue (formerly High Street) on Bailey's Hill.*

Mr. Morey was a member of the firm during nearly the entire period of its existence — from its beginning in 1841 as Smith & Morey, until he retired from active business in 1882. He died in Malden, March 31, 1885. The firm of Morey & Smith ceased operating in 1886.

Of the two other members of the firm during its pewter period, very little is known — other than that Henry White lived in East Cambridge and Reuben H. Ober lived at 24 London Street, Boston, and later boarded at 10 Sudbury Street, near the shop.

The chronology of the firm, together with the various changes of firm name and personnel, is as follows:

*This hill derived its name from Timothy Bailey, who also lived on the hill, at the corner of Main and Madison Streets, near the residence of Thomas Smith. Mr. Bailey was a man of considerable prominence in Malden, and he was, in company with James H. Putnam under the firm name of Bailey & Putnam, a manufacturer of pewter and tin ware in Malden, as will be related further on.

Fig. 1 — Haverhill Street and Haymarket Square
In 1847, Smith & Company moved their pewter business to the corner here pictured. In 1853, as Morey & Ober, the concern shifted location to the building marked *Marble Sawing*.

Fig. 4 (right) — TEAPOT BY MOREY &
    SMITH (*1857-1864*)
    Height 8½".
    Owned by Mrs. Annie L. Woodside.

1841–1842 Smith & Morey
    (Thomas Smith,
    David B. Morey)

1842–1846 Thomas Smith &
    Company
    (Thomas Smith,
    D. B. Morey,
    H. White)

1847–1848 Smith & Company
    (Thomas Smith,
    H. White, D. B.
    Morey)

1849–1851 Smith, Ober & Co.
    (Thomas Smith,
    R. H. Ober, D. B.
    Morey)

1852–1854 Morey & Ober
    (D. B. Morey,
    R. H. Ober)

in the personnel but not in
firm name — until 1886, when
it went out of business.

In the beginning, in 1841,
Smith & Morey were located
at 4 Market Street, where
they remained until 1847. In
that year they moved to 2
and 3 Haverhill Street, opposite the old Boston & Maine
Railroad depot, which stood
for so many years in Hay-
market Square. A picture of
the building, a portion of
which they occupied, is shown
in Figure 1, marked *Haverhill
St.* and *Haymarket Sq.* In 1853
they moved again, into the
adjoining building, 5 and 7
Haverhill Street, marked in
the picture *Marble Sawing*;
and later, in 1858, they moved
once more, this time further
down on Haverhill Street to
number 49, where they re-
mained until the end.

The first advertisement of
the firm that I have been able to find is that
of Smith & Company in the Boston *Directory* of 1847. This was followed in 1848 by
the illustrated announcement shown in

Fig. 5 (left) — LAMPS BY SMITH & COMPANY (*1847-
    1848*)
    Heights exclusive of burners (*left to right*) 5½", 3¼",
    3", 6".
    From the author's collection.

Fig. 6 (below) — LAMPS BY THREE MAKERS
    a. SMITH & MOREY (*1841-1842*). Height 3¾".
    b. MOREY & OBER (*1852-1854*). Height 3¾".
    c. MOREY & SMITH (*1857-1864*). Height 3¼".
    From the author's collection.

1855–1856 Morey, Ober & Co.
    (D. B. Morey, R. H. Ober,
    Thomas Smith)

1857–1864 Morey & Smith
    (D. B. Morey, Thomas Smith)

In 1862 the manufacture of pewter apparently ceased — the demand for it having
greatly diminished. The sale of glassware, in
which the firm had also been engaged for
many years, now became, with the sale of
britannia, its principal interest. So the concern continued — with some further changes

Figure 2. The reading matter in both is the same. This advertisement was continued in exactly the same form, except for the change in the firm name and the names of its members, until 1885, when the removal to 49 Haverhill Street took place and the business shifted to the sale of glassware and britannia.

The pewter turned out by this firm, under all of its various names, was of excellent quality and workmanship, and the designs were always in good taste. Coffee pots, teapots, sugar bowls, creamers, lamps and candlesticks were made. These articles are to be found marked sometimes with one firm name, sometimes with another. I have yet to find, however, a full line of pewter ware bearing the name of any one of the successive concerns. The output must have been considerable and well distributed; for, although specimens are becoming rare, they are to be found occasionally, sometimes in very remote places. I consider them worthy of a place on the shelf of any collector of American pewter.

Each of the successive firms used its own touch-mark, changing the form in accordance with its own taste or fancy. Figure 3 shows the mark of Smith & Morey as used in 1841 when the business was founded.

I do not know how many molds were used by the concern, but it would appear that the numbering of the molds remained unchanged throughout. The highest mold number that I can recall having seen is 13. This is the number of the teapot shown in Figure 4, made by Morey & Smith.

In Figure 5 are shown lamps by Smith & Company (1847–1848). The second one from the left is very rare. Three other lamps are shown in Figure 6, the one at the left by Smith & Morey (1841–1842), the middle one by Morey & Ober (1852–1854); and that at the right by Morey & Smith (1857–1864).

BAILEY & PUTNAM AND PUTNAM

The firm of Bailey & Putnam and later, after the partnership between the two men had been dissolved, Putnam, was located in Malden, Massachusetts, and was engaged in the manufacture of tin ware and pewter during the second quarter of the 1800's. The firm was first composed of Timothy Bailey and James Hervey Putnam. Each continued in business independently after the dissolution of the partnership.

Fig. 7 — LAMP BY BAILEY & PUTNAM
The rare product of a brief partnership.
From the author's collection.

Fig. 8 — MARK OF BAILEY & PUTNAM

Timothy Bailey was born in Westmoreland, New Hampshire, September 20, 1785 — the eleventh of a family of twelve children. His father was a farmer, and, like most farmers' boys of his day, Timothy worked during the summer and received such elementary education as he could secure in the little red schoolhouse during the winter.

As his father was in somewhat poor circumstances, Timothy, at the age of nine, went to live with an uncle in Tewksbury, Massachusetts. It was intended that he should learn the trade of this uncle, a shoemaker, and that he should eventually succeed to the business. But nothing came of the plan. After remaining for nine years with the uncle, Timothy rejoined his father, who, in the meantime, had moved to Andover, Massachusetts.

In the spring of 1805, being then twenty years of age and having secured his time by the payment of forty dollars to his father, Timothy went to work on the farm of Dr. Adams at Lynnfield. During the following summer while mowing in the hayfield, he suffered a severe sunstroke, which rendered him incapable of manual labor, and from which he did not fully recover for several years.

As farming was now out of the question, the young man sought Preceptor Newman of Phillips Academy at Andover, who advised him to take a course at the Academy by way of fitting himself to teach a common school in some of the back towns. The advice was followed. That Timothy succeeded very well may be inferred from the fact that, at the end of three months, the preceptor gave him so fine a recommendation that he secured a position in the school at Dracut, where he taught during the following winter.

But the pay was small — fourteen dollars a month — the season short and the total income insufficient to keep him. What to do! Should he accept the offer of Burrage Yale, the tin ware maker of South Reading (now Wakefield) and become a peddler? That did not appeal to him; for, realizing that peddlers did not have a very good name abroad, he thought he should not like the business. To this Deacon Eaton replied that it made no difference whether a man peddled tin from house to house, or whether he was a clerk and stood behind the counter and sold goods to those who came in to buy — it was the man's character that counted. And so it came about that Timothy Bailey entered into the business which he was to follow with remarkable success during the remainder of his life.

Bailey worked eight years for Yale, and it is interesting to note here what he says about it. It answers the oft asked question as to how wares found their way into such remote places. He says: "I went from town to town and from state to state peddling wares until I sold my load; then I went home for another load. I had to drive a two-wheel horse cart with a box made fast on the shafts and axletree to hold the wares. The harness for the horse to draw it with was a saddle, leather breastplate and rope tugs and a wooden whiffletree, and a bridle without reins. I had to walk beside the horse all day, hot or cold, and put up at night with private families as I could find them. I drove the same cart and harness for Mr. Yale for eight years in succession with the exception of the cold season of the winter. I walked beside my horse to average about two thousand miles a year for eight years."

In 1815 Bailey left the employ of Burrage Yale and set up in business for himself in Roxbury, making and selling tin ware. In 1817, on January 21, he married Eunice Sweetser, daughter of Paul Sweetser of South Reading, and in October, 1819, he moved to Malden and settled there permanently. He purchased the house which, at that time, stood on Main Street, southerly corner of Madison Street, but which, after his death, was moved around the corner and still stands, practically unchanged, at 20 Madison Street. Only recently did the place pass out of the family's ownership. Near by, also on Main Street, in later years stood the home of Thomas Smith; and a little further away

Fig. 9 (above) — PUTNAM PEWTER (*1835-1855*)
Height of coffee pot *11¼"*. Height of teapot *7¼"*.
Owned by Mrs. Annie L. Woodside.

Fig. 10 (below) — LAMP BY PUTNAM (*1835-1855*)
Height *8¼"*.
From the author's collection.

on High Street was that of Smith's partner, David B. Morey. It will be remembered that, on May 9, 1842, Morey married Bailey's daughter Almira; and it will be related further on that Bailey was an uncle of Putnam, so that the community of interest among these people must have been close and strong.

In the rear part of his house Timothy Bailey established his shop. Tradition still recalls the vast heap of bright shining scrap tin that was piled up in the yard back of the house. He worked hard, prospered and soon became a leading citizen of the town; and that part in which he lived became known as Bailey's Hill. In 1833 he organized the Malden Agricultural & Mechanics' Association, the first bank in Malden. Its office was installed in his house; he was elected its treasurer and so served for eighteen consecutive years. When, in 1851, the bank was absorbed by the newly organized Malden Bank, he was elected president of that institution and so remained until his death. Meanwhile, he was town treasurer from 1832 to 1840, and a member of the General Court in 1836.

The business conducted by Bailey must have been considerable. At one time he had as many as eight workmen in the shop and sixteen peddlers on the road. While he apparently confined his work to the making of tin ware, it is probable that he made pewter

Fig. 11 — PUTNAM'S MARK

also — as was the custom in those days, although I have never seen any pieces bearing his name, nor do I know of any existing. He accumulated a sufficient competence to keep him in comfort during his declining years; but he did not live long to enjoy it, for he passed away on November 19, 1852, at the age of sixty-seven.

James Hervey Putnam, the other partner in the firm of Bailey & Putnam, was born in Charlestown, New Hampshire, in 1803, the son of David and Hannah Bailey Putnam. His mother was a sister of Timothy Bailey, who was, therefore, Putnam's uncle. Very little is known of his early history, nor is it known when he came to Malden; but, from such information as I have been able to obtain, it seems probable that he came with his parents soon after Bailey settled there. It is said that he entered the employ of his uncle, serving his apprenticeship and afterward becoming a partner.

Just when this partnership was in operation I am unable to state with definiteness. The most diligent search has failed to discover any information. It is known there was such a partnership and that there are marked specimens of pewter to prove it. I fix the date tentatively about 1830–1835 — partly from hearsay evidence and partly because it could not have been before 1824, when Putnam became of age, nor after 1836, when the Massachusetts state census shows that there were two tin ware shops in Malden employing twenty hands and manufacturing goods to the value of thirty-one thousand dollars. As the largest number of hands employed by Bailey was eight, we may reasonably infer that the other twelve were employed by Putnam — for, other than these two shops, there were none of a similar kind in Malden at that time.

The business of Bailey & Putnam was conducted at Bailey's house — the partnership being, I imagine, an incident of comparatively short duration. Their output of pewter must have been of limited extent, if one may judge from the very few marked specimens of their work that are known to exist. In Figure 7 is shown a whale oil lamp made by Bailey & Putnam; and Figure 8 pictures their regular mark.

After the partnership had been dissolved, Putnam opened his own shop in the brick building which still stands at the corner of Main Street and Eastern Avenue, then called Haskins Street, while Bailey continued as before. In his own establishment Bailey seems to have done a large and prosperous business. His principal manufacture at first, like that of his uncle, was tin ware; but eventually the making of pewter and britannia seems to have become of much greater importance. The state census for the year ending June 1, 1855, records that in the one establishment in Malden for the manufacture of pewter and britannia ware (one only, for Bailey had died in 1852) the value of the goods produced as eighteen thousand dollars; the hands employed were eighteen.

On June 8, 1826, James Hervey Putnam married Mary Hill of Malden. Both were of old New England stock. Eleven children were born to them, but none of them is now living, so far as I know. One connection of the family, a son-in-law, has just died at the age of eighty-five years. He was my near neighbor and friend, an active and honored citizen whose mind was bright and clear to the last.

The pewter made by Putnam was of the usual variety. It was of excellent quality, fine workmanship and good design. In the New England *Business Directory* of 1849, Putnam is classed with Israel Trask and Eben Smith of Beverly and Roswell Gleason of Dorchester. Specimens of his work are not very difficult to find and they are well worth collecting. In Figure 9 are shown two of his pieces — a coffee pot and a teapot; and in Figure 10 is shown a whale oil lamp. Figure 11 shows Putnam's regular mark.

James Hervey Putnam died in May, 1855, at the age of fifty-two years. Several children survived him, but as they were too young to carry on the business the shop was closed.

COFFEEPOT?
TEAPOT!

By PERCY E. RAYMOND

S IR CHARLES JAMES JACKSON and John Barrett Kerfoot were the greatest authorities of their time, the one on silver, the other on pewter. But they both made errors which have been perpetuated by their followers, and which bid fair to cause endless misunderstandings.

Sir Charles got the notion from Wilfred J. Cripps that a porringer was a bleeding bowl, despite the obvious derivation of the word, and its ancient forms *potager* and *pottenger*. For some unknown reason he attached the name porringer to caudle and posset cups, and such-like drinking vessels. As I have shown in *Bulletin No. 8* of the Pewter Collectors' Club, the records of the Worshipful Company of Pewterers prove definitely that the porringer was a basin with flat, horizontal handles or "ears." I think most modern American students of silver and all writers on pewter have this opinion. However, we still see in English articles reference to the "bleeding bowls which the Americans call porringers."

Kerfoot's great misnomer was somewhat more spectacular, for he called the last phase of the making of pewter (Britannia) in America the "coffeepot era." I fear he got this idea from writers on silver. In the early days, tea was expensive. Teapots were small, pear-shaped or globular, with a capacity of a quart at most, generally less. So anything small, or squatty, or bulging, is a teapot. One could make a small quantity of strong tea and dilute it with hot water, a practice still followed by our more fastidious hostesses. But coffee couldn't be treated that way, except perhaps in Great Britain, where even to this day they have never learned how to make it. Perhaps that hell-brew of the

FIG. 1. — THREE TALL TEAPOTS. At the top, one by Eben Smith; at the bottom, one by Oliver Trask. These Beverly pewterers were among the few who indulged in a decoration, fortunately restrained. In the center, a G. Richardson, Boston, pot, with spout removed to show strainer. *From the collection of the author.*

Photographs by Frederick P. Orchard.

Near East known as Turkish coffee might be made in a small pot, but in general a vessel of generous dimensions is required. Hence, a small pot is a teapot; a large one, particularly a tall conical one of the "lighthouse" type, is a coffeepot. This seems to have been Kerfoot's idea, and, if one can judge from various books and magazine articles, is that of students of silver.

The inference, as regards pewter, is mildly ridiculous. The commonalty of our ancestors boiled their coffee. And how safe is it to put a pewter pot on a hot stove? It can be done, if the bottom of the pot rests flush with the stove-lid, provided the vessel is not allowed to boil dry. But most so-called coffeepots have the bottom raised from an eighth to a quarter of an inch, so that only a ring of metal would come in contact with the stove. This metal would inevitably melt. In fact, I have a Griswold pot which has suffered this experience and shows the scars. The problem of a cheap boiler for coffee was not solved until the tinsmiths produced the capacious vessels which used to be in every kitchen.

Tea is an infusion. One pours the boiling water over the leaves in a pot. Coffee treated in the same way, in the days before the "drip grind," was a miserable beverage. Of course, one could stew the coffee in an iron or copper receptacle, then pour it into a more elegant pot for serving at the table. Probably that was often done. But pewter coffeepots were not for the tables of the rich and showy. Pewter was for the common people who boiled the liquor on the stove.

As is well known, tea became relatively cheap and extremely popular in the days of the clipper ships. Teapots increased in capacity, for the housewife did not bother to have strong tea in one vessel and hot water in another. So teapots grew in stature till they became the coffeepots of Kerfoot.

There are two easy but not infallible ways to distinguish teapots from coffeepots. In ninety-nine cases out of one hundred, if it's Britannia, it's a teapot; I have never seen a coffeepot in pewter. The second test is to look inside, and if there is a strainer with openings from three-twentieths to one-quarter of an inch or more in diameter where the contents enter the spout, it's a teapot. The apertures in this strainer, merely holes bored in the body before the spout is attached, are so large that they would not in any degree impede the exit of coffee grounds, but they would restrain all but the smallest tea leaves.

It is true that the records show that the Britannia makers of the first half of the nineteenth century made many coffeepots. Some of them, judging from those that Calder made in Providence, were drip pots made more or less in imitation of that invented by Count Rumford of Woburn, Massachusetts. For a picture of one, see ANTIQUES, November 1936, page 210,

Figures 1 and 2. Recently I have heard these affairs referred to as dripolators, a word which does not seem to have got into the dictionaries. They were called percolators in the old days, when people made French coffee. The term percolator, as we now use it for a steam-driven kettle, seems to be of relatively modern origin.

Biggins were perhaps more common, although one finds few of them nowadays. They can be identified by the ledge inside, near the top. On this rested the ring of the shallow cloth bag which holds the coffee. In twenty years I have seen two Britannia drip pots, five biggins, and about two thousand teapots.

The biggin, named for its French inventor, was simple. The ground coffee was placed in a bag, and boiling water poured through it. The old family coffee mills produced grains of rather coarse size, but the biggins have convex strainers soldered over the entrance to the spout. These can be distinguished from tea sizes by the fineness of the mesh, the apertures being one-sixteenth of an inch in diameter. The *Gentleman's Magazine,* volume 73, 1803, says: "Mr. Biggin some years ago invented a new sort of coffee pot which has been ever since extensively sold under the name of coffee biggins." Shakespeare used the term biggin in an entirely different sense. Dickins mentioned a coffee biggin in *Little Dorrit.* But I doubt if there are a dozen people in the United States today who ever heard of a coffee biggin. I recently bought a Gleason specimen and found that it had tea leaves in it!

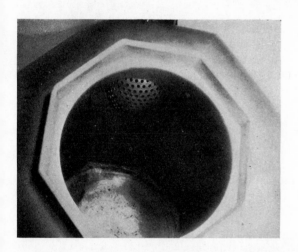

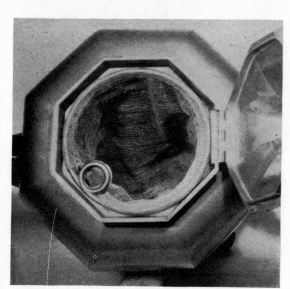

FIG. 2 — A COFFEE BIGGIN. By Roswell Gleason, Dorchester. At the left are views of the strainer, from inside, and the mesh bag with its pewter ring. Both show the ledge on which the ring rests. *From the collection of Mrs. Stephen FitzGerald.*

SOME PEWTER OF LITTLE IMPORTANCE

By PERCY E. RAYMOND

Mr. Raymond, Professor Emeritus of Paleontology at Harvard, turns to the comparatively "modern" field of antiques as a pleasant change from fossils. His special interest is in pewter, particularly English, though "that of any age intrigues me," he says.

SWEET ARE THE USES OF ADVERSITY." Those of us who are too poor to buy pewter tankards and flagons and rare plates have to browse about among the more humble things. Occasionally something unusual rewards us.

The *Norfolk Democrat* of February 11, 1848, carried an advertisement by Roswell Gleason of Dorchester, Massachusetts (ANTIQUES, August 1931, p. 89). Among other things he offered wash bowls. I bought one of them in 1946. Was I his first customer? No one else appears to have seen one. This is obviously no christening basin (*Fig. 1*), but just an ordinary washbasin, with a ring by which to hang it over the kitchen sink. Or, perhaps, over a bench in an outhouse. On my grandfather's farm there was such a bench outside the kitchen, in what, in polite modern parlance, would be called the "breezeway." On hooks above the bench hung tin washbasins and towels. It was obligatory for the "help" to perform ablutions there before entering the kitchen for dinner. Gleason added a neat little ornament to the hanger, and I've seen silver basins of poorer design than this one. Yet it is just plain despised britannia, and 1848 at that!

In the same class belongs a "spitting Bason" by Josiah Danforth. It bears his late intaglio touch (Laughlin's No. 395), and so perhaps dates from about 1835. The shape and the bear's paws which uphold it are not unattractive. And I have a suggestion for those ladies who prefer to have their cuspidors on the table instead of on the floor where they belong. Take out the funnel, replace it with a 6-inch pewter bowl, and make an arrangement of flowers, as Mrs. Chester Cook did for Figure 2.

Not new, but generally overlooked, are the cups or handled beakers circulated at the time of the campaign of William Henry Harrison for the presidency. One of them was illustrated in ANTIQUES (March 1929, p. 236) with a contemporary American flag as a background. A pair of them fell into my hands at about that time. A well-done pewter medallion is soldered to the front of a britannia cup with a capacity of a little over a half-pint (*Fig. 3*). ANTIQUES called them cider mugs, which is probable, for that was the "hard cider" campaign. The cups are not beauti-

FIG. 1 — THE GLEASON washbasin and detail of hanger. Diameter at top, 11¾ inches; of foot, 6 inches.

ful, but the broken-S handle is a little more attractive than the norm of the time. No marked example is known, but George Sweet Gibb, in *The Whitesmiths of Taunton* (p. 119), tells us that the year 1840 brought a short but vigorous trade in Harrison mugs. According to Mr. Gibb these cups not only made a profit for the company (Leonard, Reed, and Barton), but also expressed the Whig sentiments of Henry Reed.

An article which puzzles the average collector turns up now and again (*Fig. 4*). It is not a doughnut cutter or an imperfect candlestick, as some have supposed, but an adjunct to the spin-

FIG. 2 — CUSPIDOR by Josiah Danforth.

FIG. 3 — THE Harrison campaign mug, and its medallion (diameter, 1½ inches).

FIG. 4 — A DAMPER. Diameter, 3⅞ inches.

FIG. 5 — A CREAMER by Boardman and Hart. Height, 4 inches. It is obviously just a mug with a spout.

Illustrations from the author's collection; photographs by Frederick Orchard.

ning wheel. The tapered hole in the middle allows it to perch on the top of the pole. Mrs. Eaton H. Perkins tells me her researches show that its American name is "damper." It held a small amount of water, in which the housewife could moisten her fingers as she twisted the flax into thread. One which Mrs. Melville T. Nichols bought in Germany had with it a card stating that it was a *Spinn-raden*. Literally, that means distaff, suggesting the place, if not the real function of the article. Glass dampers are more common than those in metal. This one was found in southeastern Pennsylvania, is unmarked, but has the initials *M F* and the date *1865* engraved on it.

The creamer (*Fig. 5*) is remarkable only because this type seems to have been overlooked. It bears the mark of Boardman and Hart. The plebeian aspect pleases me. It is not one of those three-legged imitations of silver, designed chiefly with a view to upsetability, but a sturdy piece fitted for the kitchen table, where the pewter made at that time belonged.

Pint-size pitchers are rare. This one (*Fig. 6*) had sat on a stove at some time. Its smooth, uninterrupted curves are unusual. The handle is more like that used by Boardman and Hart than any other so far illustrated.

One cannot understand why writers ignore bedpans so completely. I do not recall having seen a picture of an American specimen. Mr. Kerfoot had a column for them in the tables at the end of his book, but there are no checks in it. One by Thomas Danforth Boardman was shown by Mrs. John Mitchell at the pewter exhibition at Springfield, Massachusetts, in May 1948. Here is its mate, with the touches of Boardman and Co. (*Fig. 7*). Doctor Madelaine R. Brown, in an article on medical pewter in *Bulletin 16* of the Pewter Collectors' Club of America, mentions having seen specimens made by the Boardmans, Samuel Kilbourn, and Spencer Stafford. These useful but unfortunate utensils have in many cases been desecrated by being converted into bowls. The handle makes a good hammer.

FIG. 6 — A PINT-SIZED cider pitcher. Unmarked. Height originally 5 inches.

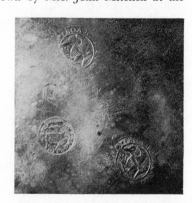

FIG. 7 — A BEDPAN and its marks. Its two large marks are *Boardman Warranted*, smaller one, *Boardman and Company*.

Samuel Pierce, Pewterer, and His Tools

By Julia D. Sophronia Snow

THE MAN

Saturday Evening, September 25th, A. D. 1790, Mr. Samuel Pierce of Middletown came with my eighth daughter, Anne, and they, in a very decent and becoming manner, asked our consent that they might be joined together in Holy Matrimony — which request of theirs we freely granted. Accordingly, the said Samuel Pierce and Anne Joyce, in the evening of Sunday following, being the 26th day of September, A. D. 1790, were joined together in Holy Matrimony at my house, ourselves being present when the ceremony was performed by the Rev. N. Abraham Jarvis.

SUCH is the record of the Joyce-Pierce nuptials, as it appears in John Joyce's Bible, which has been handed down through succeeding generations of the Pierce family, and is at present owned by the Misses Pierce, great-granddaughters of Samuel, the pewterer, whose dates and provenance have hitherto eluded the student and collector.

Mr. Kerfoot made a happy surmise when he assigned Samuel Pierce a place in the hall of fame of our American pewterers. Mr. Myers has gone one step beyond Mr. Kerfoot in localizing *a* Samuel Pierce in Middletown, Connecticut.* But the "patriotic gentleman" who he hopes may be *the* Samuel must have been the father or uncle of the pewterer. The latter could have been only eight years old at the time of enlistment in Colonel Charles Burrel's regiment; for he died in 1840 at the age of seventy-two.

But from the Pierce family Bible and deeds for land, as well as from the tools here illustrated, we are able to assign to Samuel a definite seat in Pewterers' Hall. We know that he lived in Middletown during the early part of his life; and, with this knowledge, we may, perhaps, imagine him serving his apprenticeship in the workshop of the Danforths.† But, wherever he learned his trade, Greenfield, Massachusetts, and not Middletown, Connecticut, shall claim him as hers.

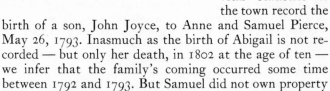

Fig. 1 — The West Hawley (Massachusetts) Communion Service
A coffeepot had to do duty as a wine flagon. Only the plates are marked.
Owned by the author.

Back in the early 1790's, report had gone abroad as to the enterprise of Greenfield. Colonel William Moore,* a pioneer from Worcester, had settled here, and through his courage, foresight, and wealth, had developed several industries, and was giving employment to a great many hands. Samuel Pierce, in the venturesome spirit of youth, unable to withstand the lure of Greenfield's prosperity, packed up his belongings, and, together with his twenty-year-old wife, and the infant Abigail, braved the broad Connecticut.

We are somewhat in the dark as to the exact day of his arrival in Greenfield, and can only approximate it from the fact that the vital statistics of the town record the birth of a son, John Joyce, to Anne and Samuel Pierce, May 26, 1793. Inasmuch as the birth of Abigail is not recorded — but only her death, in 1802 at the age of ten — we infer that the family's coming occurred some time between 1792 and 1793. But Samuel did not own property in the town until February 14, 1794.

From all appearances, Samuel Pierce was not one to precipitate himself thoughtlessly into new ventures. Before leaving Middletown, he was assured of employment in Greenfield by Colonel William Moore. Just how long he remained under Moore's jurisdiction, however, we are unable to say; but, by April, 1799, we find him engaged in the shipping business, transporting lumber, produce, and hides to points along the Connecticut as far south as Middletown, and returning with cargoes of rum, molasses, fish, tobacco, crockery, and glassware for the Greenfield merchants.†

Realizing the need for supplementing the pittance accruing from freighting on the river — for little Phebe and Anne had now joined the Pierce family—we find Samuel forming a "copartnership" with Ambrose Ames, in September, 1799, for the purpose of carrying on the "oil and salt business."‡ Although we have no actual record of his

---

*Louis Guerineau Myers — *Some Notes on American Pewterers*, Garden City, 1926, p. 62.

†A thirteen-inch, I. Danforth plate found in the Pierce house, and doubtless an inheritance from Samuel, adds color to this theory.

*Francis Thompson — *History of Greenfield*.
†Manuscript *Ledger* kept by Samuel Pierce in 1799.
‡*Franklin Gazette*, 1799.

1927

making pewter in conjunction with these other two enterprises, it is not improbable that his spare moments were devoted to his craft.

Since Samuel Pierce adhered so tenaciously to the early English custom of refraining from crying his wares publicly in the newspapers, save at times of forming or dissolving partnerships, and since surviving manuscript records are fragmentary, we are forced to rely on conjecture in spanning the wide gaps between the known facts of our pewterer's life.

During the summer of 1802, a great plague befell the inhabitants of the town of Greenfield, for two consecutive months working its destruction among young and newly-born children.* Where possible, parents sent their children away to be cared for by relatives or friends. Entire families moved to other communities in the hope of escaping contagion.

Disease is never a respecter of persons. During one month, Samuel Pierce lost three of his five children. Marking a single mound in the Federal Street Cemetery, a marble slab bears the names of Abigail, Anne, and infant Samuel. Then Samuel Pierce, with his wife and two remaining children, fled to a higher altitude — to the town of Colrain, not far from Greenfield — where the "cooper", as he was titled in a deed of 1804, bought a tract of land and a corn mill thereon, to engage in farming, milling, and, presumably, pewtering. During his residence in Colrain, the three places at his board made vacant by the epidemic, were filled once more — now by George, Henry, and Elijah.

After a five years' rural sojourn, however, Pierce sold his Colrain property, and went back to Greenfield, where he lived until the time of his death. Shortly after his return, he entered into partnership with one Hart Leavitt, a well-known merchant of the day, and, under the firm name of Pierce & Leavitt,† dispensed such wares as have always been found on the shelves of country stores the world over.

In the olden days, the principal occupation of business organizations seems to have been the making of partnerships one minute and the dissolving of them the next. Samuel was no exception; for he and Leavitt severed their business connection two years after forming it.

The next definite information we have concerning Samuel's affairs is gleaned from his diary for the years

Fig. 2 — Unfinished Items Found in the Samuel Pierce Chest
a. Teapot. *b.* Basin or porringer bearing initialed touch mark. *c.* Handle for teapot. *d.* Hinge for cover or lid. *e.* Syrup cup lid.

1816–1817. Here he records the purchase of large amounts of sheet iron, nails, steel, tin plate, and sheet and white lead from Hartford concerns. Following his rupture with Leavitt, he apparently took his eldest son, John Joyce, into partnership with him, and conducted business under the name of Samuel Pierce & Son; for, a few years later, the paper advertised the dissolution of this firm, on April 23, 1821.

Later notices tell us that John Joyce carried on the business independently for a time. In his daybook, kept between 1821 and 1826, the son records payments to his father for pewter which the latter had made and displayed for sale in his son's store. Between this date and 1830 I have found no mention of Samuel's activity as a pewterer, but, in his diary for 1831, he occasionally records having made lead aqueduct for his son, George, who had a pewtering and coopering establishment in Northampton, Massachusetts, or of having spent the day in casting teapots.

Although it is possible that Samuel worked at his trade intermittently for a few years following 1831, we assume, from his offering four cows and a yoke of oxen for sale in June, 1834, that he was no longer able to engage in either farming or pewtering, and so relinquished his trade to be perpetuated by his sons, John Joyce and George, whose careers were marked chiefly by a rapid series of making and breaking partnerships with each other and with coopers and craftsmen outside of the family.

Death finally called the father, Samuel Pierce, on the twenty-fifth day of March, 1840. His final resting place may be seen today, in the Federal Street Cemetery, Greenfield.

His Tools

Where did Samuel Pierce make his pewter? When Mr. Kerfoot set collectors agog over American Pewter, I, too, joined the hunt for specimens. My search, especially in the immediate environs of Greenfield, rewarded me with a surprising proportion of Samuel Pierce examples among those items of American origin which I found. At once I developed a "hunch", and began scanning archives. I discovered that a Samuel Pierce had made pewter here in Greenfield early in 1800.* Could it be *the* Samuel Pierce of the eagle touch mark? If so, how could I prove it? I interviewed the present generation of Pierces in the town, explained my dilemma, and, among other questions, asked if by any chance the family had preserved any ancestral tools.

Franklin Gazette, July and August, 1802.
†*Franklin Gazette*, 1811.

Franklin Gazette, April 23, 1821.

There *were* some old tools in a chest in the carriagehouse, but no one knew that any ancestor had made pewter. An uncle had been a civil engineer, and the tools were probably his. Still, it would do no harm to look.

Having some notion of what a pewterer's seal might be like, I cautioned my good friends. Two days later the telephone rang. An excited voice urged me to come at once to see what had been found. I lost no time in answering the summons. There, in the Pierce carriagehouse, in the tray of an old chest filled with strange looking, long-handled tools, lay Samuel Pierce's *eagle!* — Its discovery proved that my "hunch" had been correct.

For the benefit of the lay individual who finds it difficult to visualize a pewterer's kit, and for those who have not seen Israel Trask's set in the Beverly Historical Rooms,* I am illustrating the molds and tools found in Samuel Pierce's chest, with exception of varying sizes of the same instrument. It is regrettable that so few tools were preserved, and that none of the chucks around which the craftsman spun his metal, or his turnwheel, have as yet been discovered.

It is, further, disappointing, not to say humiliating, to confess ignorance of the names and uses of two of the tools illustrated, but they have proved enigmas to all whom I have consulted. Guessing is simple at times, but not always correct. Instead of that, pocketing my pride, I have included the unidentified items with the others in the photograph, hoping that someone, more tutored in the manufacture of pewter, will enlighten me.

Comparing the pewterers' tools enumerated by Massé† with Calder's‡ list of molds, the Danforth inventories recorded by Mr. Myers,§ and the Samuel Pierce outfit, we are enabled to approximate a fairly complete list of the instruments used by the early workers in the metal. I have appended a list of molds, and lathe and hand tools compiled from these four sources, and, by referring to the accompanying cuts, one may obtain a good idea of the appearance and size of many of them.

From the receipted Calder bill for molds, and the inventory valuations of the Danforth tools, we may realize that it required

*John Whiting Webber, *A Massachusetts Pewterer*. See ANTIQUES for January, 1924, Vol. V, p. 26.
†H. J. L. J. Massé, *Chats on Old Pewter*.
‡Charles A. Calder, *Rhode Island Pewterers and Their Work*.
§Myers, p. 22.

no small fortune to establish a man in the pewtering business in colonial times. Accordingly, we are not surprised to find pewterers sharing one another's molds, and exercising their utmost ingenuity in making the most of their tools. I would especially call the reader's attention to the roughly hewn helve of the knurl in Figure 3d, the linen padded handles of the wrought iron forceps (*Fig. 3e*) and the insulating corncob of the soldering iron (*Fig. 3h*).

Molds were made from various substances. In the case of forms for porringer handles the mold metal was *bronze* (*Fig. 4, a, b, d, e*). The dies for coffeepot spouts and handles were of *lead*; (*Fig. 4, middle row*), and the bottoms of the beakers were molded in soapstone (*Fig. 4, r* and *s*). Wood was used for casting the curious device of Figure 4, *o* and *p*. Spinning and turning tools, burnishers and rasps were made of steel; the soldering iron, forceps and turning hooks, of iron.

Two puzzles deserve special attention. Figure 3x shows one of a set of ten similar instruments, the handle, in each case, being hollow and detachable. The tool proper is made of a cylinder-shaped piece of pewter with grooves at either end and in the middle that seem solely ornamental. The two hollow brass cones shown in Figure 3 are equally puzzling. Perhaps they are no more than ferrules; but I am hoping for their exact identification.

To collectors of American pewter, Samuel Pierce's eagle touch mark needs no introduction, but I have the privilege of presenting the seal, or die, which made these impressions — Figure 4c. It is engraved in a bar of steel, five and three-quarters inches long, the intaglio being a fair specimen of the early die sinker's art. A feeling of symmetry and patriotism in design compensates for the somewhat crude delineation of the bird of freedom.

The other die used by Samuel Pierce in marking some of his pewter was not found among his tools, but an unfinished object (*Fig. 2a*), rescued from the chest, assures the doubting collector that Samuel employed this mark as well as the more common eagle touch in branding his wares. This second stamp consisted of the letter x beneath the initials s.p. enclosed in a circle. Inasmuch as the seal for this is missing, and few specimens bearing its impression have been preserved, I am of the belief that it was an early stamp, which finally gave way to the more patriotic eagle form.

The finding of these tools possesses more than cursory interest. It not only authenticates a second touch mark used by Samuel

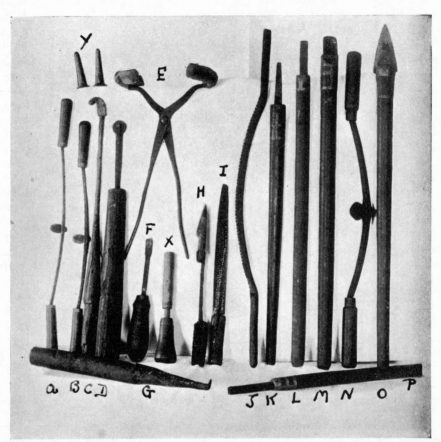

Fig. 3 — LATHE AND HAND TOOLS OF SAMUEL PIERCE FOUND IN THE SAMUEL PIERCE CHEST
a and *b*. Burnishers for two hands. *c*. Burnisher with crooked head. *d*. Knurl. *e*. Forceps. *f*. Lining tool with toothed edge. *g*. Turning hook (lying in left foreground). *h*. Soldering iron with corncob handle. *i*. Coarse file. *j*. Rasp with two handles. *k, l, m, n, o*. Cutting tools used in spinning. *p*. Grooving tool. *x* and *y*. Unknown Quantities.

Pierce, but it also dispels the mystery, hitherto surrounding the pewterer's place of abode by definitely assigning him to Greenfield, Massachusetts.

PEWTERERS' TOOLS

As listed by Massé, in *Chats on Pewter;* Myers, in *Some Notes on American Pewterers;* Calder, *Rhode Island Pewterers;* and as found among Samuel Pierce's effects.

Molds
Coffeepots and teapots — Bottoms, handles and spouts for them.
Porringers — Pint, one-half pint, and gill size; handles.
Plates — Sizes: Butter, eight-inch, nine-inch, and soup.
Basins — Sizes: three-pint, two-pint, and one-pint.
Tankards.
Cups.
Curtain ring pins.
Spoons, large size.

Lathe Tools
(NOTE—The extreme length of handle, designed to be held under the arm of the workman, facilitated precision in execution.)
Lathe, spindle and wheel.
28 Turning hooks for spinning metal on chucks on lathe.
2 Square tools.
5 Cutting or trimming tools.
2 Burnishers for two hands.
1 Burnisher with crooked head.
49 Blocks or chucks over which to spin the metal.
1 Tooth-edged tool for lining.

Hand Tools
3 Sizes planishing hammers for beating the booge of objects.
1 Rasp with two handles for scraping.
3 Sizes of files for smoothing soldered seams.
2 Soldering irons.
1 Blowpipe for soldering. (Older method.)
2 Sizes of knurls for ribbing edges.
4 Sizes of brushes for applying mixture of red ochre and egg white to molds before casting.
3 Casting ladles.
Pincers.
1 Pair of snips for cutting sheet metal.
Chisel.
Scales.
Compass.

Wire.
Borer.
Bellows.
Hone.
Set of fourquettes.
7 Cores or mandrels.
Chinole for turning molds.
Dies for twenty-four letters.
Die for touch or seal.

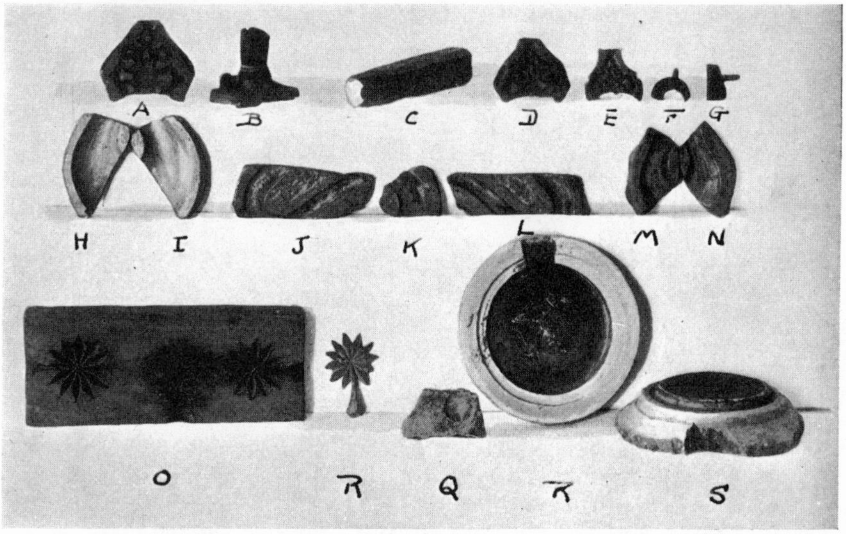

HIS PEWTER

Who, among us, honoring the maker's handiwork, would not cherish a copper teakettle, a lantern, a tin rattle-box with thistle, a "back candlestick", or even a tin "shandelier", that had come from the workshop of Samuel Pierce! But here we are only concerned with pewter. The intrinsic merits of Pierce's pewter alone would justify praise, yet its comparative rarity among American marked specimens in general lends an extrinsic element that sanctions admiration.

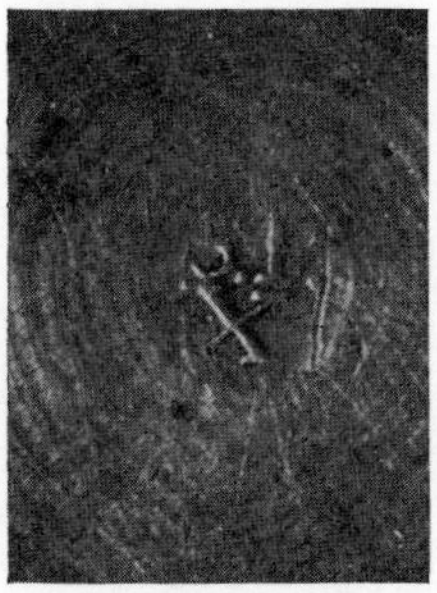

Pierce's product is characterized primarily by fineness of metal, and by a certain argental appearance. Most of his specimens extant still retain their pristine perfection, but occasionally we meet with

a trencher whose unappreciative possessor has submitted his heirloom to the corrosive abuse of rock salt or putty.

Judging from the old Pierce ledger, Samuel threw off the yoke of England's early guild laws, and wantonly bought "old pewter" from which to mold and spin his product. For this secondhand metal, he paid an average of seventeen cents a pound. Only rarely did he indulge in the extravagance of new pewter, for that cost nearly double. He doubtless added lead, tin, and antimony to suit his own fancy, but he never betrayed his formula by leaving records of the proportions of his mixture. This was his secret. Otherwise, why stamp his wares with a trade-mark?

Since so few molds were found in his chest, and the majority of his tools were those used in spinning, I am inclined to the opinion that Samuel's wares were largely a product of the lathe. Furthermore, most of his specimens bear the concentric rings which typify spun objects. Whatever his method, he was a master craftsman, whose pewter needed no advertising.

Although his branded pieces have been found in greatest quantity in the vicinity of Greenfield, I have never sighted a large flock of Samuel's eagles soaring in any one locality (unless it be New Jersey). Most of these fowl seem to have alighted on eight and eleven-inch plates and platters. The eight-inch basin was also a favorite perch.

Pierce's initialed touch is rare. Once I found it hiding in a quart mug. Mr. Myers speaks of its appearance on beakers as well. But these are the only places where his marks have been discovered. The fact naturally raises the question, "Did Samuel ever make any other pieces?" For one answer, look to the communion service illustrated in Figure 1. Only the plates bear the Pierce eagle; but, from the general feeling and appearance of the cups and the flagon — (Pardon the sacrilegious coffeepot! The little church in West Hawley was too poor in the early days ever to afford the more costly flagon. The sect is still poor, or was, until it sold its ecclesiastical plate in order to raise money for paintng the meeting house. That is how I happen to be its privileged possessor) — and from the fact that the pieces were always used in the same parish, there is no possibility in my mind of their being the work of any other pewterer. Furthermore, the bottom of the beaker fits rather conclusively into one of the soapstone molds of Figure 4.

Albeit no porringers, tumblers, or teapots bearing Pierce's touch have been

Fig. 6 — LATER MARK OF SAMUEL PIERCE

Fig. 4 — MOLDS AND SEAL OF SAMUEL PIERCE FOUND IN THE SAMUEL PIERCE TOOL CHEST
Top Row (left to right) Bronze Molds.
a and *b.* Face and back of large porringer handle mold. *c.* Eagle seal. *d* and *e.* Smaller porringer handles. *f* and *g.* Two sections conical shaped mold for coffeepot handle.
Middle Row Lead Molds.
h and *i.* Two halves of base of coffeepot spout. *j, k, l.* Three sections of teapot handle. *m* and *n.* Two sections of base of teapot spout.
Bottom Row
o and *p.* Wooden mold and ornament. *q.* Soapstone mold for lead balls. *r* and *s.* Halves of soapstone mold for bottoms of beakers.

Fig. 5 — EARLY MARK OF SAMUEL PIERCE

found — to my knowledge — the following list of items, together with their selling prices, is positive proof of his having made these other forms.

Porringers	.06, .12, .13, .14 each	Tumbler	.10
Coffeepots	.75 — 1.50	Basin (quart)	.40
Teapots	1.25	Basin (pint)	.25
Quart cup	.92	Platters	.92
Pint cup	.25	Curtain pins	.13 for ten pins
Shaving cup	.25	Wash pans	.42
Mug	.20		

The unfinished teapot-handle and syrup-cup lid found among his tools (*Figs. 2 d* and *e*) are additional testimony.

Through Samuel's failure to set his seal upon all his pewter, the unauthenticated pieces of his handiwork have lost their identity, and have thus enhanced present-day values of the surviving authenticated specimens to heights widely disproportionate to their original costs.*

*The list is derived from John Joyce Pierce's ledger in which occur entries of items purchased from Samuel.

Samuel Pierce, Jr., and the small eagle die

BY MARION AND OLIVER DEMING

Small iron die marked with an eagle and the name SAMUEL PIERCE, found among the pewterer's tools and now on display at the Hall Tavern, Old Deerfield. This illustration shows the die much enlarged. *Photograph by Taylor and Dull.*

As PEWTERERS GO, Samuel Pierce of Greenfield, Massachusetts (1767-1840) is somewhat more notable than many of his contemporaries—not so much for his pewter, however excellent in quality and form, as for his tools. These were discovered more than thirty years ago by Julia D. Sophronia Snow and reported on by her in an article (ANTIQUES, February 1927, p. 124) described by Ledlie I. Laughlin in *Pewter in America* as "the most absorbing article on American pewter that it has ever been my good fortune to read." Mr. Laughlin purchased the tools (which include the only pewterer's eagle die known to exist) and presented them to Old Deerfield. Today they are displayed there in a replica of a pewterer's shop (ANTIQUES, September 1956, p. 256), not too far from the place where they were originally used.

The life and the pewter of Samuel Pierce were described by Miss Snow and Mr. Laughlin in the works cited. The three recorded Pierce touches are his initial (No. 407 in Laughlin), thought to be his earliest; a large and very scarce eagle with his name (L-405); and the small eagle of similar design (L-406) shown here. Both eagles have been found separately with the initial touch, but so far as is known never together on a single piece of pewter. Except for a pear-shape teapot which Charles F. Montgomery has seen and the six-inch plate illustrated here, both with the initial touch, no Pierce pewter has been found in forms other than those listed by Laughlin. But in recent research we have uncovered some facts about his sons, the youngest in particular, which we believe to be of real significance to the story of Pierce pewter.

Several years ago, while compiling material on the life of the primitive painter George Washington Mark of Greenfield (ANTIQUES, July 1952, p. 43), we came across some advertisements of Samuel Pierce, Jr., who seemed to be a son of the pewterer (one of these advertisements was dated after the known pewterer's death). These aroused our interest, since we had understood that though a son named Samuel Pierce, Jr., had been born to Anna and Samuel Pierce, he had died in infancy. A check of the town records revealed that, following a not unusual custom of their time, the parents gave another son, born on October 11, 1812, the same name.

Samuel Pierce, Jr., was one of ten children, six of them sons. Three children (one of them the first Samuel, Jr.) died of plague in the summer of 1802; two sons died in their mid-twenties; and the three surviving sons, John Joyce, George, and Samuel, Jr., eventually became active in the business and community life of Greenfield and Northampton, Massachusetts, forming and dissolving partnerships with each other or with contemporary craftsmen which are recorded in advertisements and announcements in the *Franklin Gazette* and the *Northampton Gazette*.

When Samuel, Jr., was twenty-one he entered the business field as a partner of one G. W. Johnson; their specialty was tinware. After three months this firm was dissolved and Samuel joined his brother John. Their advertisement states "we manufacture and keep constantly for sale a general assortment of wares," pewter included. In the fall of 1835 John formed a partnership with William Wilson, and Samuel continued alone. An announcement in the spring of 1838 says that he "Keeps on hand a full assortment *and* manufactures to order (wholesale and retail) ware made of pewter, tin, brass, sheetiron, copper and zinc." In 1840 he makes it known that he has sold his tools and stock in connection with the sheetiron, copper, and tin business to his brother George. Rejoining John in 1844, he was once more by himself a year later and decided to seek greener pastures. He and his sister Phebe, both unmarried, had lived in their own residence not too far from the old family home, but patent records show that in 1846 Samuel was in Peekskill, New York, and in Troy, New York, in 1851, where he applied for patents for coal stoves. When he finally moved to Tabor, Iowa, Phebe followed him there and it is thought that his brother George did too. In 1855 Samuel and Phebe sold their Greenfield farm. Phebe died in Iowa in 1858, leaving all her property to Samuel. Records show that he was still living in 1860, but where or when he died and where he is buried are unknown.

Judged by the standards of their day, the Pierces were successful men. Primarily they were tinsmiths, sheetiron workers, and coppersmiths. Their accomplishments varied considerably as did their stock. Even though pewter was supposedly a part-time trade for the elder Samuel, it undoubtedly proved worth while, and in most of his son's advertisements it heads the list of goods for sale. Because of this, one is led to believe that the father was a silent partner, serving in an advisory capacity and as financial backer for his sons' partnerships. The terms of the elder Pierce's will support this assumption.

Ledgers kept by the father and the son John for the years 1821-1825, which a surviving member of the family has kindly permitted us to examine, record pewter occasionally but mostly old pewter metal. Large quantities of this, possibly surplus or of inferior quality, were sold to others. Later diaries kept by the father mention making pewter for his son George, and another entry records the fact that he spent the day casting teapots.

If one takes the many advertisements literally, the sons made pewterware or had a hand in the making of it. Certainly they could have served apprenticeships to either the father or an elder brother. There is the likelihood, too, that the father after casting forms allowed his sons to finish the pieces. If this was the case it explains the lack of marked specimens, especially teapots, which required assembling and further lathe and burnishing work after the parts were cast.

A pewterer's die, with a few exceptions, is the equivalent of his personal signature; it is incontestable evidence that he made a particular piece of pewter. Yet when two men had the same initials or name in a family of pewter workers, there is likely to be some difficulty in making positive attributions. This confusion has been resolved to some extent in relation to the Richard Lees, the Francis Bassetts, and the Danforths, among others. But in some instances further proof is required—and this is the case with the two Samuel Pierces, father and son.

The records show that Samuel Pierce, Sr., helped to

Selected references to ANTIQUES

COVERS OR FRONTISPIECES showing American pewter, and editorial comment on the pieces shown, were published in ANTIQUES in January 1926, December 1926, March 1927, February 1928, April 1938, February 1939, June 1945, and October 1945.

Articles of particular interest to collectors of American pewter appeared in November 1922, p. 209; January 1923, p. 17; April 1923, p. 173; July 1923, p. 27; September 1923, p. 132; November 1923, p. 226; January 1924, p. 26; March 1924, p. 122; July 1924, p. 24; April 1925, p. 192; October 1925, p. 212; January 1926, p. 19; May 1926, p. 315; February 1927, p. 124; March 1927, p. 190; January 1928, p. 28; June 1928, p. 493; October 1928, p. 331; March 1930, p. 242; May 1930, p. 437; August 1930, p. 144; November 1930, p. 399; February 1931, p. 97; August 1931, p. 87; September 1931, p. 150; July 1932, p. 8; September 1932, p. 92; May 1934, p. 189; January 1935, p. 23; June 1936, p. 239; November 1936, p. 209; April 1938, p. 188; November 1938, p. 248; March 1939, p. 130; June 1940, p. 300; July 1940, p. 26; April 1941, p. 191; May 1942, p. 315; April 1943, p. 171; December 1943, p. 292; August 1944, p. 75; June 1945, p. 326; October 1945, p. 204; April 1947, p. 253; June 1947, p. 394; January 1948, p. 60; March 1948, p. 196; November 1948, p. 340; January 1949, p. 40; September 1949, p. 179; April 1950, p. 274; January 1951, p. 57; July 1951, p. 51; February 1952, p. 178; June 1953, p. 521; May 1954, p. 388 and 412; March 1955, p. 230; January 1956, p. 55; September 1956, p. 256.

establish his sons in business. It seems natural that a father would particularly wish his namesake to learn a trade that he himself enjoyed, and that as an incentive he might have allowed the son to use the small eagle die. If such was the case, it is probable that the initial touch was used solely by the elder. Since neither that touch nor the larger eagle die was with the tools when they were discovered it is assumed that they had been removed some years earlier—or if the elder gave the tools to his namesake, he may have given him only the small eagle die.

In 1838, when Samuel, Jr., advertised that he manufactured pewter it was but two years before his father's death, a period when pewter, especially plates and basins, was declining in use. It is significant that many of the eight-inch plates and quart basins bearing the small eagle touch are found in virtually mint condition,

and that on these apparently later pieces the die was often struck off-center, as though by another hand.

The tools were found in a building belonging to John's descendants which had been erected some years after the elder Pierce's death, but they could have been given to Samuel, Jr., when he was active in business and when, according to advertisements, he manufactured pewter; and he may have entrusted or given them to John, with whom he seems to have kept in touch, when he went to Iowa. Legally, the tools were his if they were still the property of his father at the time of the latter's death, as Samuel, Sr., left certain lands and buildings to John and George, but to Phebe and Samuel, Jr., he left "all the rest and residue and remainder of my estate, both real and personal."

All in all, we believe the evidence is in favor of Samuel Jr.'s having used the small eagle die.

Unmarked 2¼-inch porringer whose handle fits one of the Pierce molds (no marked Pierce porringer is known), and a 6⅛-inch plate with Pierce's initial touch, formerly in the author's collection. *Photograph by Robinson Photographic Laboratories.*

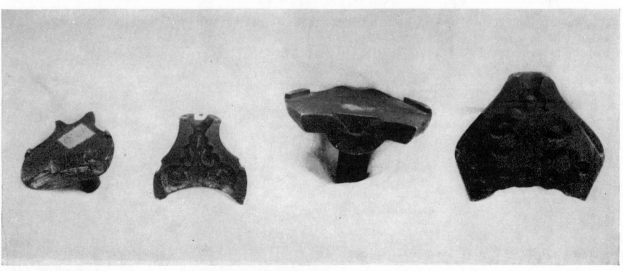

Pierce porringer-handle molds. *Old Deerfield; photograph by Robert Bliss.*

William Calder, a Transition Pewterer

By Percy E. Raymond

EVERY trade has its aristocracy, its bourgeoisie, and its peasants. It is not always easy to define these castes, but Mr. Kerfoot did it for American pewterers. To his mind, the eight-inch plate is its maker's badge of honor; the "coffeepot" the symbol of a hopeless plebeian. The middle classes, who made both plates and "coffeepots," Mr. Kerfoot denominates transition workers. Most of the last group started life as aristocrats, making more plates than "coffeepots." Once they yielded to the temptation to produce the latter articles, their Avernal descent appears to have been rapid. Perhaps the only way to estimate the place of a transition worker in the social scale of pewterdom is to determine the ratio between his "coffeepots" and his plates. If it is no higher than fifty-fifty, I think the candidate is entitled to a seat among the aristocrats.

Judged by this criterion, William Calder deserves a very good seat indeed. Fortunately for lovers of pewter, his daybook, with entries from January 1, 1826, to November 15, 1838, has been preserved. It was inherited by the late Charles A. Calder, a grandson, who became the historian of Rhode Island pewterers. Through the kindness of his widow, Alice D. P. Calder, I have been permitted to study this book, in which I find that, during the period covered, Calder sold about as many plates as coffeepots. In fact, he seems to have exercised remarkable self-restraint, for apparently he disposed of only twenty-four coffeepots in 1826, eighty-four in 1831, and as few as thirty-five in 1838.

For him, and perhaps for other pewterers, this period was really a teapot era, during which Calder produced 3,103 teapots, over fifty per cent of his total recorded output. I say recorded, for the entries in the daybook seem not to include cash sales. Most customers probably said, "I'll see you at the end of the week," for there are many entries amounting to less than one dollar each. Throughout the book, but chiefly before 1830, individual entries are recorded in shillings, but totals in dollars and cents. It is rather disconcerting for one who was brought up to believe that a York State shilling was worth just half the twenty-five cents of the Connecticut shilling, to learn that real New England shillings ran six to the dollar!

As told by Charles A. Calder in his interesting little book, *Rhode Island Pewterers and Their Work*, William Calder was born in Providence, Rhode Island, in 1792, and died there in 1856. He learned his trade during an apprenticeship to Samuel E. Hamlin, and appears to have gone into business for himself in January 1817, when he traded a plot of land valued at $109 to Josiah Keene in exchange for a set of molds. These molds the young master listed as follows:

One quart pot mold, with mold of bottom and handle; one nine-inch plate; one eight inch; and one butter plate mold; one large pint porringer mold; one wine pint, and one half pint ditto; with three handle molds.

No suggestion of coffeepots here! Keene himself is certainly above suspicion of making such things. So far as we know, he is represented now by one porringer and one plate. Keene did not altogether go out of business when he passed on his molds to Calder. Perhaps these items were out of date and he was glad to get rid of them. On November 21, 1827, Calder sold him 6 pigs of tin, weighing 398 ½ pounds. The last entry in which Keene is mentioned is dated March 3, 1832, and is a credit for 7 ¼ pounds of pewter. It would appear that Keene was more interested in other parts of his business than in the manufacture of pewterware, and that he probably renounced this branch of his trade when he sold his molds to Calder. This seems more likely than that he was a founder who manufactured pewter molds, as Mr. Myers has suggested. This is also the published opinion of Dr. Madelaine R. Brown, the owner of the one marked Keene plate.

According to his daybook, in 1826 Calder sold 1,876 pieces of hollow- and flatware, 42 dozen tablespoons, and 1 ½ dozen teaspoons. For this output he received $1,174.68. Ignoring the spoons, teapots represent 64 per cent of the production, porringers 13 per cent, and small plates 7 per cent. The climax in the demand for spoons seems to have been reached in 1831, when he sold 194 dozen tablespoons and 49 dozen teaspoons. In this year, however, teapots were still best sellers, accounting for 60 per cent of the total. Porringers were a very poor second.

Calder's business must have expanded rapidly during this period, for the list shows thirty-five varieties of articles, as compared with twenty-four in 1826. During the last year covered by the book (*1838*), 2,408 pieces of hollow- and flatware were sold. Curiously, the spoon trade appears to have dropped to zero; but 2,454 spindle caps are a sign of the development of the machine age in the cotton industry of Rhode Island. The total amount of business entered was $1,731.76. In this same year teapots constituted only 42 per cent of the volume. Tumblers and cups were second (35 per cent) in importance; porringers came third.

I have listed, in the order of the number of pieces sold, all the

Fig. 1 — Coffee Percolator Assembled
This example is not marked, but is believed to have been made by Calder. Formerly in the Charles A. Calder collection, it is now in that of the author. *Height*, 12 inches.
This and other photographs by Boecker

articles charged in 1826, 1831, and 1838. The varying positions of articles in this list are of some interest. For instance, in 1826 first place is occupied by quart teapots; in 1831 by three-pint teapots; whereas in 1838 *two-quart* teapots were in demand, although only second in the list. What are we to infer from this gradual increase in the size of the family teapot? Were families growing larger, or spinsters more numerous, or was tea cheaper? The last explanation is the most plausible.

Other trends are of more obvious significance. Eight-inch plates were fourth in 1826, fifteenth in 1831, and twenty-seventh in 1838. On the other hand, tumblers were sixth in 1826, third in 1831, and first in 1838. Coffee-pots were thirteenth in 1826, seventh in 1831, and dropped to sixteenth in 1838.

Not the least interesting of Calder's entries are those relating to the purchase of raw materials. His dealings were exclusively with Phelps and Peck. From them, between December 20, 1826, and July 16, 1833, he purchased about 12,920 pounds of tin, and about 1,020 pounds of antimony, or about 8 per cent

Fig. 2 — PERCOLATOR DISASSEMBLED
The upper strainers served to distribute the water over the surface of the coffee

Fig. 3 — PAIR OF CYLINDRICAL WHALE-OIL LAMPS AND FIVE-BOTTLE CASTER
All marked by Calder. One of the lamps has the *Providence* stamp shown in the accompanying detail. This has not been previously pictured.
Lamps from the collection of Mrs. Bertha B. Hambly; caster from the author's collection

or pigs. We may, then, only guess at what may have been his formula for pewter. The best britannia, according to Massé, was about 6 per cent antimony and a little less than 2 per cent copper. Judging from the hardness of some of his later pieces, Calder probably stressed the antimony a bit.

Whatever the actual composition, Calder himself obviously recognized a difference between britannia and pewter, and was just making the transition from one compound to the other in 1826, although articles in britannia ware had been advertised in Providence at least fifteen years earlier. Thus, in 1826, Calder's only mention of britannia is in the sale of 8 teapots (out of a total of 1,193), 12 tumblers, and 4 lamps. Incidentally, during this year he sold three "block tin" ladles, the only mention of the use of this metal in the book. Britannia and pewter tumblers are clearly distinguished in an entry during 1827; britannia spoons are first mentioned in 1828; and britannia plates and cups in 1829. After the last-named date, distinctions are seldom made. I think it is safe to infer that, by 1830, britannia had virtually super-

as much of the latter as of the former. The figures are not exact, for some entries are incomplete, and the weights have to be estimated. The tin most used was English. A small amount came from India, and even less from Spain. English and Indian tin cost the same, from 17 to 19 cents a pound, whereas the Spanish was cheaper, approximately 14 ½ to 15 cents. Antimony maintained a 23-cent level, except in 1827 when it once rose to 27 cents.

Strangely enough, Calder seems not to have bought any great amount of copper, brass, or lead. He occasionally acquired small amounts of these metals, in the form of junk, but no ingots

seded pewter in the making of household wares. Incidentally, britannia articles brought higher prices than those made of "common" pewter.

Space does not permit enumeration of all the types of articles made by Calder. The total, which may possibly involve duplications because of the employment of different names for the same objects (especially among teapots, where thirteen kinds seem to be listed), appears to be 69, of which 45 are not on the list for 1826.

The most significant trend during the period covered by the Calder daybook is toward the production of articles for use in churches. Flagons and church cups are first mentioned in 1830. In one instance samples were sent out, to be returned if not sold. In 1833 church cups were on general sale, and a new variety with a handle was added to the list. Christening bowls appear in 1834, a Communion basin in 1837, and ten-inch and twelve-inch plates in 1838. During these same years we note a constant increase in the sale of tumblers, cups (probably what we usually call beakers), and handled cups. Worth observing is the fact that, whereas the demand for porringers

Fig. 4 — PAIR OF SAUCER WHALE-OIL LAMPS AND A HANDLED CUP
All marked by Calder. Handled cups were among the pewterer's specialties in 1838.
Lamps from the collection of E. V. Spooner; cup from the collection of Dr. Madelaine R. Brown

of other sizes dropped steadily until 1838, the small (presumably gill) size sold well in the last-named year, indicating that it was used as a drinking vessel. The demand for articles associated with church ceremonies obviously coincides with a period of church expansion into new, and poor, frontier communities.

Throughout most of the period covered by his book, Calder seems to have worked alone. Apparently he made sporadic attempts to obtain help, for one E. Leslie is debited with enough lost time during 1827 to indicate that he was an employee. Finally, early in 1828, he earned a dollar, and, satisfied, retired to private life. On September 11, 1829, one Charles Plumly was credited with $60.03 for "Finishing spoons up to Date, etc." and debited with $20.50 for board since July 8. On December 3 of the same year Charles' job appears to have promised "15 dols per mo," but his castle crashed on December 11, when he received $8.32 as "Ballence on Settlement."

Collectors may find some of Calder's entries helpful in the proper naming of certain pewter articles. Kerfoot, for instance, mentions Calder as one of the

Fig. 5 — THE WELL-KNOWN CALDER EAGLE TOUCH
An unusually clear impression, appearing on a porringer handle.
From the author's collection

very few makers of marked "courting" or "sparking" lamps. These same utensils appear in the book, less romantically, as "nursing lamps." Certain entries also seem to answer Mr. Myers' query as to whether the vessels nowadays usually denominated "coffeepots" were actually used for the preparation of coffee, or were no more than tall teapots.

At first blush, the mention of coffeepots seems to indicate that collectors have correctly identified these tall but none too handsome vessels. Nevertheless, as I have already observed, Calder made few coffeepots, whereas the articles so designated by Kerfoot are so abundant as to be almost commonplace. Furthermore, several entries afford details regarding the coffeepot of the Calder era. Such are: "1 small coffee percolator," "1 percolator, as a sample," "1 Biggin $3.25," "2 Coffee Biggins $6.00," "2 French Coffee pots."

These notes indicate that, at the time, coffee was made by the French drip system, a method which probably did not involve the application of heat to the bottom of the pot. Whether Calder used the terms percolator, biggin, and French coffeepot as synonyms is not clear. I have never seen a biggin in either pewter or britannia. Such a pot should, of course, have a ledge within the lip to support the ring which holds the coffee bag. The percolator of that day was a drip pot, as we know from the rather long-winded essay of the versatile Count Rumford, *Of the excellent qualities of coffee and the Art of making it in the highest perfection.* Some cite the Count as the inventor of the percolator, but he himself says that the origin of the utensil is obscure. His chief contribution seems to have been the determination of the exact amount of coffee to be used per cup, and the invention of a sort of plunger-strainer (the one with a rod in Figure 2), to be used in smoothing and packing the coffee so as to retard the passage of the hot water.

The question remains: were all the coffeepots of the day percolators? Two lines of evidence in the daybook indicate that they were. One is their high price, as indicated above. Another entry quotes them at $20 per dozen, whereas the most expensive teapots were only $13 per dozen. Still more convincing is the popularity of two-quart teapots in 1838. If any owner will take the trouble to measure, he will find that Calder's large pots hold from a gill to a half pint more than two quarts, just enough for a margin of safety, whereas his teapots are all of less capacity. When one comes to think it over, it is obvious that coffee could be made in pewter only by employing the "French" or "drip" system. Hence all *real* coffeepots in pewter or britannia may have been in two parts. What we now call coffeepots were intended to harbor vast brews of tea.

In closing: a few hints to collectors. Of course we do not know what Calder made between 1838 and the time of his death in 1856, but it is possible that some unique items may survive. He made "1 Gall Coffee pot" for "Nich Sheldon" in 1831, and a two-quart mug for John Calder's shop in 1835. He records the sale of only one pair of candlesticks, perhaps the curious lamp candlesticks now in the Calder Memorial Collection at the Rhode Island Historical Society. Only four nursing bottles appear in his list; only one gravy dish, two sugar bowls, and two creamers. He also made "mouth-pieces" for ear trumpets. Did your great-aunt have one?

George Richardson, Pewterer

By Lura Woodside Watkins

Note. This article is based on data assembled by my late father, Charles L. Woodside. To his notes I have added such material as I could obtain, together with information received after the reading of a paper on Richardson before the Pewter Club. I wish to express my thanks to those members of the Club who so kindly lent me their pieces to be photographed. — *L. W. W.*

THAT George Richardson was a Boston pewterer is well established by documentary evidence corroborated by his own mark. The supposition that he lived and worked in Rhode Island is based wholly on the touch GLENNORE CO. — CRANSTON, R. I. that appears on some of his pieces. The most diligent search has discovered no substantiating data. Nevertheless, the town mark leads to the almost inevitable conclusion that at one time or another Richardson plied his trade in Cranston. J. B. Kerfoot in his *American Pewter*, and William Calder, author of *Rhode Island Pewterers*, agree in this judgment. On stylistic grounds they place Richardson in the period around 1825.

The purpose of this article is to summarize what we do know about Richardson, and to outline for future students what has been done in the effort to prove that he was, indeed, a resident of Rhode Island at one period in his life.

Some of the Richardson pewter bears the mark G. RICHARDSON BOSTON. A search through Boston directories reveals the fact that George Richardson worked in the Hub from 1818 to 1828, the last date when his name is listed. It has been surmised that he moved to Cranston after that time. As a matter of fact, he did nothing of the kind. By 1828 he was an old man, probably ill and unable to keep his shop; for he died in Boston, April 10, 1830, at the age of eighty-three. He was buried in Lot 106 of Copp's Hill Burying Ground, within sight of the Old North Church.

Richardson first appeared in the city as a partner of Samuel Green, who had already been established for twenty years or more. Why the two elderly men joined forces we may only guess. At the time Green was sixty-three and Richardson seventy-one. For a short period they conducted their trade in a shop on Hawley Street. Later in the year, an advertisement in the Boston

Fig. 1 — OLIVER PLACE, BOSTON
The second archway from the right is Number 4, where Richardson spent the last five years of his life

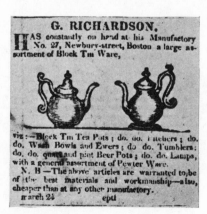

Fig. 2 — ADVERTISEMENT IN THE "COLUMBIAN CENTINEL," MARCH 28, 1821

Commercial Gazette (November 13, 1818) indicates a change of address. It reads as follows:

> Boston Wholesale and retail Block Tin Tea Pot Manufactory Nos. 5 & 9 Marlboro' Place.
> Green and Richardson take this opportunity of returning thanks &c &c.
> N. B. All kinds of Pewter Ware manufactured at the shortest notice.
> Cash and the highest price given for Old Pewter.

Nothing is known about the factory and its output, for no pewter marked with the names of both Green and Richardson has been found. According to Kerfoot, only one marked specimen of Green's work — an especially fine plate — has survived, although many unmarked pieces representing his industry must be in existence.

In 1820 Green was back in Hawley Place, and Richardson's name is not mentioned in the directory. The partnership must have been unsatisfactory. The next year Green continued the business at Marlboro' Place, while Richardson set up shop alone at 27 Newbury Street. Here he rented a house or building owned by Samuel Hastings. In that day, Newbury Street was the section of our present-day Washington Street between what are now Winter and Boylston Streets. Number 27 was probably opposite the present location of Jordan Marsh's store. The Boston tax list gives the total value of Richardson's property at this address as $400. This sum, representing personal property only — doubtless the craftsman's tools and stock on hand — indicates that he did not own a house or other real estate.

An advertisement in the *Columbian Centinel* for March 28, 1821, announces that "G. Richardson, Has constantly on hand at his Manufactory No. 27, Newbury-street, Boston a large assortment of Block Tin Ware," and, after listing a number of articles for sale, concludes, "The above articles are warranted to be of the best materials and workmanship — also, cheaper than at any other manufactory."

Richardson's name appears at the same address in the 1822 directory — the following year not at all. In 1825 he was still listed as a pewterer, living and working at 4 Oliver Place. By some rather roundabout investigation, we are enabled to follow him during the next five years until his death. Oliver Place was a new street, which had just been laid out through land owned by Ebenezer Oliver. It ran south from Essex Street, skirting the property of the Boston Crown Glass Manufactory to Oliver's Wharf on the waterfront. This was a short distance, as the South Cove had not yet been filled. Oliver, who lived around the corner on Essex Street, had erected four brick dwellings on the new place. They are mentioned in the inventory of his estate drawn up after his death in 1826. This inventory is worth quoting in full as showing what possessions were most valued by a gentleman of the period.

2 dwelling houses in Essex Street and four small brick houses in Oliver Place with the land under the same and thereto belonging, and the Wharf adjoining $21,000

Pew in King's Chapel	500
Tomb under "	150
Large brass kettle	5
2 pr Candlesticks in kitchen	2
Brass warming pan	1
Clock	10
Lamp	10

Surrounded by tall modern business buildings, the little houses are still standing and were photographed by my father a few years ago. They look much the same as they did in Richardson's time. With their old-style arched doorways, they have a pleasingly quaint air, reminiscent of London. Richardson lived in the second house from the right (*Fig. 1*). The Oliver accounts show that in 1827 he paid a rental of $237.

George Richardson continued to be listed as a pewterer until 1828. After that, he was undoubtedly out of the running. Nonlisting in the directory is no indication that he had left town, for inactive men living at home were not invariably included. Samuel Green, who died in Boston in 1833, was given no notice in the directories after 1825.

Richardson was not a citizen of great influence or valuable possessions, but he had a skilful hand and a rare understanding of form. Mr. Kerfoot dubbed his covered sugar bowl the "Miss America" of native pewter. In other words, although that authority believed that such pieces were made as late as 1830, he still considered them the finest achievement of their kind in American pewter. Since Richardson was eighty-three at the time

Fig. 3 — Teapots and Pint Beer Mug, Marked "G. Richardson Boston"
Heights, 6 ¼ inches; 11 ¼ inches; 4 ½ inches.
From the collections of Percy E. Raymond (left), and Dr. Madelaine R. Brown (centre and right)

Fig. 4 (*right*) — Mark in Beer Mug of Figure 3
The teapot, Figure 3 (*centre*), bears the same interior bottom mark

of his death in 1830, it now seems likely that his excellent bowls were designed at a much earlier period. Indeed, he was old enough to have been a skilled pewterer before 1770.

Before discussing the types of Richardson pewter, it may be well to review what has been done in the way of investigating the pewterer's supposed residence in Rhode Island. In the early days Cranston was a part of Providence, and it is in Providence County that Cranston's vital statistics are to be sought. Among these, however, Mr. Calder never found any reference to Richardson, nor did he anywhere run across advertisements of Richardson or the Glennore Company. Ledlie Laughlin, likewise, has delved among the files of deeds and land conveyances of Providence County, but without avail. My father learned from state records that the Glennore Company was never incorporated in Rhode Island. In Cranston he found no trace of it as a fire, military, or business company. Richardson's name is not included in the vital records of either Providence or Cranston. If the pewterer did live in Cranston, it was certainly before his advent in Boston. At that time there were no Cranston town records. It may be that the Glennore Company was an eighteenth-century concern and that the sole evidence of its existence is the pewter mark.

As to Boston, Richardson was neither born nor married there, and no inventory of his estate was filed in Suffolk County following his death. Richardson genealogies and the vital records of numerous Massachusetts towns leave us still in the dark as to his antecedents.

Fortunately, we have some knowledge of what Richardson made in Boston. Not

Fig. 5 — Sugar Bowls with Richardson's Cranston Mark; Teapot Marked "G. Richardson — Warranted"
Sugar bowls a pair, except for slight variations in covers. *Height*, 5 ¼ inches; *diameter*, 6 ½ inches. *Height of teapot*, 10 ½ inches.
From the collection of Mrs. Melville T. Nichols
Fig. 6 (*right*) — Mark on Teapot of Figure 5

144

Fig. 7 — TEAPOT WITH CRANSTON MARK
Height, 8 ¾ inches.
From the collection of Miss Bessie R. Jacobs

Fig. 8 — RICHARDSON PITCHER
A fine example, shape of early 1800's. Height, 7 ¼ inches.
From the collection of Chester Wing

only did he produce teapots, examples of which are now far from rare, but he also turned out washbowls and ewers, tumblers, quart and pint beer pots, and lamps. The last item is the most important, for it places the American pewter lamp much earlier than students have hitherto believed. Kerfoot, for example, placed all the lampmakers after 1825, and probably not earlier than 1830. Yet we find the obscure and mysterious George Richardson making lamps in 1821 and possibly earlier. That these articles were the regular, closed-reservoir, whale-oil lamps cannot be doubted, since lighting devices of that type in other metals are known to have been in use for twenty years or more before that time. He also advertised a "general assortment of Pewter Ware."

During the Boston period the mark used was G. RICHARDSON BOSTON, or simply G. RICHARDSON. without other device. One rare example has come to light with the word WARRANTED under the name (*Fig. 6*). This mark substantiates the maker's advertised guarantee of quality and low price. Teapots with the Boston marks far outnumber other specimens. The beer mug in Figure 3 also has the Boston imprint.

Richardson's handsome covered sugar bowls have a more elaborate touch. In addition to the name are the words GLENNORE CO. in a curved line above, CRANSTON, R. I. in a curve below, and a neat small eagle. A small imprinted NO. 2 also appears. For a time these pieces were the only known examples of Richardson's presumptive Cranston period. It has been suggested that the Glennore mark is merely an indication of ownership quite unrelated to the place where Richardson pursued his trade. Until we have definite proof to this effect we are hardly justified in drawing such a conclusion, and must consider the Cranston mark as evidential. In this connection, it is interesting to note that Richardson's name, with CRANSTON, R. I. but without GLENNORE CO., seems not to have been used.

Several other forms bearing the same touch have recently come to my attention.

The teapot in Figure 7 is one example. This piece is stamped NO. C, where the sugar bowls are numbered 2. A pint pot with the Glennore mark may also be seen in the Calder collection at the Rhode Island Historical Society.

Most important is the pitcher shown in Figure 8. It is hard to express adequately the æsthetic satisfaction which one experiences in looking at this piece. Unlike the ordinary pewter water jug, it has no spreading foot or base, but follows the lines of English earthenware pitchers made during the second decade of the nineteenth century. It is strongly built, with a prominent seam at the body joining. Its simplicity and dignity place it in the same class and probably in the same period with the sugar bowls. The pitcher is stamped NO. I., and with the familiar Cranston touch. It is a matter for speculation whether such numbering designates grades of quality, or particular molds.

The eagle touch is suggestive of the eighteenth century, rather than of somewhat later, when it became the custom to stamp pewter with the maker's name only. At least, it places Richardson in the period of transition between plate- and porringer-making to the "coffeepot" era. Knowing that Richardson's Cranston pewter could not have been made after 1818, we must still conjecture how far back to date it. Both form and workmanship point to the period around 1810. It is possible that the pewterer who chose a Scotch name for his trademark was not a native American, in spite of his eagle, but may have drifted here, a stranger from the old country, to ply his trade in sugar bowls and pitchers of unique form.

Note. Since writing this article, the author has explored Oliver Place, hoping to find the erstwhile home of Richardson and to pay respect to his memory. But, alas! the little houses have disappeared, and the narrow way is now a filthy alley almost buried in refuse and garbage thrown out by the Chinese who inhabit it. The accompanying photograph seems to be the last record of its better and cleaner days.

—*L.W.W.*

Fig. 9 — MARK ON PITCHER OF FIGURE 8

GEORGE RICHARDSON, PEWTERER

By EDWARD H. WEST

FOR MANY years pewter collectors have tried to solve the riddle of George Richardson of Cranston, Rhode Island, and his Glennore Company. The various magazine articles written about him have been mainly speculative, as it was admitted that, aside from a few pieces of pewter bearing his touch mark, no records existed which would throw any light on the man or his enterprise. It was not until 1939 that an article[1] was published showing a picture of his old factory, whose walls, though standing in 1885, are now not much more than a pile of rocks. In that article was quoted a statement, made by a lady who had known one of the Richardsons, that George Richardson had failed in his business. It was noted that a George W. H. Richardson had been listed in the 1860 Tax Book of Cranston. However, the 1860 census of Cranston shows this Richardson to have been born in 1816, much too late to have been the pewterer. Besides, this man was a farm laborer, and earlier directories of Providence show that he worked at times as brewer and laborer.

However, the 1840 census of Cranston shows a George Richardson, 50 to 60 years of age, with one son 20 to 30, another 15 to 20, and three younger, a wife 40 to 50, and six daughters, three of the family being engaged in manufacturing. Although the 1840 census has a manufactures schedule, only machinery, cotton, and woolen goods are itemized, while all the rest are lumped under the heading, *Other manufactures*. Thus the listing is of no assistance in proving that the Richardsons were engaged in the manufacture of pewterware.

Although no other mention is made of George Richardson in any census of Cranston, further records of him appear in the 1847/48 directory of Providence, Rhode Island:

George Richardson Agent   Providence Britannia Ware 207 High
George B. Richardson   Providence Britannia Ware 207 High
Francis B. Richardson   Providence Britannia Ware 207 High

It seems safe to assume that these were the three men engaged in manufacture in Cranston in 1840. George Richardson, failing in business in Cranston after 1840, possibly employed the subterfuge of "Agent" in running a britannia ware company in Providence. The 1850 census of Providence fails to show George Rich-

ardson, the elder, but does show George B. Richardson, age 31, britannia ware manufacturer, born Massachusetts, wife Amey Ann, and two children born after 1845. It lists also Francis B. Richardson, age 28, britannia ware manufacturer, born in Massachusetts, wife Mary, and two children born after 1845. The ages of these two men compare favorably with the ages of the two elder Richardson sons in the 1840 census of Cranston.

The Providence death records show that George Richardson died July 15, 1848, at the age of 66. Eliza, widow of George Richardson, was born in Boston and died March 23, 1884, age 88. George B. Richardson, son of George and Eliza, was born in Boston and died September 29, 1890, age 71. If George B. Richardson was born in Boston about 1819, George Richardson of Cranston, his father, might well have been in Boston at that time and even earlier. Is it not possible that George Richardson, pewterer, of Boston 1818–1828, afterwards moved to Cranston, taking with him his son George B. and probably his younger son, Francis B. Richardson?

It has been suggested that George Richardson of Boston died there in April 1830, at the age of 83.[2] What proof have we that it was the pewterer who died then? Two Boston newspapers record the death of a George Richardson, age 83, on that date, but do not call him pewterer or anything else. True, the pewterer does not appear in the directories of Boston after 1828, but neither does another George Richardson, a housewright, who appears in the same Boston directories from 1800 to 1828. As this housewright appears in both the 1810 and 1820 census records of Boston as over 45 years of age, it is certainly possible that he, not the pewterer, was the George Richardson who died in 1830.

Doubt is also cast on the statement that Samuel Green, age 63, and George Richardson, age 71, went into partnership in 1818,[2] a statement which on its face seems improbable. Although such a thing is not impossible, it was no more likely in 1818 than in 1940 that a man of seventy-one would start a business or go into partnership. It is much more credible that Samuel Green, having passed three score years, needed a younger man in his business and chose Richardson, who had probably learned his trade in London. The work of the two men was entirely different, as

FIG. 1 — PINT PEWTER MUG BY GEORGE RICHARDSON. Bearing the *Boston* mark shown in the inset, below. *From the collection of Doctor Madelaine R. Brown*

FIG. 2 — PINT PEWTER MUG BY GEORGE RICHARDSON. Bearing the *Glennore Co. / G. Richardson / Cranston* mark shown in the inset, at right. *From the Rhode Island Historical Society*

Green made flat ware while Richardson seems to have made only hollow ware, to judge from surviving pieces. Possibly this fact, and the differences in their ages as well as in their nationalities, brought their partnership to its speedy close.

Where Richardson went after he left Boston is, as yet, unknown. Taunton at that time had begun to make pewterware, and as the Taunton Britannia Manufacturing Company was started in 1830, Richardson may perfectly well have gone there. This is mere conjecture — he does not appear in the 1830 census.

Both Calder[3] and Kerfoot[4] say that George Richardson's work was done about 1825, and that certainly ware marked *Boston* was made not later than 1828. Ware with the mark of the *Glennore Company*, however, was made much later, just how much later cannot now be told. One of the reasons why no Rhode Island record of George Richardson was found by the pewter collectors in their search may well have been that they were looking for a much older man. He was, in fact, a few years older than William Calder, the pewterer of Providence, and there can be no doubt that the two men knew each other.

In the opinion of a genealogist (although he is not a pewter collector), it is impossible for a man to turn out such work as did Richardson, acknowledged by all to be of superior design and workmanship, and yet leave no other trace of his life. It was on this assumption that I searched the records and, in the light of facts and probabilities, have partly reconstructed the life of George Richardson. He probably arrived in this country from London, shortly before 1818, being then about thirty years of age. He must have been married shortly after his arrival and then entered the Boston partnership with Samuel Green, when he started his "Block Tin Tea Pot Manufactury."[2] Although this partnership did not last long, Richardson continued to make his teapots. The fact that his name does not appear in all issues of the Boston directories is no proof that he was not in that city, as the books were not always complete. Until a piece of pewter is found bearing Richardson's touch and the name of some other town in which it was made, it will be well to assume that this pewterer had but two factories of his own. He may have worked for some other manufacturer between 1828 and the unknown date on which he arrived at Cranston; but in that case his name would not appear on the pewter, and all trace of him, through his work, would be lost.

It is fitting to close this article with an obituary printed in the *Republican Herald* of Providence, July 15, 1848, in which we may find the final proof of the identity of our subject:

Died: On the 14th inst. George Richardson, Esq., a native of London, England, aged 66 years.

Mr. Richardson started the first teapot manufactory in the United States at Boston, Massachusetts, and has engaged in the business until his decease. His funeral will take place at his late residence, No. 27 Knight Street, tomorrow, Sunday at 1 o'clock. Boston papers please copy.

REFERENCES

1. Madelaine R. Brown, M.D., Rhode Island Historical Society *Collections*, January 1939
2. Lura Woodside Watkins, ANTIQUES, April 1937
3. Charles A. Calder, Rhode Island Historical Society *Collections*, July 1924
4. J. B. Kerfoot, *American Pewter*, 1924

Note. As this information has all been obtained at Washington, D. C., it is probable that much more can be added to it by further search in Providence. If there were bankruptcy proceedings, the books of the creditors might show just when the Glennore Company was started at Cranston. As Richardson sometimes used an eagle in his mark, it would be interesting to learn if he was ever naturalized. Then, too, some records of the Providence Britannia Ware Company might be found which would throw further light on this story. George B. Richardson, the son, worked in Providence, where he remained until his death. During this time he was continually listed in the directories as a britannia ware worker, except in the last few years of his life, when he was a japanner of metal. Francis B. Richardson removed to Boston shortly after 1850, where he appears for many years as a britannia ware manufacturer.

— *E. H. W.*

Fig. 1 — FLAGON AND LAMPS
Made by Israel Trask. *From the author's collection.*

A Massachusetts Pewterer

By JOHN WHITING WEBBER

BEFORE the elaborate "elegancies" of the Victorian Era reached this country, the composition metal workers of America devoted themselves to making articles which should be useful and practical. Incidentally they created work which often had a certain beauty. Later, when "doyleys" and "whatnots" bedecked the parlor of every hooped lady, it was thought that the sombre surface of pewter must be embellished with decoration; and, from that time, the sturdy shapes characteristic of the ware lost their simple and unconscious grace.

Not only the lines of various objects changed, but the dead lustre of the old pewter plate was scorned, and alloys which would have more sheen were sought. In the eighteenth century, the English sometimes added antimony, copper and zinc to their composition, finding that a harder and more brilliant material resulted, which, to distinguish it from the other kinds of pewter, was called Britannia metal. This term, however, has since been used for alloys of appearance quite different from the original Britannia.

When we pick up the old volume called Stone's *History of Beverly* we wonder just what composition the author referred to, in 1843, when he wrote that

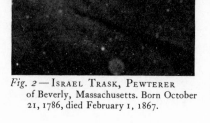

Fig. 2 — ISRAEL TRASK, PEWTERER
of Beverly, Massachusetts. Born October 21, 1786, died February 1, 1867.

"the manufacture of Britannia ware in this country was commenced in 1812 by Mr. Israel Trask." Previous to that time, and subsequently as well, Trask worked in pewter; and, as pieces bearing his mark vary from whale-oil lamps and tankards of dull, leady alloy to shiny, ornate casters, it is impossible to know just what his earliest Britannia resembled. Certain of his tools among the treasures of the Beverly Historical Society help us to discover the processes by which he worked at one period of his long life, but as to the exact proportions of metals used at different times, we are considerably in the dark.

The embargoes of the turbulent period of our second war with England changed the course of the industries of young America, and Trask's business was affected with the others. One day, while Trask was selling his spoons in Boston—according to an article in an old local newspaper*—a lady entered and asked the proprietor of the store for a teapot. But there were none to be had, as the supply from England had been shut off. Trask, however, who had overheard the conversation, spoke up: "Mrs. Ball," said he, "if you will give me a sack full of old teapots, I will melt them up and will make you as fine a new tea-

Beverly Citizen, February 7, 1897.

Fig. 3 — SHEFFIELD TEAPOT
Used as a model by Israel Trask in making the pewter teapot illustrated in Figure 4. *Owned by Mrs. Jesse Trask.*

Fig. 4 — PEWTER OR BRITANNIA TEAPOT
Made by Israel Trask and bearing the mark *I. Trask*. The pot was designed after the one illustrated in Figure 3. *Owned by Mrs. Jesse Trask.*

pot as ever came from old England." The metal was taken to Beverly, melted in the kiln, cooled on iron plates, rolled to the desired thickness and made into oval-shaped teapots. The result must have been satisfactory, as, at a later time, an order for one hundred dozen was given.

As this increase in business proved too much for Trask and his one helper, the services of his two brothers, George and Oliver, were required. George, though apparently enjoying his apprenticeship to his "saintly brother," as he later wrote,* forsook this work for the ministry and the anti-tobacco cause. Oliver, however, kept to his trade, although leaving his brother and setting up a separate shop in Beverly. It was this brother, Oliver, who made the

Autobiographical Sketch, Rev. George Trask, Fitchburg, 1870.

handsome pewter flagon now in the Boston Museum of Fine Arts, although it appears to be identical with one in my own collection bearing Israel Trask's mark. After his brothers left him, Israel's business became of larger proportions; in fact, the Boston Art Museum's list of American pewterers gives the years 1825 to 1842 as the period during which Israel Trask was producing pewter.

By 1831 the business had become so large that Trask decided to invest $325 of his savings in a lot of land on Cabot Street where he erected a stone shop, still standing, and behind it another stone building in which the metals were worked. In a document* written the following year, he is referred to as a goldsmith, though it is doubtful that

* Will of Edeth Wallis, March 16, 1832.

Fig. 5 — COMMUNION SET
Made by Israel Trask. *Owned by the author.*

he carried on that craft to any great extent. During his later years he seems to have made mostly Britannia tableware. Casters were a specialty, the bottles probably being obtained either from Sandwich or from the glass works at East Cambridge. One of these casters is now in the collection of the Essex Institute at Salem.

Humble pewter whale-oil lamps made by Israel Trask, and teapots of good proportion and line, are occasionally seen in New England collections, and several specimens have remained in the hands of his descendants. At one time I came across a diminutive bedroom lamp with an ingenious false bottom. Being inspired by curiosity, I learned that there was a legend that this *objet d'art* had been turned out for his beloved by a love-sick youth at the Trask pewter shop. He had hidden his daguerreotype in the compartment within the metal, and given the lamp to the damsel. The story, however, fails to state whether this sentimental gift succeeded in its mission.

A novel way which Trask invented, or rather happened upon, for making teapot spouts, or *snouts* as they were then called, is also recounted in the newspaper article referred to above. Previously the pewter was molded separately for each half of the spout and later the pieces were soldered together, more or less securely. One day while Israel Trask was engaged in heating the moulds by pouring into them molten metal, an alarm of fire was sounded. Putting the two moulds together in his haste, and grabbing the leather bucket which hung above his bench, he rushed off to the fire. When he returned and

Fig. 6 — Rubbings of Pewter Marks
That on the left is the mark of Israel Trask; that on the right, of his brother, Oliver Trask.

Fig. 7 — Britannia Coffee-Pot
Made by Israel Trask and given to Mrs. Martha Trask in 1840. *Owned by Miss Kate Studley*

separated the moulds, to his surprise he found that enough metal had adhered to them so that a perfect spout was formed. Time was thus saved, and, for the future, the housewife was less likely to find drops trickling from a leaky seam as she poured her tea.

The pieces which Trask made during the latter part of his long life followed the tendency of the times towards over-decoration. He apparently used different recipes for mixing his alloy, although the appearance of the surface may have been altered by heating the articles in baths of cream of tartar, acids or oils. His grandson once told me that he believed the mixtures were made up each time according to the judgment of Mr. Trask rather than by definite weights and, consequently, that they varied considerably.

On most of this pewterer's work there appears a small indented rectangle reading *I. Trask*. The brother's stamp, *O. Trask*, was similar, though somewhat larger. It has been maintained* that a composition worker named John Trask, who is listed in the Boston directories from 1822 to 1826 at various addresses, manufactured pewter articles, but, though I have examined large numbers of pieces, I have never been able to identify any of this man's work.

Among his contemporaries, Israel Trask was known as the maker of "improved" and "up-to-date" tableware. At present, however, there is little interest in these later examples. The present-day collector seeks out rather the sturdy and substantial earlier products of this Essex County pewterer, leaving his later work for later appreciation.

* See *Pewter and the Amateur Collector*, Edwards J. Gale.

Fig. 8 — Britannia Coffee-Pots
The third from the left was made by Oliver Trask, the other three by Israel. *Owned by the author.*

Three Maine Pewterers

By Charles L. Woodside and Lura Woodside Watkins

Illustrations, with the exception noted, from the Woodside collections

Fig. 1 (above) — Lamp Marked a. porter" (*1830–1835*)
Of pewter, for burning whale oil. Mark reproduced at
right below.
Height: 5 inches

Fig. 2 (right) — Lamp Marked "a. porter" (*1830–1835*)
Of pewter, for burning whale oil.
Height: 6 inches

THE story of American pewter-making is still so far from complete that nothing more is known of many of the pewterers than the names of the towns where they worked; and, in some instances, even those locations have been wrongly assigned. The three men whose histories we here bring to light are Allen Porter, Freeman Porter, and Rufus Dunham. Information concerning them comes, for the most part, from Frederick Dunham, one of the sons in the old-time firm of Rufus Dunham & Sons, of Portland, Maine. Mr. Dunham has further given us a picturesque tale of a group of pewterers, tinsmiths, brush and comb-makers, and tin peddlers — not in Southington, Connecticut, or in Westbrook, Connecticut, where the Porters are supposed to have worked, but in Westbrook, Maine, now a part of the city of Portland.

Because the story of Allen Porter and his brother Freeman antedates that of Rufus Dunham, it is important to relate first the few facts we have been able to obtain about this earlier pair. It is thought that Allen Porter came from Connecticut to Westbrook, Maine, a township about three miles west of Portland, incorporated in 1815. At that time the place included a district — later set off as the city of Deering — that was annexed to Portland some thirty years ago. In this Deering section of Westbrook, in a village known as Stevens Plains, Allen Porter settled about 1830. It is possible that he manufactured pewter somewhere in the Nutmeg State before his departure for Maine, but we have been unable to find any evidence to that effect. Mr. Dunham further assures us that, though he has consulted records in Southington, Connecticut, he has found no reference to Porter or to any other pewterer.

Fig. 3 — Pewter Pitcher Bearing F.
Porter's Mark
Height: 6½ inches.
In the collection of Mrs. Watkins

deaths. The place Mrs. Porter lived to just before 1900. Of his further relation-nothing more is thirties he was in met and talked with Forbes, whom he persuaded to go to Westbrook as a foreman in Freeman Porter's factory. The daughter of Mr. Forbes believes that Allen never thereafter returned to Westbrook. According to Mr. Dunham, he sold out to his brother, and probably returned to Connecticut. Freeman Porter continued the business until the Civil War. During his later years he suffered ill health, a circumstance that may account for his abandonment of pewter-making. In 1868 he was a town selectman.

Freeman Porter first appears as his brother's bookkeeper at Westbrook in 1832 or 1833. From an article on Westbrook by Leonard B. Chapman in the Deering *News* of July 25–28, 1900, we learn that this younger man was born in Colebrook, New Hampshire, July 1, 1808 — though because of the lack of early records in Colebrook the date cannot be verified. Freeman was only twenty-four or twenty-five years old when his connection with the pewtering business began. Two years later — March 16, 1835 — a partnership between the brothers was announced, and in the *Eastern Argus* of Portland on April 20, 1835, appeared the following notice (*Fig. 11*):

"Allen Porter has associated himself with his brother Freeman Porter, under the firm of A. & F. Porter, for transacting Mercantile and Manufacturing Business, at his old stand on Stevens' Plains, Me."

On July 1, 1835, Freeman Porter married Mary Ann (Buckley) Partridge. The couple began housekeeping in a dwelling on Stevens Avenue, where they remained until their is still standing. a ripe old age, dying Allen Porter and ship with the firm known. In the late Hartford, where he a certain Elizur B.

Rufus Dunham

The account of Rufus Dunham begins with his birth in Saco, Maine, May 30, 1815. He was of the ninth generation in descent from John Dunham, who came to Plymouth in 1630. At the age of nine, compelled to earn his own way, he went to live with a farmer, who beat and otherwise illtreated him. One day, in a drunken frenzy, the man gave the boy an unusually hard flogging with a harness strap; whereupon the lad ran away to Portland. There he found a job in the United States Hotel as handy boy about the billiard room and bar. Young Dunham had something fine about his make-up. The atmosphere of drinking and gambling that surrounded him made no unfortunate impression on his character. He was always looking forward to better circumstances. Meanwhile he attended night school and in that way managed to obtain a rudimentary education.

Concerning his father, Frederick Dunham says: "One Sunday with a companion he strolled in the country to Stevens Plains, Westbrook, three miles from Portland. At that time the place was very much alive, since it was the headquarters for one hundred or more peddlers whose markets were in northern New England, Canada, and along the coast of Maine, New Brunswick, and Nova Scotia. The windows of the different factories where were made high-back horn combs, brooms, tinware, decorated japan ware, brushes, and pewter ware so fascinated him that, in the following week, he asked for time off so that he might see the works in operation.

"On this second visit he bound himself as an apprentice for three years to Allen Porter. His wages were to be two suits of clothes per annum, his board, and fifty dollars in cash. This was in 1831. At the end of two years, he broke his contract on the ground that he had not received the pay due him for overtime work."

Boston was his next goal. Since there were no railroads or steamboats, he made his way by sailing packet. Once in the city, he secured work in Dorchester with the pewterer Roswell Gleason. Here, and in Poughkeepsie, he spent the time between 1833 and 1837. By the latter year he was making plans for a business of his own, and the attraction of Westbrook drew him once more. He had saved eight hundred dollars and had secured molds and tools in Poughkeepsie. In 1837 he opened a shop in Stevens Plains with his brother John as helper. The following year he exhibited his wares at the Mechanics' Fair in Portland, and received a silver medal for the best specimen of *block tin ware*, as pewter was sometimes called at that time. The Portland *Transcript* of September 29 thus briefly mentioned him: "R. Dunham of Westbrook presented some elegant Britannia Ware."

For power he at first used a foot lathe. Later, as business warranted, a horse, walking in a circle, replaced the foot power. Still later Dunham installed a steam engine. It is said that he had the distinction of being the second man in Maine to use steam for motive power.

"He sold his first product to Eben Steel, a crockery dealer in Portland, and he was very much elated to find that he could *sell* as well as *make* his wares. The winters were long and the highways impassable, save for the road to Montreal via Crawford Notch, Lyndonville, Derby Line, and Coaticook, Quebec, which was kept open by a long line of four- and six-horse vans transporting freight from Canada to Portland, for reshipment by water to Boston. Consequently, the peddlers could do no business, and most of the Westbrook shops shut down for want of trade.

"Rufus Dunham, however, filled a wagon with his goods and went north to barter pewter wares for furs, hides, sheep pelts, yarns, stockings, mittens, oxtails, hogs' bristles, and cattle horns. The hides and pelts he forwarded to Portland — a welcome cargo for the teamsters to spread over their winter loads while on their way to the coast. On arrival these articles were sold to local tanners and wool pullers, the bristles and oxtails to brush-makers, the horns to comb-makers. The furs, yarns, stockings, and mittens were taken to Boston and turned into cash among various merchants of the Hub.

"By thus opening a winter market, Dunham was able to give

Fig. 4 (above) — LAMP MARKED "F. PORTER WESTBROOK NO. 1." *(after 1835).*
Except for the reservoir, similar to the lamp of Figure 1. Mark reproduced at the left.
Height: 6 inches

Fig. 5 (left) — LAMP ASCRIBED TO F. PORTER *(after 1835)*
Though unmarked, this pewter whale-oil lamp is the same as a known F. Porter specimen.
Height: 3½ inches

his men year-round work. As he usually paid cash wages, the best workmen were attracted to his shop. He employed from twenty-five to thirty helpers, many of whom worked for him during their whole lives."

Dunham continued his business in Stevens Plains until 1861, when his buildings were burned and he leased new quarters in Portland. In 1876 his sons Joseph S. and Frederick were taken into the firm, which remained as Rufus Dunham & Sons until 1882, when it was dissolved.

Mr. Dunham was twice married; first, to Emeline Stevens of Westbrook, by whom he had two children; second, to Emma B. Sargent of Portland, who became the mother of nine little Dunhams. His home was on Stevens Avenue, almost directly opposite that of Freeman Porter. After the second Mrs. Dunham's death, the house was purchased by the Bishop of Portland, and is now used as the rectory of Saint Joseph's Church. Rufus Dunham was always a highly respected citizen in his community, and one who was accustomed to extend lavish hospitality to his friends and to notables who passed through the town. It is said that, on one occasion, he entertained thirty-two persons in his home overnight. For many years he was a trustee of Westbrook Seminary. The All Souls Universalist Church of Portland is a memorial to him and to his wife.

Stevens Plains

The statement that one hundred or more tin peddlers were congregated in Stevens Plains suggests to the imagination a scene of

Figs. 6 and 7 — WHALE-OIL LAMPS MARKED "R. DUNHAM"
The mark is shown at left.
Height: 6 inches and 8 inches

enormous activity. What with the shops turning out the useful and decorative articles that filled the peddlers' carts, the arrival and departure of the vans, and the sorting of the goods taken in exchange, it was the centre of a varied and colorful life.

The decoration of tinware was in itself an industry. This work was done almost entirely by women. Trays, teapots, matchboxes — all the many objects japanned and painted in gay colorings — came forth from the shops of Westbrook. The tin box illustrated in Figure 8 was purchased from Mrs. O. H. Perry, granddaughter of Zachariah B. Stevens, a tinsmith, who sent out many cartloads of gaudy tin to be bartered for rags. The long building where these rags were sorted remained standing until nearly 1900, when it was pulled down and its only remaining cart was destroyed. Thus vanished the last vestiges of the once-flourishing industries of the Plains.

A note in the Deering *News* mentions Thomas Brisco as another decorator of tinware. "He was a peddler and the driver of his own horse and cart. His goods consisted of japanned tin ware, japanned and ornamented by his wife, aided later by five orphaned nieces. Undoubtedly, he was the first tin ware manufacturer and peddler of the Plains." Rufus Dunham bought a share of Brisco's property.

Walter B. Goodrich and his son Walter F. Goodrich are named as tinsmiths by Miss H. A. Forbes. The term is applied indiscriminately to makers of pewter, britannia ware, and tin. It would be interesting to know whether any real pewter, other than the products of the Porters and Rufus Dunham, came from Stevens Plains. Further research might reveal the names of additional makers. At least one clockmaker — Enoch Burnham — belonged to the community.

Fig. 8 — Tin Box from Westbrook
Made in the shop of Zachariah B. Stevens. Bright yellow, with red and green flowers

Wares of the Porters

Mr. Kerfoot briefly dismisses Allen Porter, saying that the only specimen of this pewterer's work that he has seen is a lamp belonging to Louis G. Myers of New York. This is presumably one of the two shown in Mr. Myers' *Some Notes on American Pewterers*, opposite page 46. No comment concerning them occurs in the text. It will be observed that these lamps have flat wicks, such as were used for lard oil. Miss Forbes states that her father — the Elizur B. Forbes who came to work for Freeman Porter in the late thirties — was the inventor of this type of burner, with its little toothed barrel wheel for turning up the wick.

The only known pieces of Porter's pewter are lamps. It is interesting to note that the three examples in the Woodside collection have stems that must have been made in the same mold. Freeman Porter, no doubt, continued to use his brother's molds when he took over the business.

Mr. Kerfoot mentions lamps, candlesticks, water pitchers, and coffee pots by Freeman Porter, who "shares

with R. Dunham and William McQuilkin the task of keeping American collectors supplied with open-topped pitchers," of which he made at least a third of the number now in existence. A pitcher (*Fig. 3*) brought from Maine by Mr. Woodside's grandmother, bears the mark *F. Porter Westbrook No. I.* It was always spoken of as the britannia pitcher, though it is of pewter. The significance of the *No. I* and *No. II* in Freeman Porter's marks is unknown.

Wares of Rufus Dunham

In a letter from Frederick Dunham to Mrs. Samuel G. Babcock, published in the Boston *Evening Transcript,* Saturday, March 19, 1927, some interesting sidelights are thrown on nineteenth-century methods of pewter-making. Speaking of his father, Mr. Dunham says:

"He bought his first metal of James Ellerson of Boston — tin, copper, antimony, and bismuth. The mixture when melted was cast in molds — the body of the pot, cover and bottom, spout and handle. After being turned, using a hand lathe, the parts were soldered together, the handles japanned, and they were ready for market. So far as I know, all pewter was cast in molds. With the advent of rolled metal, the word pewter was dropped, and Britannia was the new name adopted.

"In the 1860's there was a revolution in the pewter business. Teapots and what is called 'hollow' ware were made from rolled metal and spun on lathes into shape and called 'white metal.' For the more particular trade such articles were electro-silver-plated. The unplated goods were known as Britannia ware. [The beginning of rolled britannia ware antedates 1860, however. The first sheet of such metal was produced with a pair of jeweler's hand rolls in Taunton, Massachusetts, as early as 1824.]

"About 1870 there was a demand for copper bottom teapots, as . . . they were more serviceable than those made entirely of pewter. These wares were usually stamped *R. Dunham & Sons, Portland, Me.*"

Rufus Dunham manufactured Communion ware, coffee and tea urns, rolled and cast metal coffee and teapots, ale and water pitchers, ale mugs, both plain and with glass bottoms, soup tureens, soup ladles, teaspoons, tablespoons, castor frames, salts, peppers, and mustard cups, whale-oil and fluid lamps, candlesticks, and other small articles.

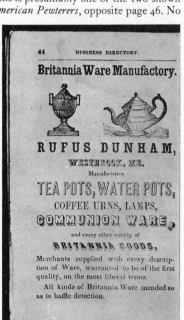

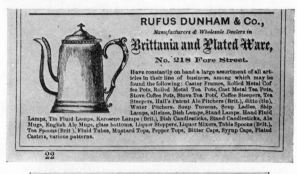

Fig. 9 (*left*) — Portland Directory Advertisement (*1844*)

Fig. 10 — Portland Directory Advertisement (*1866–1867*)

Fig. 11 — Partnership Notice, "Eastern Argus" (*April 20, 1835*)

Fig. 1 — Specimens of Sellew and Company's Products (1834-1860)

Ohio and Missouri Pewter Data

By J. G. Braecklein

Illustrations from the author's private collection

Author's Note. — The making of good pewter and britannia wares in the heyday of their popularity was by no means confined to the eastern seaboard of the United States. Communities well to the westward were likewise competently served by local craftsmen. The failure of these pewterers to receive due meed of appreciation from recent writers is attributable, not to any inferiority in skill and artistry on their part, but solely to the circumstance that, hitherto, no student from their part of the country has been willing to devote himself to the research essential to discovering their identity and the evidences of their accomplishment. The aim of the following notes is to make at least a beginning in the right direction, by offering some fresh information concerning certain early pewter and britannia manufacturers of Ohio and Missouri. It is hoped that others, encouraged by these preliminary blazes along the trail, will be stimulated to further and far more complete exploration. One important circumstance may, however, hamper their progress: namely, the extraordinary scarcity of specimens of ware which might offer some preliminary clue to a course of investigation. This circumstance — in so far as Missouri is concerned—may perhaps be due to the fact that, during the Civil War, great quantities of household pewter were melted into bullets at the Jefferson Barracks near St. Louis.

For assistance in the preparation of these notes acknowledgment should be made of valuable assistance rendered by Antoinette Douglas of the St. Louis Library, by Sophie M. Collman of the Art Department of the Cincinnati Public Library, by Joseph T. Homan, President of the Homan Manufacturing Company of Cincinnati, and by Professor Dains of the University of Kansas, an ardent devotee of pewter.—*J. G. B.*

IT is interesting to note that the manufacture of pewter, which had been for so long a time confined to the Atlantic seaboard, followed the western tide of migration, and appeared in the growing city of Cincinnati, Ohio, during the early 1830's, and in St. Louis, Missouri, before 1845.

SELLEW AND COMPANY

In the Cincinnati Directory for 1834, the name of Sellew and Company appears, in an engraved advertisement, as that of an established firm (*Fig. 4*). Since the name is lacking in the Directory for 1831, it would seem probable that the firm was founded in 1832 or 1833. In the Directory for 1836–7 Sellew and Company (Sellew, Enos & Osman) appear as a britannia ware company. Evidence of subsequent prosperity is to be found in a certificate of the Ohio Mechanics Institute, dated July 22, 1839, which states that specimens of britannia ware from the factory of "Messrs. Sellew & Co." were "much admired as good work, well finished and of handsome pattern."

In 1841 the firm employed eight hands, with an annual product valued

Fig. 2 — Teapot by Sellew and Company
(*probably of the 1830's*)
The form of the piece indicates a relatively early date.

The eagle mark, shown at the right, is known only on this single specimen of Sellew's output.

Fig. 3 — Pitchers by Sellew and Company

In general form these follow the ample and inviting lines of Roswell Gleason's pitchers; but their handles are considerably more ornate than those applied by the eastern pewterer or his local contemporaries.

at $12,840, quite a sum in those days. Cist, in his *Sketches and Statistics of Cincinnati*, 1851, remarks:

Sellew and Company manufacture britannia coffee and tea sets, pitchers, cups, lamps, etc. The establishment is of long existence and is constantly enlarging its business, which finds a market throughout the entire west and southwest.

The firm maintained operations until sometime in the late seventies; but probably discontinued the manufacture of pewter about 1860, or a little before. Its wares bear, as a mark, the imprint *Sellew & Company, Cincinnati.* Recently, however, I found a pewter teapot marked *Sellew & Company*, with an eagle (*Fig. 2*). This example must be of extreme rarity, since it is the only one of Sellew's products with an eagle device upon

SELLEW & CO.

MANUFACTURERS OF

BRITTANIA AND PEWTER WARES,

Which they offer at wholesale or retail, as low as can be obtained from the east of equal quality. They also keep an assortment of Communion Furniture, consisting of Brittania Metal Flagons, Goblets, Beakers, Plates and Baptismal Founts, which they will sell in sets or separately.

Fifth street, between Walnut and Vine,

CINCINNATI.

N. B. All kinds of Brittania wares repaired at short notice.

Fig. 4 — A Sellew Advertisement
From the Cincinnati Directory of 1834.

it which has thus far been discovered.

The shape of this teapot and the stamp upon it are reminiscent of Boardman and Company, New York (*1825–27*), and suggest the possibility that Sellew may, at one time, have been connected with the Boardmans before going west to try his fortunes. A Sellew coffee pot is strikingly similar in design to a Boardman pot illustrated by Kerfoot. One might even venture the hypothesis that Sellew carried westward with him some of the Boardman molds, and that he added to the eagle, which characterizes the mark of so many eastern pewterers, his own name, to assure the individuality of his touch.

While some of the Sellew Company's pieces, furthermore, strikingly resemble those of Israel Trask

Fig. 5 — Specimens of Sellew and Company's Products (*1834-1860*)

Fig. 6 — Specimens of Homan and Company's Products (*1847-1864*)

(*1825-42*), notably the high-shouldered, or pigeon-breast, teapot, of Figure 237, in Kerfoot's *American Pewter*, the Cincinnati pewterers soon struck out upon lines of their own, and their pitchers, especially, are known for their excellence of form, sincere craftsmanship, and fine quality of metal (*Fig. 3*).

FLAGG AND HOMAN

The Cincinnati Directories of 1842-43, and of 1846, list Asa F. Flagg as a britannia ware manufacturer. In 1847 this same Flagg, an English pewterer, who was popularly known as "Pewter Flagg," and Henry Homan, an American, began the manufacture of pewter and britannia ware in the Ohio city. In 1854 Mr. Flagg retired, and Henry Homan continued the making of pewter until 1864, when he gradually changed the business into the manufacture of electro silver-plated ware. The present Homan Manufacturing Company of Cincinnati, the President of which is one of the sons of the original Henry Homan, has in its possession the original catalogues issued by the founder, as well as his tools and other equipment; and is preparing to revive the manufacture of pewter as it was first made by the firm of eighty years ago.

Many good specimens from Homan's factory are still in existence (*Fig. 6*). The author has a five-piece set which formerly belonged to General Grant's father, when the latter lived in Bethel, Ohio. A syrup jug of britannia ware by Homan was shown at the Twentieth Century Club Exhibit of American Pewter, in Boston, in 1925, and is illustrated in ANTIQUES for April, 1925.* It is also pictured in N. Hudson Moore's book.† It bears the mark *H. Homan*.

Any history of American pewter must recognize the fact that

*See ANTIQUES, Vol. VII, p. 196.
†*Old Pewter, Brass, Copper, and Sheffield Plate*, New York, 1905, Fig. 41.

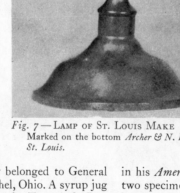

Fig. 7 — LAMP OF ST. LOUIS MAKE
Marked on the bottom *Archer & N. E. Janney, St. Louis.*

the two firms, Sellew and Company, and Henry Homan, were making high-grade pewter and britannia ware in Cincinnati at least between the years of 1832 and 1864, and that their work was of quality equal to that achieved by eastern pewterers during the transition and coffee-pot eras.

N. E. JANNEY AND COMPANY, AND BENJAMIN ARCHER

The first St. Louis, Missouri, Directory, published in 1845, lists N. E. Janney and Company, importers of and wholesale dealers in britannia and German silverware. In 1847 the Directory lists Benjamin Archer, britannia ware manufacturer. The oil lamp pictured in Figure 7 is marked, on the bottom, *Archer & N. E. Janney, St. Louis.* This would, perhaps, indicate that Archer made the lamp for N. E. Janney & Company.

T. SAGE AND COMPANY

The St. Louis Directory of 1847 carries the firm name of T. Sage & Co., manufacturers of britannia ware, at 62 Green Street. In the Directory of the following year, Timothy Sage appears, at 68 Green Street, as a manufacturer of britannia ware. A teapot stamped *T. Sage, St. Louis, Mo.*, was found by me recently in Washington Court House, Ohio. Mr. Kerfoot, in his *American Pewter*,* mentions the firm of Sage and Beebe, two specimens of whose pewter, together with the firm's mark, he reproduces. Whether or not the Sage of this concern is identical with the recently discovered T. Sage of St. Louis, is a question which is yet to be answered.

I have failed to find record of any pewter manufacturers in the south or in Chicago, Illinois.

*Page 175.

Index

Aaronsburg, Penn, 102-103
Albany, N.Y., 64, 65, 69, 71, 98-99, 105
Alderson, Thomas, 33
Angel figures, Austrian, 14
Archer, Benjamin, 156
Archer & N.E. Janney, 156
Austin, Nathaniel, 65, 68
Austin, Richard, 63
AW, mark, English, 36, 37, 38, 39, 43

Badger, Thomas, 63
Bailey, Timothy, 125-127
Bailey & Putnam, 123, 125-127
Baltimore, Md., 59
Baluster measure, English, 21-22, 27-28; Scottish, 21, 30; *see* also measure
Basin, American, 105, 119, 130; baptismal, 55; *see* also bowls
Bassett, Francis, I, 71, 85, 94-97
Bassett, Francis, II, 94-95
Bassett, Frederick, 54, 55, 68, 70, 72, 94-97
Bassett, John, 70, 94-97
Beaker, American, 59, 64, 67, 132; *see* also cup
Bedpan, American, 131
Belcher, Joseph, 69, 75
Belcher, Joseph, Jr., 69
Biberon, Austrian, 14
Biggin, coffee, 129, 142
Boardman, Sherman, 64
Boardman, Thomas Danforth, 54, 64, 75, 109, 131
Boardman & Co., 60, 155
Boardman and Hart, 131
Boston, Mass., 55, 59, 60, 65, 69, 84, 123-125, 128, 143-147
Bottle, baby's, 54, 142; dram, 114, 115
Bowl, American—66, 102-103; baptismal, 60, 104-105, sugar, 60, 105, 107, 109, 116, 125, 142, 144; English—27-38; font, 19; Scottish —rosewater, 25
Box, American, writing, 64

Boyd, Parks, 58, 60, 72
Boyden, Richard, 26
Boyle, Robert, 63, 97
Bradford, Cornelius, 56, 83-84, 100-101
Bradford, William, 56, 100
Bradford, William, Jr., 63, 71, 83, 84, 100
Brigden, Timothy, 88, 98-99
Bristol, England, 77, 83
Brittania ware, 56, 127, 129, 141, 146, 148, 150, 153, 154, 156
Buffalo, N.Y., 60

Calder, William, 129, 140-142
Can, American, 69, Swiss, 34
Candlesticks, American, 125, 142; English, 20, 21, 26, 27-28, 33; German, 13
Carnes, John, 69
Carter, A., 32
Casey, Samuel, 70
Caster, American, 141, 150
Chalice, American, 66, 87, 88, 89, 93, 98-99, 102-103, 105, 106-107, 116, 132, 149; English, 34; Irish, 34; Scottish, 34
Channel Islands, 31
Charger, English, 25
Chuckatuck spoon, 53, 55, 80-82
Ciborium, Dutch, 13
Cincinnati, Ohio, 154-156
Coffeepot, American, 58, 60, 125, 126, 128-129, 132, 140-142, 150
Coldwell, George, 86-87
Collecting, basic factors, 14
Coney, John, 84
Copeland, Joseph, 53, 80-82
Creamer, American, 105, 106-107, 125, 131, 142
Cup, American, 140, 142; English, 27-28, 34; Irish, 26; Scottish, 25
Curtiss, D., 65
Cuspidor, American, 130

Damper, American, 131
Danforth, Edward, 64
Danforth, John, 74
Danforth, Josiah, 69, 130
Danforth, Samuel, 54, 60, 61, 64, 109
Danforth, Thomas, 74
Danforth, Thomas, III, 59, 60, 64, 73
Day, Benjamin, 65, 70, 76
DB, mark, English, 22
de St. Croix, John, 32
Dish, American, 54, 86, 96-97, 98-99, 142; Austrian, 16, British, 16, 18, 27-28, 33, 34
Dolbeare, Edmund, 85
DS, mark, American, 101
Duffield, Peter, 27
Dunham, Rufus, 151-153
Dunham, Rufus & Sons, 151-153
Dyer, Lawrence, 34

East Anglia, 18
Eddon (Eden), William, 16, 27-28
Edgell, Simon, 54, 56
Edinburgh, Hammermen's Incorporation of, 25
Edinburgh, Scotland, 25, 34
EE, mark, English
Elsworth, William, 85
Emes, John, 23-24
Ewer, American, 102-103, 104-105; English, 33; see also pitcher

FB, mark, American, 70, 94
FE, mark, English, 22
Flagg, Asa, 156
Flagon, American, 85, 88, 89-93, 98-99, 102-103, 105, 107, 110-112, 113-116, 148, 149; Austrian, 13, 16; Dutch, 15; English, 23-24, 25, 26, 27-28; German, 14, 17, 110, 116; Scottish, 25; Swedish, 111-112; Swiss, 13
Flask, French, 14
Funnel, American, 94

Gilbert, Edward, 27-28
Gleason, Roswell, 56, 129, 130, 152, 155
Glenmore Company, 144
Green, Samuel, 143
Guild sign, German, 17

Hamlin, Samuel E., 140
Hammermen's Guild of Ludlow, England, 47-50
Hartford, Conn., 54, 56, 60, 61, 64, 109
Haward (Howard), Thomas, 18-19
Hera, J.C., 113
Heyne, Johann Christoph, 54, 105, 108, 110-112, 113-116
Hincham, A., 22
Hindersson, Erik, 112
Hitchman, James, 33
Homan, Henry, 156
Homan and Company, 156
Hopper, Henry, 65
HS, mark, English, 37, 43
HW, mark, English, 18-19, 20

IB, mark, American, 70, 94-95
ICH, mark, American, 105, 110, 113-114
IDSX, mark, English, 32
IG, mark, American, 60
IHK, mark, Continental
Ingles, Jonathan, 26
Inglis, Archibald, 25
IS, mark, American, 63, 65
IW, mark, American, 74; English, 36, 37, 43

Jamestown, Va., 80-82
Janney, N.E. & Co., 156
Jenison arms and crest, 25
Jones, Gershom, 54, 65, 73
Jones, Robert, 33
Jug, American, syrup, 156; English, beer, 33; French, 14

Keene, Josiah, 67, 140
Kelk, Nicholas, 16
Kilbourn, Samuel, 59, 131
Kirby, William, 68, 71, 85
Kirk, Elisha, 60, 76

Ladle, American, 108, 118
Lamps, American, 124-127, 141-142, 145, 148, 150, 151-153, 156
Lancaster, Penn., 54, 105, 108, 110, 112, 113-115
Lavabo ewer, Austrian, 14
Lawrence, Edward, 46
Lawrence, Samuel, 43, 46

Leddell, Joseph, 55, 56, 85, 87, 97
Leddell, Joseph, Jr., 84
Lee, Richard, Jr., 63, 75, 117-119
Lee, Richard, Sr., 63, 74, 75, 117-119
Leonard, Reed, and Barton, 130
Lewis, Isaac C., 75
Liddell, Joseph, 63
Loan Exhibition, 1939, Metropolitan Museum of
    Art, 62
London, England, 32, 33, 34, 37, 39, 40, 43, 46, 47
Lowes, G., 20, 21
Ludlow, England, 47-50
Lupton, Thomas, 24

Malden, Mass., 123-127
Mann, John, 81
Marnell, Samuel, 112
McEuen, Malcolm, 100
Measure, Austrian, 16; Channel Islands, 31-32; En-
    glish, 21, 24; German, 17; Scottish, 29-30, 34; see
    also *baluster measure*
Melville, David, 65, 69, 76, 78
Meriden, Conn., 75
Michel, André, 68
Middletown, Conn., 69, 132
Mollins, Robert, 27
Monteith, 16
Morey, David, B., 123-124
Morey & Ober, 124
Morey, Ober & Co., 124
Morey & Smith, 123-125
Mouthpieces, American, 142
Mug, American, 56, 57, 60, 62, 65, 68, 85, 101, 105,
    108, 130, 144, 146; *see* also cup and beaker
Müller, H., 110, 113, 116

Newcastle, England, 20
Newham, John, 27-28
New London, Conn., 69
Newport, R.I., 64, 65, 69, 70, 75, 76, 77
New York, N.Y., 54, 55, 63, 64, 65, 68, 69, 71,
    83-87, 96-97, 100-101
New York Society of Pewterers, 47
Noren, Petter, 111, 112
Norham, England, 25
Norwich, Conn., 74

Ober, Reuben H., 123

Palethorp, John Harrison, 66
Paschall, Thomas, Sr., 83
Pennock, Samuel, 59, 60
Percolator, coffee, American, 140, 142
Pettiver, William, 25, 27-28
Pewter Collector's Club of America, 16, 53, 67, 78,
    128, 131, 143
Philadelphia, Penn., 54, 56, 57, 59, 64, 65, 72,
    76-77, 83, 100, 104, 106-107, 108-109, 111
Pierece, Samuel, Jr., 137-139
Pierce, Samuel, Sr., 64, 132-136
Pitcher, American, 65, 102-103, 104-105, 131, 145,
    151, 155; Swedish, 111; *see* also ewer
Plate, American, 54, 55, 63, 66, 68, 69, 101, 118,
    132, 137, 139, 140; Austrian, 14; Dutch, 15; English,
    18-19, 26; Romano-British, 18; Scottish, 25
Platter, German, 15
Porringer, American, 54, 56, 59, 60, 64, 67, 69,
    73-79, 117, 119, 139, 140; English, 33, 35-46, 73;
    French, 45
Porter, Allen, 151, 153
Porter, Freeman, 151, 153
Portland, Me., 151-153
Price, F.G. Hilton, 18
Providence, R.I., 54, 64, 65, 67, 73, 140, 144
Pschorn, Heinrich Gottfried, 111, 112
Putnam Co., 125-127
Putnam, James Hervey, 125-127

Ramage, Adam, 34
RB, mark, English, 21, 25
Reed and Barton, 105
RI, mark, English, 24, 33
Richardson, George (Boston), 59, 60, 128, 143-147
Richardson, George (Cranston, R.I.), 143-145
RL, mark, American, 117-119
Romano-British pewter, 18

Sage, T. & Co., 156
Sage, Timothy, 65
Sage and Beebe, 156
St. Louis, Mo., 65, 154, 156
Salem, Mass., 85
Salt, American, 106; British, 16, English, 20, 26;
    Prague, 17

Salver, French, 14
Saur, Carl, I, 112
Seagood, Henry, 23
Sellew and Company, 154-156
Smith, Eben, 128
Smith, Henry, 37, 39-41, 43, 46
Smith & Company, 123-125
Smith and Feltman, 105
Smith & Morey, 123-125
Smith, Ober & Co., 124
Smith, Thomas, 26
Smith, Thomas, Jr., 123
Smith, Thomas, Sr., 123-124
Smith, Thomas & Company, 124
Society of Pewter Collectors, 78
Soup pot, German, 15
SP, mark, American, 76
Spindle caps, American, 140
Spoon rack, English, 20
Spoons, American, 53, 55, 60, 80-82, 140; English,
    19-20, 26
Stafford, Spencer, 71, 98-99, 131
Stettin, Germany, 111
Stevens Plains, Me., 151
Stockholm, Sweden, 111-112
Stone, Thomas 27-28

Tankard, American, 55, 56, 63, 67, 68, 70-72, 83,
    84, 91-92, 98, 101, 107, 108-109; English, 16,
    21, 23, 26; French, 14; German, 15; Swedish,
    111-112
Tasters, American, 75
Taudin, Jacques, 26
TB, mark, American, 98-99
Tea caddy, American, 86-87
Teapot, American, 57, 60, 62-63, 65, 67, 86, 98-99,
    104-105, 108, 124, 125, 126, 128-129, 137, 140,
    142, 144, 149, 150, 154

Tea set, American, 105
Tools, 133-135, 137-139
Tough, Charles, 27-28
Trask, Israel, 65, 148-150, 155
Trask, Oliver, 128, 149-150
Tumblers, American, 140
TY, mark, American, 98-99

Waite, John, 39-41, 43, 46
Walley, Allen, 40
Warford, Anthony, 40
WB, mark, American, 79; English, 25
Webb, Richard, 34
Weir, Richard, 25
WG, mark, English, 27
Wharton, Arthur, 40
White, Henry, 123
Whitehouse, E., 60-61
Whitmore, Jacob, 69
Whyte, Robert, 34
Wiggin, Abraham, 38, 39-41, 43
Will, Henry, 56, 64, 69, 71, 88, 93, 97, 103, 108
Will, John, 55, 56, 62, 63, 70, 74, 83-85, 89-93, 108
Will, Philip, 85, 89
Will, William, 54, 56, 57, 58, 60, 65, 66, 67, 72, 83,
    88, 90, 91, 93, 102-105, 106-107, 109
Williams, O., 60
Wingod, Joseph, 32
WK, mark, American, 71
WN, mark, American, 73, 79
Worshipful Company of Pewterers, 25, 26, 38, 44,
    47, 48, 53, 55, 56, 81, 128

York, England, 40
York, Penn., 60, 76
Young, Peter, 64, 67, 71, 85, 88, 91, 93, 98-99, 103